MAKING #CHARLOTTESVILLE

Media from Civil Rights to Unite the Right

ANIKO BODROGHKOZY

UNIVERSITY OF VIRGINIA PRESS
Charlottesville and London

University of Virginia Press
© 2023 by the Rector and Visitors of the University of Virginia
All rights reserved
Printed in the United States of America on acid-free paper

First published 2023

9 8 7 6 5 4 3 2 1

Library of Congress Cataloging-in-Publication Data

Names: Bodroghkozy, Aniko, author.
Title: Making #Charlottesville : media from civil rights to Unite the Right / Aniko Bodroghkozy.
Description: Charlottesville : University of Virginia Press, [2023] | Includes bibliographical references and index.
Identifiers: LCCN 2022050638 (print) | LCCN 2022050639 (ebook) | ISBN 9780813949130 (hardcover) | ISBN 9780813949147 (paperback) | ISBN 9780813949154 (ebook)
Subjects: LCSH: Unite the Right Rally, Charlottesville, Va., 2017.—In mass media. | White supremacy movements—United States—History—21st century. | Right-wing extremists—Virginia—Charlottesville. | Civil rights movements—United States—History—20th century. | Civil rights movements—United States—History—21st century. | Riots—Virginia—Charlottesville—History—21st century.
Classification: LCC P96.U55 B63 2023 (print) | LCC P96.U55 (ebook) | DDC 305.8—dc23/eng/20221129
LC record available at https://lccn.loc.gov/2022050638
LC ebook record available at https://lccn.loc.gov/2022050639

Author royalties from sales of this book will be donated to the Jefferson School African American Heritage Center, Charlottesville, Virginia.

MAKING #CHARLOTTESVILLE

In memory of
Eva Parzenczewska Majerczyk
January 15, 1925, in Lodz, Poland, to May 15, 2021, in Montreal, Canada
She prevailed over Nazis

CONTENTS

Acknowledgments	ix
Introduction	1
1. Choosing the Set	15
2. Being Media-Savvy: The Alt-Right	26
3. Being More Media-Savvy: Charlottesville Antiracist Activists	53
4. A12: Iconic Images	86
5. Viola/Heather and Annie/Veronica	112
6. "This Is What Community Looks Like!"	129
7. Four Presidents	153
Conclusion: A12 to J6 and Beyond	175
Afterword: My Summer of Hate—A Personal Narrative	189
Notes	197
Index	235

ACKNOWLEDGMENTS

This is not a book I ever thought I would write—or could write. I'm a media historian focused on the 1960s and don't stray too far from that turbulent era in my scholarship. But after the shocks of what Charlottesville folks call "the summer of hate" or simply "A12" I couldn't think about much else. My way of dealing with the trauma of what we as a community went through was to talk and engage obsessively about it. This work evolved slowly and with hesitation. Digging into my analytical toolkit as a media studies scholar, I found tools that seemed to help me make some sense of it. The work grew from there. And grew and grew. A planned article became a book, written and revised largely during the early period of the Covid pandemic. I happened to be on sabbatical in 2020—that timing was either lousy or invaluable depending on my mood or the day. But an entire book got drafted that year, a feat I don't expect ever to repeat.

This book deals with recent events that I participated in, so I have little emotional distance from the subject matter. The research and writing were often just plain painful. Using the comparative historical framework that structures the book, I was able to find some analytical distance. But as an historian, I'm used to having bounds around my objects of study provided by historical periodization. However, the present and near-present refuse to stand still.

I barely had a draft together before I knew I needed to address new, monumental incidents and happenings that connected to, or issued from, what had happened in Charlottesville in 2017. When the unprecedented uprising of protest following the police killing of George Floyd swept the country and the world, I knew I'd have to dip back into the book's chapter on Charlottesville antiracists and try to make some comparative meaning of it all.

I drafted a chapter comparing how three presidents and one presidential candidate responded in televised addresses to media events concerning the struggle against white supremacy. Would Democratic candidate Joe Biden prevail over Trump? The book went out to peer reviewers with no conclusion to the chapter because the 2020 election hadn't happened yet. The draft went out with a bunch of question marks.

One hopeful culmination of the Charlottesville struggle we all waited for: would the Confederate statues come down? Would that happen before this book went into production? It would be healing for the community and would give this book a provisionally happy ending. And then who could have predicted insurrection at the Capitol, with some of the very same groups that rioted in Charlottesville under the Unite the Right banner doing so under the Stop the Steal banner on January 6, 2021? As I sat watching the wall-to-wall coverage, the horrifying linkages back to what had happened in Charlottesville were obvious. I scrambled to make some sense of it. And then the *Sines v. Kessler* case unfolded later in 2021, which put the organizers of the Unite the Right violence on trial in Charlottesville for conspiracy to commit racially motivated violence, concluding with guilty verdicts. I've tried to plug in updates where I could, but at a certain point, with events relevant to this book's concerns continuing to unfold, I've had to stop, impose a boundary line, and leave it to future scholars, chroniclers, and historians to continue the necessary process of documenting and understanding the struggle against resurgent white supremacy in twenty-first-century America.

This book would not have come together as cogently as I hope it has if it wasn't for my indispensable editor at the University of Virginia Press, Nadine Zimmerli. She understood the book's potential even before I was sure there was a book here. Nadine is the kind of editor every writer wants and that few academics publishing with university presses are lucky enough to find. She provided multiple close readings of the entire manuscript, with sharp insights and advice that have made this a better book. Nadine was an intellectual partner and cheerleader through the entire process. This book mattered to her, and I'm so grateful for her commitment to helping me get it right—and putting up with me when I got bullheaded about taking some of her entirely appropriate suggestions. She also demystified aspects of publishing that this author of three books still didn't quite understand.

UVA Press provided a safe and encouraging environment for this project—I couldn't imagine publishing this book anywhere else. The Summer of Hate happened to many people who work at the Press, and some were, like me, activists on the street standing up against the forces of white supremacy. I was comforted knowing that everyone at the Press wholeheartedly supported this project—it's personal to us all—and participated in making it the highest-quality book possible. And because this is such an image-rich work, I'm grateful for the design and production team's meticulous work in making this a visually striking book—even as the images are ugly, violent, and brutal. Thanks to Wren Morgan Myers and their project team. I'm especially grateful for the smart and careful copyediting Wren's project team provided.

Historians need archives and archivists are among our favorite people. I've gotten to know the staff at UVA's Small Special Collections library over the years as I bring my classes there for sessions using archival materials. I happened to be in Molly Schwartzburg's office some years ago and noticed a bunch of tiki torches in the corner. Special Collections librarians had pulled the torches out of a garbage can following the infamous torch parade. Staff collected other physical artifacts, but also, because we live in a digital media age, they carried out bulk scraping of social media platforms to gather material related to the Unite the Right rally and community response. Titled "The University of Virginia Collection on the Events in Charlottesville, VA August 11–13, 2017," this compendium of analog and "born digital" materials will be a necessary archive for scholars and historians. I didn't end up making much use of the "born digital" materials. The library was closed because of Covid restrictions so I couldn't get hands-on training from staff about how to "rehydrate" the social media materials that might be useful. (I never got the image of a watering can out of my head.) I did my own, more limited scraping of social media. Scholars more adept at social media research will, I'm sure, improve on my modest efforts here. Along with Molly (now departed to Harvard), thanks to Krystal Appiah and Joseph Azizi for all their assistance.

Some of the key themes and ideas that undergird this book, such as the concept of "historical rhymes," first got a working-out in a class I began teaching in 2018 on media and protest of the 1960s. Many thanks to the students who helped me explore these ideas, see their utility and well as their limits. Teaching UVA students has always been a pleasure. I'm lucky to have such enthusiastic and intellectually curious young minds to engage with.

Charlottesville's community of antiracists, named and anonymous, have so inspired me and have supported and assisted this work. An anonymous activist centrally involved in the organizing throughout 2017 generously read over and fact-checked my chapter on Charlottesville antiracists. Any errors or faulty analysis remains mine. Jalane Schmidt, an inspiring and indispensable antiracist leader in this community, along with being a notable scholar in UVA's Department of Religious Studies, has also been a supportive colleague and wise teacher. She graciously read my chapter on white antiracist martyrs, providing much helpful response. Lisa Draine—whose brilliant idea of a photography installation for the second anniversary of the Summer of Hate, to honor those doing antiracist work in this community, forms the subject of chapter 6—gave of her time to read over that chapter, as did Kristen Finn who contributed some of the photography work. While I didn't end up interviewing activists about their use of media tools for this book, I want to send shout-outs to those I have gotten to know and admire both before and since the summer of 2017: Lisa Woolfork, Ben Doherty, Walt Heinecke, Mimi Arbeit, Dan Doernberg, Dolly Joseph, Rosia Parker and Katrina Turner, Don Gathers, Ézé Amos, Rabbi Rachel Schmelkin, Rabbi Tom Gutherz, and my partner in "care bear" duties on the day of A12, Cora Schenberg.

I also want to thank Susan Bro, who continues to inspire with the wisdom and clarity of purpose she has acquired through the unimaginable grief of losing a daughter to racist terrorism. Susan agreed to read and comment on my chapter about media treatment of her daughter's death, a remarkably generous act for which I am humbled. That chapter also deals with media treatment of another white female martyr to white supremacist terror. Fifty-plus years later, the children of Viola Liuzzo still grapple with their unending grief. I know that my work has added to their pain, as some of Mrs. Liuzzo's children have read the chapter and dislike what I have written. I apologize for causing distress. What happened in Selma may be "history," but it's still recent enough that the trauma continues to bring suffering to the living. What happened in Charlottesville is also ongoing trauma, and I fear that release of this book, with its copious imagery of racist violence, may also prick at community members' wounds that will likely never heal.

My academic colleagues have provided important feedback and suggestions for this work as it developed. At the end of August 2017, Nick Davis and Pamela Wojcik, on behalf of the programming committee of the Society for Cinema and Media Studies, let me hastily pull together two roundtable panels on "Mediating Charlottesville" on very short notice for the 2018 SCMS conference. Thanks to them and to panelists Jennifer Petersen, Emily Blout (both at the time UVA Media Studies colleagues), Eric Pierson, Michael Kackman, and Anna Everett. I gave a number of Zoom presentations on the book-in-progress during the pandemic and got helpful feedback. Thanks to Yeidy Rivero for the opportunity to speak to the University of Michigan Department of Film, Television, and Media. Big thanks to Oxford University's Sage Goodwin and Cindy

Ma, who organized the "Race and Racialisation" conference and put me on a panel in dialogue with Jessie Daniels. The pandemic had forced cancelation of the original conference, retooling it as a virtual event. But I still got to engage with Jessie Daniels's work, which so informs this book. I eventually managed to fulfill my dream of visiting Oxford and presented chapter 4 in a seminar at the Rothermere American Institute. It was gratifying to hear feedback and responses from non–media historians. Thanks to Stephen Tuck (Go Pembroke!) for helping to make that happen.

I'm lucky to have wonderfully supportive colleagues in the Department of Media Studies at UVA. Siva Vaidhyanathan provided a platform for this work and yet another opportunity for Jessie Daniels and me to discuss media and white supremacy on Siva's podcast with History Department colleague Will Hitchcock, "Democracy in Danger." (The episode, available online, is titled "White Power on Trial.") The chair of Media Studies, Andrea Press, has been a staunch ally and advocate. She miraculously found departmental funds that I desperately needed to offset the significant costs of clearing rights to use the many photos reproduced in this book. Thank you, Andrea!

The office of the Dean of Arts and Sciences also came to my aid with generous subvention funds to help with the expenses of publishing such an image-rich book. Thanks especially to our former Dean Christian McMillen for his support.

Peer reviewing is the foundation of good scholarly publishing. I was lucky with the two (no longer anonymous) scholarly reviewers of my book. Julian Hayter at the University of Richmond provided exactly the tough but encouraging review I needed. A bit daunted at first, I quickly realized how his requests and suggestions would immeasurably improve the book and navigate me away from weak spots. Allison Perlman at UC-Irvine also helped shape this into a hopefully more coherent and thematically connected book. I also thank the anonymous community reviewer for their helpful comments.

My daughter, Aviva, a member in good standing of Gen Z, understands the world of contemporary social media far more than her mom's generation ever will. As a communication and media studies scholar in her own right, she did me the great favor of reading the chapter on the alt-right with an eye for any bad gaffes in my attempt to understand the alt-right's use of Discord and memes. She also helped me better understand #Gamergate. All remaining gaffes and errors are mine.

The advice and counsel of my husband, Elliot, are all over this work. He assiduously read every word of the manuscript, gave unfiltered advice (the best kind), and helped me with the gargantuan task of dealing with all the images. Writers' spouses live with their partners' book projects, and Elliot dealt with my obsessive talking and thinking and pandemic writing about #Charlottesville from the moment I returned home the late afternoon of August 12. This has not been an easy project to live with for more than four years. Thank you, Elliot.

This book is dedicated to Elliot's mother, Eva Majerczyk, a Holocaust survivor. She passed away as I was revising the volume, and her loss remains an indelible hole in my heart. So few survivors remain, and their lived memory of what fascism does is more necessary than ever. Surviving Nazis in Poland, she had to witness, via media coverage, neo-Nazis marching in her son and daughter-in-law's town. Let me end with a heartfelt acknowledgment to her by telling some of her story.

Eva was fourteen when she, along with her fifteen-year-old sister, Ruth, were forced to leave their middle-class Hasidic family in Lodz, Poland, late in 1939. The girls thought their parents and two brothers would follow a few days later. Their father wept as the girls departed; Eva had never seen him shed tears before. And she never saw her family again.

Eva and Ruth began an orphaned life that included about a year in the early Warsaw Ghetto, where Eva contracted typhoid fever. Had the family she and Ruth roomed with sent her away to the ghetto hospital, where patients were packed two to three in one bed, she would have perished. Hidden in their rented back room, Ruth nursed her sister back to health. A well-connected uncle eventually found a smuggler to get them out of the ghetto. First sneaking Eva out, the middle-aged smuggler and Eva had to pretend to be a married couple, a life-or-death gamble since the very skinny teenager with long black braids looked considerably younger than her years. On the first leg of a journey that would end at her uncle's town in Silesia, the smuggler unexpectedly left Eva alone at a train station in a town unfamiliar to her while he journeyed back to get Ruth. It was barely dawn, and all Eva had was an address located inside the town's Jewish ghetto but no idea how to find it. As a Jew with no papers, no mandatory star on her clothing, and outside the confines of a ghetto, Eva was in a dangerous predicament. She saw a group of workmen nearby and overheard one man asking his companions, in a tone of concern, what such a young girl was doing out alone so early in the morning. Deciding he must be a kind human being, she asked him for directions even though doing so would reveal she was a Jew, as no non-Jew would have a reason to venture into the ghetto. Her instinct was correct. He was kind and brought her to the address inside the ghetto.

Eventually Ruth was smuggled out as well, and the girls were reunited with their uncle and his family after more arduous and risky travels. But the girls were fugitives from the Warsaw Ghetto with no documents, and that placed their relatives in danger. All could be shot by the Nazis. The sisters' solution to their dilemma: willingly go into a slave-labor camp.

Over the next three years, the sisters worked in a series of increasingly harsh and punishing camps, surviving on one small ration of food a day: a piece of brown bread and some watery soup. The camp slave-labor force was almost entirely made up of young people; girls in one barrack and boys in another. Group solidarity kept them alive. Forming themselves into bands of about six girls, each one buoyed up the others, sharing food, clothes, blankets, everything. They made sure everyone washed and kept their bodies, their clothes, and their sleeping areas clean. Eva quickly noticed that laborers who didn't use every means available to stay clean inevitably declined, got sick, and then got shipped off to Auschwitz. The slave laborers knew what happened at Auschwitz.

Teenagers being teenagers, even in a Nazi slave-labor camp, romance sometimes blossomed. And for Eva, who secured work in the camp kitchen, a German cook served as an unlikely matchmaker. The cook, who had taken a shine to her, repeatedly joked, "Eva, where is your Adam? I'll find your Adam." New contingents of male slave laborers came into the camp regularly. One day, the cook proclaimed, "Eva, I've found your Adam." He pointed to a blond youth in the latest grouping. At first embarrassed at being matched like this, the boy and the girl eventually began chatting across the barbed wire that separated the male and female barracks.

In 1944, Eva, Ruth, and her contingent of slave laborers were summarily ordered to pack up, herded onto a cattle car, and traveled three days not knowing their destination. They disembarked and immediately saw a large chimney belching smoke. Despite their fears, it was not a death camp but an ammunition work camp. For the first time Eva encountered SS guards. They were female, and they were vicious. Labor duties were especially awful, as the enslaved worked with yellow powder that clung to everything, causing sneezing, coughing, and eye irritation; their skin seemed permanently yellow. After twelve hours of work, the laborers endured a five-kilometer trek back to barracks. Some girls slept as they walked with companions on either side holding up the slumbering one. Group solidarity kept them going.

Eventually the work stopped, the SS guards disappeared into the night, and food became even more scarce. A campmate who had been a pharmacist assured them that the dandelions sprouting around the camp were edible. Finally in May 1945 they were liberated. One month later, Eva and her Adam (real name Haim, Polish nickname Shlamek, English name Henry), having found each other, got married.

Because Eva and Ruth had survived, they hoped that their parents and brothers may have also. But their father, Jehiel Parzenczewski and older brother, Jakow, had perished in the Lodz Ghetto. Their mother, Malka, and younger brother, Nahum, were murdered at Auschwitz following the liquidation of the Lodz Ghetto; they'd believed—or willed themselves to believe—that they were going to be resettled. Their uncle, Haim Zilberberg, who had managed to save his young nieces, ended up in the Theresienstadt concentration camp, but survived. He couldn't save his wife and two daughters; they died in Auschwitz.

With few blood relatives left, Eva and her Adam built new extended families around their campmates. The bonds of solidarity that kept Eva and Ruth alive during three years of slave labor to the Nazi war machine became the foundation of a full and rich, if wounded, life thereafter. They had children and lived to see grandchildren and great-grandchildren. Eva and Ruth became revered family matriarchs. They prevailed.

MAKING #CHARLOTTESVILLE

INTRODUCTION

Place names can be powerful. Consider these three: Charlottesville, Selma, Birmingham.

Since 2017, "Charlottesville" has come to mean something besides a Jeffersonian college town in central Virginia. In media discourse and even everyday conversation (for people who don't actually live in Charlottesville as I do), the name connotes the rise of a visible, violent, aggrieved, and emboldened white nationalist "alt-right" in the age of Trump. The small city became a hashtag: #Charlottesville.

As a media historian looking at an event that is not yet history, I want to understand what happened in my town during the tumultuous summer of 2017 through an historical lens. "History doesn't repeat itself, but it often rhymes." The quote is typically attributed to Mark Twain. In the weeks and days before August 12, 2017, I started noticing parallels and resonances to the civil rights era in our community's preparation for the Unite the Right (UTR) onslaught. (I provide a narrative of my personal experience of the events examined in this book in the Afterword.)

Having written and taught about the civil rights era for many years, I may have been more primed than others to see—or look for—linkages. An activist clergy group sent out an appeal to faith leaders around the country to come to Charlottesville and stand in solidarity with local antiracist activists. Just like what Martin Luther King Jr. did during the Selma campaign in 1965. A nonviolent direct-action trainer came to Charlottesville to conduct workshops for activists planning to put their bodies on the line. Just like during the sit-in movement and just like before other campaigns, including Birmingham in

1963. Charlottesville community members and activists congregated in a local church and sang freedom songs before the anticipated confrontation with white racists. And then the church got put on lockdown because it was the evening of August 11 and right across the street white supremacists were congregating with torches, potentially threatening everyone in the church. Inside the sanctuary rumors spread that racists with guns were nearby. Just like what happened in Montgomery in 1961 to Freedom Riders and their supporters who found themselves locked down in a prominent Black church while right outside, racists congregated and threatened to invade.[1] And then on August 12, at what most everyone thought was the end of the truncated rally, a white female antiracist marcher was murdered by a neo-Nazi in a car attack. Just like the end of the Selma-to-Montgomery march when four Klansmen in a car killed a white female volunteer ferrying marchers back to Selma.

National and local media outlets in 2017 circulated a set of narrative themes and visual tropes echoing those that had dominated coverage during the civil rights years. And in an audacious and alarming twist, the alt-right forces turned Charlottesville into a stage set for their demonstrations trumpeting white supremacy, flipping a script perfected by the civil rights movement that had turned Birmingham and Selma into stage sets—and media events—for powerful battles to vanquish white supremacy. A half century on from the successes of the civil rights era, a new generation of white racists felt emboldened enough to pursue maximum media visibility. They did so for a media campaign meant to normalize and make compelling and attractive a worldview that the Black empowerment movements of the 1960s appeared to have thoroughly delegitimized.

Like Charlottesville in 2017, "Selma" in 1965 has come to symbolize not just a specific campaign of the Martin Luther King–led push for Black voting rights in 1965 that led directly to the passage of the landmark Voting Rights Act. In the popular imagination it sometimes signifies the entire civil rights movement. When President Obama in his second inaugural address spoke of "Seneca Falls and Selma and Stonewall," the assumption was that listeners understood what he meant by invoking that Alabama town in his alliterative list of place names.[2]

If we play counterfactual history and imagine Twitter existing in the early to mid-1960s, #Selma would have been trending all over social media in 1965. And two years before that civil rights watershed event, #Birmingham would also have blown up a 1963 internet, with viral video of dogs attacking young people and high-powered water hoses pulverizing them as they demonstrated for racial integration in the other major civil rights media event of the era. That one led directly to the passage of the landmark Civil Rights Act of 1964.

The place name "Birmingham" may not function readily as a verbal signifier of the civil rights movement, like "Selma" does; "Portland" and "Berkeley" likewise don't tend to instantly remind people of alt-right confrontations that happened there, like the mere naming of "Charlottesville" does. Consider how "Ferguson" became the hashtag for the rise of the Black Lives Matter (BLM) movement, not "St. Louis." In 2020 when the police killing of George Floyd spawned a worldwide and broad-based movement against police brutality and racism, Minneapolis, the scene of the event and days of uprising, got massive media attention; the city didn't quite become "#Minneapolis." Smaller towns and cities with fewer already-extant sets of meanings and associations may be more likely to become—and stay—our shorthand references for major events that happened in them.

Why lump together the Birmingham and Selma campaigns with what happened in Charlottesville in 2017? What does the Unite the Right rally and its attendant mayhem have to do with these two seminal moments of the civil rights era? All three put white supremacy and the struggle against it into sharp relief. All three were major media events that communicated something about American racism. They have become verbal shorthand. And what happened in Charlottesville, as I'll be arguing in the chapters ahead, had surprising echoes, resonances, and outright similarities to the events in Birmingham and Selma, as well as other civil rights flash points a half century earlier, revealing both the abiding power, but also the alarming pressures on, civil rights era accomplishments with their attendant broadening of democratic access. Startling correspondences are displayed, at times in reverse-mirror ways, in each era's media coverage of the confrontations as well as the means used by activists to marshal their own media tools.

1965: Before and After

Iconic moments in the struggle against white supremacy that become media events are part of a longer through line in American history that ultimately reveals the extent to which democracy and diversity have flourished—or can flourish—in this country. *New York Times* journalist Nikole Hannah-Jones zeroed in on this history in her Pulitzer Prize–winning lead essay for her 1619 Project, which reframes American history by centering slavery and its legacy as well as the contributions of Black Americans. Her provocative argument: "The truth is that as much democracy as this nation has today, it has been borne on the backs of black resistance."[3] She frames the 1960s civil rights era as the second mass movement, following the 1865-to-1877 Reconstruction period in the aftermath of the Civil War, to advance rights and freedoms not just for Black people but for other disadvantaged and disempowered groups. The Southern white backlash against Reconstruction's enshrining of Black civil and voting rights into the Constitution effectively rendered the American South a nondemocracy—a white ethnostate. It took the legislative triumphs of the 1960s Black empowerment movement, which dismantled Jim Crow segregation and forced the passage of powerful legislation on voting rights, to make good on those Reconstruction Amendments.[4]

The high media visibility of the 1963 Birmingham and the 1965 Selma campaigns served as triggering moments. As worldwide media events, they forced the White House and Congress to act and, in remarkably short order, to pass those pieces of landmark legislation. Those statutes, in turn, provided a degree of legal protection for an extended period of expanding rights and democratic access in the decades to follow. Additionally, as Hannah-Jones notes briefly, and other historians and legal scholars have explored, the moral arguments of the civil rights movement and the legal force of the Civil Rights Act provided the impetus for another piece of landmark legislation that remade America: the Hart-Celler Immigration Act.[5] It dismantled the racist 1924 Johnson-Reed Immigration Act, which had excluded immigrants from Asia and severely limited those from southern and eastern European nations whose populations, including Jews, weren't deemed suitably white. Along with the Voting Rights Act, and the monumental wave of President Lyndon Johnson's Great Society and War on Poverty programs, the new immigration act signed into law in October 1965 capped a seismic year for progressive and democratically expansive federal lawmaking.[6]

That year has proven to be monumental for alt-right adherents as well. Scholar Alexandra Minna Stern argues that it has been a fixation in the alt-right's "reactionary timescape." For white nationalists, 1965 stands "as the decisive year when the White Republic was lost."[7] She quotes a participant on a podcast of Identity Evropa, a key white nationalist group centrally involved in the Unite the Right rally, observing, "1965, MLK, all that, that's year zero."[8] In the wake of those consequential legislative acts, Black people achieved at least some degree of political and social power, as did women since the Civil

Rights Act included sex in its categories protected against discrimination. The second-wave feminist movement would soon flourish, as would other rights struggles—by gays and lesbians, by Latinx peoples, by Native Americans, by the disabled, and by trans and nonbinary people. And the US would become less and less demographically white.

When alt-right marchers chanted "You (and Jews) will not replace us" in Charlottesville, they were obviously reacting to this fifty-year rights expansion and demographic transformation, seeing themselves as America's newest disempowered minority. They also enacted in a hypervisible way the ultimate logic of Trump's "Make America Great Again" campaign slogan. For his largely white and aggrieved base of voters, when had America last been great? Certainly before the nation had elected an African American president. In a MAGA timescape, America was great before 1965.

If "Birmingham" and "Selma" were seminal media events signaling how a social change movement could push the United States to begin repairing its racist and antidemocratic past, "Charlottesville" portended the rise of a potentially potent alternative social change movement and a political landscape committed to the reversal of those progressive gains. As we'll see, a forceful movement of antiracists successfully pushed back, and the resultant media narrative suggested defeat and failure for the "Unite the Right" cause. Democratic presidential contender Joe Biden rode to victory wielding the media imagery of #Charlottesville amidst a summer of unprecedented antiracist activism and protest. But another transfixing media event that made the stakes for inclusive democracy crystal clear unfolded on January 6, 2021. Trump supporters, including some of the very same aggrieved white males who marched under the Unite the Right banner in Charlottesville, violently invaded the US Capitol to stop the certification of Joe Biden's presidential election. White supremacy and its antidemocratic impulses were far from vanquished. The maximum visibility achieved by the insurrectionists and their attempted coup may have galvanized a right-wing extremist movement that seemed to have failed in the streets of Charlottesville. In 2017 the slogan was "you (and Jews) will not replace us!" In 2021 it was "stop the steal." Antidemocratic white grievance connected them both.

The beleaguered Voting Rights Act that civil rights activists had struggled and sacrificed so much for sat at the heart of these latter-day threats to democratic process. Republican leaders and legislators, asserting concerns about voter fraud and insecure elections, attempted to make voting more difficult, especially for voters of color. They could do so only because in 2013 a conservative majority on the Supreme Court hollowed out the 1965 Act by taking away a key provision that required federal authorization for any changes to voting regulations made by a state or locality with a history of voting discrimination.[9] These assaults on the Voting Rights Act, along with years of purposeful weakening of the guardrails of democracy, so precisely detailed by Harvard University government scholars Steven Levitsky and Daniel Ziblatt in their bestselling 2018 book *How Democracies Die,* culminated with Trump's incendiary refusal to recognize a free and fair election defeat.[10]

In that through line of America's push-and-pull history around overcoming white supremacy and expanding democracy and diversity, media events like Birmingham and Selma a half century ago, along with Charlottesville and most recently the January 6 Capitol insurrection, serve as signal moments compelling consideration about the state of American race relations and democratic ideals. The fact that they all received intense press coverage, particularly on highly visual media outlets such as television news and photojournalism, has been a key reason for their power to captivate wide attention—attention that continues way past the traditional "news cycle." But why focus on the ways these events were mediated? How are we to understand them as media events, and what utility does that framework of analysis provide?

Media Events

In the early 1960s, Daniel Boorstin, a historian and future Librarian of Congress, tried to make sense of a relatively new phenomenon: an activity, event, or happening specifically designed to elicit the attention of the media for publicity purposes. He called them "pseudo-events" in an acclaimed and much discussed book, *The Image.* For Boorstin there were real events—and then there were those "planned primarily (not always exclusively) for the immediate purpose of being reported or reproduced." The pseudo-event was "arranged for the convenience of the reporting or reproducing media. Its success is measured by how widely it is reported."[11] In an era of public relations experts, mass media, and the new medium of television, Boorstin lamented the loss of the real, or what later generations of scholars and intellectuals might refer to as the "unmediated."

Were the Birmingham and Selma demonstrations pseudo-events? They certainly were planned and arranged by civil rights and voting rights activists to garner media attention.[12] And because they achieved worldwide coverage from the press, they surely could be deemed successful. The image of white segregationist brutality the news media disseminated wasn't in any way inauthentic, but it wasn't spontaneous either. Boorstin found himself grappling with the fundamental shifts in the media ecosystem of his day—which coincided with the civil rights movement—but without the analytical tools that theorists would soon provide for diagnosing the new postmodern era of media ubiquity and its attendant collapsing of "the real" and its representation.[13] He could point to the new phenomenon of the media event without entirely grasping what he was witnessing.

It's important to have a robust definition of "media events" for this project, and media scholar John Fiske in the 1990s succeeded in doing what Boorstin in the early 1960s gestured toward. Fiske moved past what by then was a clearly untenable distinction between a "real" event happening over here and its mediated representation reproduced over there. For media events, Fiske argued, "their reality included their televisuality."[14] In his theorization, "media events are sites of maximum visibility and maximum turbulence."[15] Suddenly and sharply visible because of blanket mass media coverage are struggles and contestations around meanings and power dynamics that have bubbled and churned within the body politic but have remained more or less unseen or ignored. The contested issues haven't grabbed public attention forcefully until a specific media story commands massive amounts of journalistic oxygen. The media event, bringing these struggles into heightened visibility, "invites intervention" and serves as "a site of popular engagement and involvement."[16]

In the early to mid-1960s, Martin Luther King's organization, the Southern Christian Leadership Conference (SCLC), perfected a strategy for dramatizing the injustices of Jim Crow segregation and white racism, using marches and demonstrations to bring to maximum visibility the struggle against racial discrimination—the tools for achieving that maximum visibility included a new medium, network television news, as well as photojournalism. The SCLC exploited the affordances of visual media to galvanize engagement and involvement by Americans whose opinions could be swayed, mostly outside the Deep South, and by elected officials in Washington who could be pressured to put forth and pass ameliorative legislation. Historian Adam Fairclough notes that the SCLC "sought to evoke *dramatic* violence rather than *deadly* violence," relying on the presence of reporters and photographers to restrain racists from the extremes of brutality that Southern Black people were all too familiar with.[17]

When the strategy worked, as it did in Birmingham with the dogs and fire hoses, this kind of segregationist violence "inflicted no serious injuries, but gave the press dramatic images to splash across the front pages."[18]

Of course, the strategy did not always save activists from the deadly peril of white supremacist violence. In Birmingham some months after the successful "Project C for Confrontation," racists detonated a powerful bomb at the Sixteenth Street Baptist Church where many marches were organized; four young girls perished. Despite the media presence in Selma, three activists were murdered. The point, nevertheless, was to generate visually powerful and narratively compelling images and stories that exploded into a media event, which then would command maximum and sustained attention for the formerly unseen and their grievances. In the midst of a major media event, audiences find themselves compelled to engage.

What the SCLC did in Birmingham and later in Selma, the alt-right wanted to do in Charlottesville. The difference was that the alt-right didn't make much of a distinction between dramatic versus deadly violence.[19] Far more than previous battles in Portland and Berkeley, which certainly garnered media attention, Unite the Right organizers designed Charlottesville to become a media event. It was meant to bring to maximum visibility the cause of white male grievance, fears of "the Great Replacement," and the struggle against multiculturalism, feminism, immigration, and all the gains by people of color in the decades since the social justice movements sparked by the civil rights era. Seeing themselves as an increasingly oppressed soon-to-be-minority in their own country, the organizers wanted to use the inevitable confrontations and clashes with antiracist counterprotesters to invite involvement and engagement with other aggrieved white males. The point was to galvanize a social change movement. Before #Charlottesville, organizing had occurred mostly in specialized and hidden venues online. Generating media events, like the Black empowerment movements of fifty years ago had, would be a great way to gain recruits and start the process of changing American race politics and civic representation back to the "White Republic" that existed before Birmingham, before Selma, before 1965. In other words, Unite the Right organizers used civil rights–era tools, only they flipped the script first deployed by civil rights organizers.

The media landscape of 2017 was, of course, markedly different from that of the 1960s. Back then, three broadcast TV networks, CBS, NBC, and ABC, along with the major nationally distributed newsmagazines such as *Time*,

Newsweek, and *U.S. News & World Report* as well as the popular photography-oriented *Life* and *Look* all operated on an ideology of "moderatism" and presented news, as CBS's president of news in the 1960s and '70s blithely declared, "from *nobody's* point of view."[20] The news media, in general, were trusted by broad swathes of the American public, with CBS anchorman Walter Cronkite famously considered the most trusted man in America.[21] National news media were not partisan or opinion-driven like they have become in the new millennium. They were, of course, entirely dominated by white men, and most of them unreflexively believed themselves to be reporting objectively rather than from a very specific standpoint. In the social media environment of the 2010s, news consumers could more easily curate their own information flows, ensuring highly delineated points of view and far more ideologically driven news feeds. The traditional gatekeeping function of major journalistic institutions and their staff, which in the mass media age determined what was newsworthy, has weakened significantly. It's given way in a user-generated media age to a free-for-all, with technology companies like Twitter and Facebook becoming algorithmic gatekeepers of information.[22] This environment has made the dissemination of disinformation, propaganda, and lies far easier.

The major media event, however, is what cuts through—then and now. For an extended period, days or even weeks, all major media outlets and their audiences become fixated on a particular incident or phenomenon, particularly one that is visually compelling, dramatic, or provocative. Even in the cluttered and cacophonous environment of contemporary social media, there's not much escape. At the dawn of the twenty-first century's new media landscape, television historian Lynn Spigel noted how in the aftermath of the 9/11 terrorist attacks "for a moment the nation returned to something very much like the old three-network system" as cable channels all broadcast the same programming as the over-the-air network stations for about a week.[23] Yet in an even more fragmented and politically divisive media environment, sixteen years on from 9/11, a major media event can still, for a brief moment, recreate some of the features of the mass media era and its mass audiences. During the "breaking news" moment, whether it's the 9/11 terrorist attack, the mayhem of neo-Nazis marching in a bucolic Southern college town, or insurrectionists swarming the nation's Capitol, the "shock of the news" and the initial incomprehensibility of the astonishing images tend to send even ideologically oriented news outlets scrambling merely to report. And in the case of both #Charlottesville and the

January 6, 2021, insurrection at the US Capitol, initially pundits and politicians stood up for traditional norms of democracy and excoriated the violent extremists as un-American.[24]

This initial unified chorus of condemnation did not persist. And that's how #Charlottesville became a media event in Fiske's definition: as the US has become more divided along axes of social difference, events that dramatize and make visible those fissures in the body politic grab the public imagination. There is no disentangling the dramatization and visualization provided by media representation from a nonmediated "real" event such as Boorstin, back in the 1960s, wanted to cling to. In a postmodern era characterized by media being everywhere, the media event provides clarity, as Fiske argues, "to murky anxieties and political differences" and "serves as a public arena wherein the American people engage with urgent political debate and in sometimes effective political action."[25] Birmingham and Selma led to such politically effective action; #Charlottesville brought clarity and debate to the attempt to obliterate those actions.

Mapping the Book

To begin making sense of #Charlottesville as a media event, chapter 1 explores how maximum visibility was achieved by the careful choosing of locations for dramatic confrontation. For the civil rights movement, Birmingham and Selma provided the right set of characteristics and personages expected to generate conflict that would lure media outlets. Echoing the civil rights movement script, Unite the Right organizers, two key ones being University of Virginia graduates, knew Charlottesville had a compelling set of features and figures that could be exploited for drama, conflict, and violent confrontation. It was no accident that it all came together in this town.

By staging campaigns in locales like Birmingham and Selma, civil rights organizers displayed high levels of media savviness, particularly with respect to the new media ecosystem of their day. Network television news was that era's newest form of journalism, one with a uniquely wide-ranging, national reach. The white supremacist antagonists of the Southern Black empowerment movement never managed to match that media savviness. But, as we'll see in chapter 2, their progeny a half century later did command the new media landscape of their day quite expertly, using social media platforms and especially creating and disseminating memes, to craft edgy, rebellious, and visually striking materials well designed to build a new age racist movement. The alt-right actually had much in common with the second coming of the Ku Klux Klan in the 1920s, which also displayed remarkable facility with the new media of their day in order to build an almost mainstream political movement.[26] In the run-up to the Unite the Right rally, organizers encountered a relatively accommodating local press willing to provide a ready platform for white nationalists who made good copy and who effectively mobilized "free speech" and First Amendment arguments.

On the other hand, as we'll see in chapter 3, local media tended to treat with hostility and disparagement the activists organizing in opposition to the white supremacists, Klan members, and alt-right figures descending on Charlottesville throughout the spring and summer of 2017. Nevertheless, antiracist activists managed to outmaneuver alt-right leaders, using social media tools in creative ways to mobilize the community, thereby undermining, infiltrating, and prevailing over the Unite the Right organizers. Charlottesville's activists modeled the kind of social change movement "muscle" that media studies scholar Zeynep Tufekci argues has been hard to sustain in the twenty-first-century era of digital tools, which make quick organizing efficient but can hamper the ability to build robust movements like the civil rights movement of the 1950s and '60s.[27] Charlottesville's antiracist mobilization served as a harbinger of antiracist uprisings to come, especially during the "Summer of George Floyd" in 2020.

National media reporting about civil rights–era campaigns as well as Charlottesville's Summer of Hate all resulted in powerful images—films and still photos that communicated disturbing narratives about race relations, white power, hatred, and intolerance. As we'll see in chapter 4, among the vast number of photos and films of these heavily documented events, only some achieved enduring exposure, circulating widely and getting reproduced in multiple outlets. The Birmingham and Selma campaigns produced some of the most iconic images of the civil rights movement. Some of the most reproduced images of #Charlottesville echo iconic civil rights–era photos in striking ways. Media treatment of all three of these flashpoints in the struggle against white supremacy tended to play in a melodramatic key, visually narrating stakes that trace all the way back to Harriet Beecher Stowe's *Uncle Tom's Cabin*.[28] The echoes in dominant media visualizations of the struggle against white supremacy across a half century and more suggest an enduringly limited palette in figuring whiteness and blackness and power.

The civil rights movement produced, tragically, many martyrs to the cause of racial justice. Of all those murdered by white supremacist violence in the civil rights era, only one was a white woman: Viola Liuzzo, murdered by Klansmen at the end of the Selma-to-Montgomery march. Similarly, at the end of the Unite the Right rally, Heather Heyer was killed by a neo-Nazi who plowed his car into a crowd of antiracist marchers. Both women received voluminous media attention, and each would be further victimized by misogynistic vilification by white supremacists on their media platforms. Chapter 5 explores how we can understand the similarities and differences in the representation of these two martyrs—and what their status as white women means for their sanctification and denigration. Media treatment of African American women activists in Selma and Charlottesville differed, perhaps not surprisingly, from coverage given these white martyrs. Much may have changed in the status of white women since 1965; the relative invisibility of Black women has changed much less.

Chapter 6 explores how, in the aftermath of a major media event, a local community grapples with the ways it has been defined by major media narratives. Both Birmingham and Selma have created very different kinds of monuments to what happened in their towns in the civil rights era. Birmingham uses statues in a public park to both evoke its iconic media images but also to reframe the story told by the famous photos. Selma has turned the Edmund Pettus Bridge into a civil rights monument even as it's still a functioning piece of transportation infrastructure. The Charlottesville confrontations were, of course, significantly organized around the question of monuments. As the community and its activists in the short years following #Charlottesville attempted to grapple with the enduring media narrative of tiki torches, marauding neo-Nazis, and a horrifying terrorist car attack, they monumentalized an alternative narrative about the Summer of Hate using a large-scale photography installation. Like citizens in Birmingham, they also tried to use public space to tell a different story—their story—about activism and the struggle for racial justice.

In the aftermath of the events in Birmingham, Selma, and Charlottesville, four very different presidents felt the need to go before the television cameras to frame for the nation the significance of these eruptions of racial violence and struggle, as chapter 7 explores. John F. Kennedy and Lyndon Johnson in the wake of Birmingham and Selma gave moving televised addresses about what was at stake for America in confronting white supremacy and racial injustice, along with the need for decisive action. Both embraced the activists' cause and even their language. So did Joe Biden as he launched his campaign for the

Democratic presidential nomination, using #Charlottesville as the reason he felt he had to run. Donald Trump did something very different in his three televised addresses responding to the situation in Charlottesville. Unlike those other political leaders, he refused to categorically condemn white supremacists. The chapter explores how it matters the way a president (or aspirant to the position) uses the bully pulpit of the office to engage racial justice and the fight against white supremacy—and what it means when a president refuses. Trump went down in ignominious defeat—but not before unleashing his most fervent followers, including white supremacists like contingents of Proud Boys and Oath Keepers, some of whom had also marched in Charlottesville, in an insurrectionary mob at the Capitol. That Trump wasn't merely an outlier in the history of modern presidential response to racism but a fundamental threat to American democracy was first brought to maximum visibility in his Charlottesville responses. And as the conclusion will explore, January 6, 2021, served as a kind of companion media event to that of #Charlottesville in dramatizing the threats posed by organized white nationalism in the most shocking images.

Birmingham in 1963 and Selma in 1965 are seminal events in twentieth-century American history, chronicled and investigated voluminously by historians and documentarians, popularized and mythologized by Hollywood filmmakers and best-selling authors.[29] That both were such powerfully *visual* media events—using the affordances of photography and television as well as other forms of mass communications to amplify struggles around white supremacy, democratic inclusion, and the resistance movement against it all—has much to do with the durability of these events in the American imagination. It may be too soon to affirm Charlottesville 2017 as a twenty-first-century seminal event in American history, yet its rhymes and echoes with these civil rights–era events, and the fact that Hollywood filmmakers, documentarians, pop music luminaries, and aspiring presidents have gravitated to its images and Manichaean struggles between racists and antiracists suggest #Charlottesville is a watershed moment.[30] It's an event that, like Birmingham and Selma before it, dramatized in the starkest terms possible the stakes in America's abiding struggle against the never-defeated, always-regrouping forces of white supremacy. But like Birmingham and Selma, #Charlottesville showed how to engage the fight. January 6 made clear the necessity of doing so.

1

CHOOSING THE SET

"They picked Selma just like a movie producer would pick a set: you had the right ingredients." So said Joe Smitherman, the mayor of Selma, in a mid-1980s interview for the groundbreaking documentary about the civil rights movement, *Eyes on the Prize*. "They" meant Dr. Martin Luther King Jr.'s Southern Christian Leadership Conference (SCLC); "the right ingredients" included, first and foremost, Sheriff Jim Clark, a notorious quick-tempered racist and staunch segregationist known for his brutality towards Black people. The movement King led may have practiced strict nonviolence, but it fundamentally needed violence from white supremacists and segregationists.[1] White racist violence—the unmerited suffering that King argued was redemptive—brought the TV cameras and the photojournalists. TV news thrived on drama and provided a relatively new form of uniquely national journalism. Civil rights movement leaders and activists knew they needed significant national news media coverage in order to arouse the conscience of the nation and thereby lead to necessary legislation in Congress addressing segregation and disenfranchisement.[2] King's approach to activism required drama, confrontation, and an antagonist who would act out violently when cameras were there. It also required an activated community with large numbers of local residents willing to go into the streets, put their bodies on the line, and stand up to the forces of white supremacy.

A half century later, the organizers of the Unite the Right rally came to Charlottesville and flipped the civil rights movement's script. They picked the central Virginia college town because it had a set of ingredients that were useful for their movement and likely to encourage lots of media attention. Drama, confrontation, and violence were certainly part of the script. The big difference from the SCLC's strategy was that the alt-right forces had no intention of practicing nonviolence and had no assumption that physical aggression would come only from their antagonists and opponents. The white supremacists, neo-Nazis, and assorted aggrieved men planning to demonstrate in Charlottesville came expecting to foment violence themselves. But like Selma and like Birmingham before it, Charlottesville also had an activated local community willing to stand up to the forces of white supremacy. The script had been flipped, but the struggle and the stakes remained distressingly the same.

The Media Campaign Template: Birmingham

The script got its first effective enactment in the streets of Birmingham in 1963. Alabama's biggest city, and its most notoriously and violently segregated one, became the civil rights movement's most successful stage set to date for enacting an ongoing drama of the vicissitudes of Jim Crow and the organized struggle against it. And while media coverage at the time, and popular memory in the decades after, focused on the leadership of Martin Luther King Jr., Birmingham had an activated local movement long before King's SCLC agreed to conduct a high-profile campaign in the "Magic City."

Local firebrand Rev. Fred Shuttlesworth headed a militant organization, the Alabama Christian Movement for Human Rights (ACMHR) that garnered much disdain from the city's traditional Black leadership class, which advocated a more accommodationist approach with whatever "moderate" local white business leaders seemed available.[3] Birmingham also had an activated student movement, initially inspired by the sit-ins of early 1960. The brutal treatment meted out to Shuttlesworth and the students peaked media attention, leading most consequentially to Harrison Salisbury of the *New York Times* coming to town to investigate. He famously diagnosed the city's "emotional dynamite of racism enforced by the whip, the club, the knife, the mob, the police, and many branches of the state apparatus."[4] That indictment in turn sent CBS News cameras down to investigate further. Correspondent Howard K. Smith happened to be on the spot to witness the brutal beating by KKK hooligans of Freedom Riders disembarking at Birmingham's Greyhound station.[5] Smith used the nationwide platform of an hour-long prime-time network news report to confirm what Salisbury had found.[6]

Eugene "Bull" Connor embodied white supremacist brutality. As the city's

Commissioner for Public Safety, he'd conspired with the Klan thugs in advance of the Freedom Riders' arrival, promising to keep police away from the bus station for fifteen minutes so that the racists could have their way with the integration activists. Smith spotlighted Connor, quoting his patently ridiculous excuse that his officers were all on leave for Mother's Day and therefore unable to respond promptly. So before Martin Luther King and his SCLC associates set up camp at the Gaston Motel across from Kelly Ingram Park and close by the 16th Street Baptist Church early in 1963 for their "Project C" (for "Confrontation"), "Birmingham" already signified violent white supremacy and the struggle against it in American national media.

Because of the strength and resiliency of the local movement—students had been pursuing what they called a "selective buying" campaign against segregationist merchants (calling it a boycott risked arrests)—the SCLC agreed early in 1963 to join forces with the mobilized activists and, as civil rights historian Glenn Eskew notes, "suddenly the isolated local movement was linked to the large world of the national movement."[7] Birmingham would now become a stage set for the playing out of nonviolent resistance to the system of Jim Crow segregation. Over a month in April and May, the movement organized mass marches, lunch counter sit-ins, boycotts of local shops, nonviolent civil disobedience, and mass jailings. King also went to jail, using his time there to pen a letter pushing back against local moderate clergy who criticized the street demonstrations and suggested the courts as a preferable venue to address the issue of segregation.[8] King's response to the charge of leading an "unwise and untimely" protest became one of the civil rights movement's most powerful and widely disseminated documents.

The street protests culminated in early May with a "Children's Crusade." Fewer and fewer adults were willing or able to face jail time, so the movement made the consequential decision to use children in its mass marches and direct actions against Bull Connor's law enforcement structure. And that's when Connor fully committed to the role the movement had cast for him. Right in front of the television and print media's cameras, he performed the brutality of white supremacy, orchestrating his men in a display of racist violence against mostly youthful Black marchers. The photos and news film that resulted remain to this day the most heavily reproduced images of the civil rights movement.[9] When Connor unleashed dogs and high-powered fire hoses on those marchers—high school kids and younger—the resulting images, now iconic, were quickly transmitted across the nation and around the world. The power of those images finally compelled a formerly reluctant Kennedy administration to fully embrace the movement and shortly thereafter put forth robust civil rights legislation—what became the landmark Civil Rights Act of 1964.[10]

The visuality of television—and also of photojournalism highlighted in national newsmagazines like *Life*—were crucial resources for the civil rights movement. The lessons learned: for a protest event to matter, for it to have political impact, the media had to show up, and the media would more likely show up if there was drama, conflict, and even violence. John Lewis, head of the Student Nonviolent Coordinating Committee (SNCC), who had been clubbed during the Freedom Rides and would suffer a concussion after being beaten with other voting rights marchers on Selma's Edmund Pettus Bridge, referred to it as "that cycle of violence and publicity and more violence and more publicity that would eventually, we hoped, push things to the point where something—ideally, the law—would have to be changed."[11]

Perfecting the Media Campaign: Selma

Two years later, the issue was the disenfranchisement of Black people throughout the Deep South. Selma was no more or less egregious in keeping Black people off the voting rolls than cities and counties in Alabama, Mississippi, or other Southern states. It certainly didn't seem to meet the SCLC's "strategic requirements" for a major campaign, being far from airports and television stations.[12] Reporters wouldn't be able to get in and out of town easily, fly their film and photos for processing in New York or other media production centers, or broadcast reports from local radio or TV stations. News packaging and dissemination would inevitably be more cumbersome, making Selma a less obvious stage set for a media event.[13]

But Selma had other compelling features. First and foremost, Selma had the volatile Sheriff Clark, visually striking with his white pith helmet, swagger stick, and an anti-integration "Never" button he frequently had pinned to his uniform. The city also had recently elected a very young and inexperienced mayor. Additionally, Selma had an activated Black community, just as Birmingham had before King and the SCLC came to town. Mrs. Amelia Boynton, one of the town's only registered Black voters, headed the Dallas County Voters League. Her voting rights activism inspired SNCC organizer Bernard Lafayette in 1962 to set up a grassroots campaign in town.[14] Regular marches to the courthouse ensued, with Sheriff Clark responding with cattle prods. In 1964

Mrs. Boynton, with a mostly female committee, journeyed to SCLC's Atlanta offices to request King's help. Despite Selma's isolation, as SCLC Executive Director Andrew Young noted in his memoir of the movement: "In little Selma, more people were committed to the movement before Martin's arrival than after months of organizing and two weeks of daily demonstrations in Birmingham. The people's commitment made it the right place for us."[15] By the time King and the SCLC set up operations, all the elements for a dramatic campaign were in place.[16]

Violent confrontation was expected; it was required. Stirring the conscience of the nation and using the outrage from media accounts of brutal violence against nonviolent marchers were the levers for federal action. That was the lesson of Birmingham. Once Bull Connor had unleashed the police dogs and high-powered fire hoses with national and international media outlets recording the mayhem, the road to the Civil Rights Act was cleared. Selma, too, ended up obliging. On Sunday, March 7, network television cameras captured what happened when hundreds of voting rights activists tried to march out of Selma to the state capital, Montgomery, to protest not only the disenfranchisement of Black voters but the recent killing of a local activist, Jimmie Lee Jackson, by a state trooper after a night-time demonstration. With SCLC's Hosea Williams and SNCC's John Lewis at the head of the march, they faced off against Governor George Wallace's state troopers and Sheriff Clark's posse of men at the foot of the Edmund Pettus Bridge. The troopers advanced, plowing over the marchers, beating and tear-gassing them mercilessly, resulting in maximum visibility of white supremacist brutality. The news film interrupted prime-time Sunday programming and quickly galvanized an outpouring of outrage—and volunteers from around the country, who descended on Selma to stand with the assaulted marchers.[17] The local pressure, activism, and marching continued, culminating in the five-day Selma-to-Montgomery march, with hundreds of Black and white activists striding the fifty miles down Highway 80, swelling to 25,000 as they amassed at the state capitol building on March 25 with massive international media coverage and a cowering Governor George Wallace furtively peeking through the windows at the throng in front of him. The landmark 1965 Voting Rights Act sped through Congress five months later.

The civil rights movement perfected a confrontational protest template that would serve as a go-to strategy for social change movements around the world in the decades to follow. The Vietnam antiwar movement of the later 1960s drew from the civil rights playbook, even as some of that movement's youthful activists may have strayed from the nonviolent philosophy of confrontation.[18] Into the 1970s, the women's and gay liberation movements also drew from the civil rights era, with AIDS activists in the 1980s in particular mobilizing civil disobedience.[19] But the Martin Luther King approach to organizing for direct-action confrontation was not the exclusive purview of left and politically progressive movements. From the 1980s and on, the antiabortion movement took a leaf from King's book in its approach to organizing direct-action protests in front of women's reproductive health clinics, overtly linking their cause to the civil rights movement. So whether it was ACT UP shutting down the Food and Drug Administration in 1987 around access to AIDS drugs, or Operation Rescue with its 1991 "Summer of Mercy" actions against clinics in Wichita, Kansas, the point was to set a stage for protest with bodies on the line, to change policy but also to garner as much national media attention as possible to change viewpoints and bring allies to the movement.[20]

Charlottesville, 2017: The Alt-Right Appropriates the Template for a Media Campaign

In 2017, Charlottesville became a set, like the Birmingham and Selma templates, chosen for having the right ingredients. In this case alt-right activists Jason Kessler and his fellow University of Virginia (UVA) alumnus Richard Spencer picked it for their "Unite the Right" gathering of white nationalists, neo-Nazis, antisemites, and miscellaneous aggrieved and disaffected white men, along with an assortment of gun-toting Second Amendment militia groups.

Spencer himself coined the term "alt-right" and "alternative right" in 2008 when he was head of a white nationalist think tank, innocuously named the National Policy Institute. Breaking with then-dominant conservatism and the Republican Party, the alt-right embraced "identitarianism," which advocates for racial homogeneity, disdaining all non-northern European immigration and refugee settlement. The ultimate goal was the creation of a white ethnostate. Some factions of the movement have emphasized antisemitism more forthrightly than other factions. As we'll see in chapter 2, this new generation of white nationalists were particularly adept at using the internet and new social media tools to recruit, particularly among young males. While notoriously fractured along some ideological and tactical lines, this new phenomenon, which began getting massive media attention at the same time Donald Trump launched his bid for the presidency in 2015, was grounded in fears of white political disempowerment. Trump's surprise electoral win emboldened and further energized alt-right adherents, galvanizing a drive to unify the movement.[21]

But why organize a confrontation media event in Charlottesville, beyond the fact that both Kessler and Spencer were University of Virginia alums and thus knew the town and the university well? Why was this town the stage set for a violent playing out of white nationalist grievances and hatred? The ostensible motivating rationale was the city's decision to remove two monuments to the Confederacy: statues of Robert E. Lee and Stonewall Jackson in the middle of two downtown parks. But New Orleans, after a protracted two-year process, had already dismantled four Confederate monuments in May 2017. While the decision resulted in protests, New Orleans did not become the showcase for a major alt-right rally. Baltimore, similar to Charlottesville, had set up a commission to review what to do with its Confederate statues, leading to a recommendation to remove some and add signage to others. Following the taking down of the New Orleans statues, the Baltimore mayor in May 2017 indicated she was exploring how to do the same thing.[22] Baltimore did not become the stage set for the Unite the Right rally either. Charlottesville, however, had a compelling set of "right ingredients."

On January 31, 2017, Mayor Mike Signer declared to a gathering of hundreds on the town's pedestrian downtown mall that Charlottesville was "a capital of the resistance." The rally was in response to the just-inaugurated Trump and his recent executive order banning travel from seven predominantly Muslim countries.[23] Also at the rally was Khizr Khan, a Charlottesville resident, Muslim, and father of a young US Army officer and UVA graduate, Humayan Khan, who was killed in a suicide attack in Iraq. As a Gold Star father, Khan had become instantly famous for challenging Trump at the 2016 Democratic National Convention by holding up a pocket-sized copy of the US Constitution and asking the Republican candidate, "Have you even read the United States Constitution? I will gladly lend you my copy."

The point of Signer's rally was to highlight what Charlottesville could do to protect immigrants and refugees. Nobody spoke about Confederate monuments. Nevertheless, the mayor wanted to signal a very particular identity for a town generally more well known at that time as a top destination for retirees, as the "happiest city" in America (at least in 2014, when it was so designated by the US National Bureau of Economic Research), and as the home of Thomas Jefferson's great university, whose central grounds are a World Heritage Site.

Like many college towns, Charlottesville had a liberal reputation as a spot of blue in a politically red surrounding rural area. Signer, in his well-publicized speech, seemed to want to recast Charlottesville as a progressive hub pushing against everything that Trump and Trumpism stood for.

White supremacist websites saw Signer as an enemy months before organizing of the Unite the Right rally began. "Left-wing activist from a New York Jewish family leads push in a Southern town to eliminate symbols of its native White ethnic group and welcome in large numbers of non-White immigrants to re-populate the area." That's how Occidental Dissent, a prominent hate site, characterized Signer in a May 14, 2017, post.[24]

Vice-mayor Wes Bellamy also appeared at the "capital of the resistance" gathering. A young, vocal African American man, he was an even more ideal adversary for the alt-right. Bellamy, at age thirty, was the youngest person ever elected to Charlottesville City Council and at the time its only Black member.[25] When an African American high school freshman, Zyahna Bryant, started a Change.org petition in March 2016 requesting that the city council remove the statue of Robert E. Lee and change the name of Lee Park, Bellamy quickly took up the fifteen-year-old girl's cause.[26] Bellamy became the most visible proponent of the campaign to remove the statues, with a city council–created Blue Ribbon Commission on Race, Memorials, and Public Spaces spending a fractious seven months and seventeen public meetings before, with some difficulty and contestation, coming to its recommendations.[27] Bellamy's visibility as a Black politician, and especially as one who waded into fraught issues of racism and race relations, made him a lightning rod. Within alt-right circles online, Signer and Bellamy were often lumped together: the "Jew Mayor and his Negroid Deputy."[28]

Jason Kessler, the individual most responsible for arranging Charlottesville as the stage set for an empowered white nationalist movement to assert itself, also happened to be at the "capital of the resistance" gathering. A white University of Virginia graduate, Kessler had been involved with the city's Occupy protests in 2011 before getting booted out of an encampment in Lee Park because of his violent rhetoric. He then migrated to white nationalist politics. Wes Bellamy became the object of Kessler's white rage and the center of his bids for public attention, fueling his growing media skills. In November 2016 on his heretofore little-known blog, Kessler accused the vice-mayor of antiwhite bigotry, homophobia, and misogyny, using as evidence a series of tweets Bellamy had posted years earlier that Kessler found after scouring Bellamy's Twitter account. A huge story in Charlottesville, the incident got a certain amount of national coverage and suddenly Kessler had a platform and attention.[29] Kessler may have cared little about the tweets' slurs on gays or women; he wanted to discredit the city's most visible—and notably African American—proponent of taking down Confederate statues. City Council and significant parts of the community rallied around the contrite and repentant Bellamy, who nevertheless refused to resign from his political position. Bellamy, with his strong embrace of Black Lives Matter politics, had become another suitable enemy for the alt-right movement that was now seeing Kessler as an asset.

Richard Spencer, who was attempting to mainstream white racist politics, was also responsible for seeing Charlottesville as a stage set for a media event. With Kessler's participation, Spencer organized two back-to-back demonstrations in the city on May 13, 2017. Following a daytime rally in Jackson (soon to be renamed Justice) Park, and in a harbinger of events three months hence, Spencer's group materialized in Lee Park that evening hoisting torches and chanting, "You will not replace us."[30] In the speech he delivered that day, Spencer declared: "This is the beginning of a movement. This is the beginning of an awakening here in Charlottesville, an awakening that is going around the entire world."[31] Clearly Spencer wanted to use the town as a platform. The pretext was Confederate statues, but these alt-right figures were after something much bigger.

Movements often generate manifestos. Sometimes they bear the names of the places where they were composed. The 1960s saw the writing of the Sharon Statement, the Port Huron Statement, and most famously, "Letter from Birmingham Jail."[32] In the midst of the 1963 Birmingham campaign, the SCLC-led movement was in some disarray and financial stress, with many activists in jail, little bail money, and much concern that the campaign might be faltering, as had been the case the previous year in Albany, Georgia. Martin Luther King penned his statement on scraps of paper while he sat in Bull Connor's jail. His defense of nonviolent direct action, and the need to press urgently against the segregationist status quo rather than wait for moderate forces to prevail, elegantly and eloquently laid out the movement's rationale, goals, and moral vision. It was printed in magazines and as a pamphlet following the successful end of the Birmingham campaign, then immortalized in King's widely circulated book about Birmingham, *Why We Can't Wait*.[33]

Richard Spencer was probably not thinking about "Letter from Birmingham Jail" as he, along with fellow extremist Augustus Sol Invictus, penned a manifesto of the alt-right movement, which was released just before the Unite the Right rally and strategically named "The Charlottesville Statement."[34] Its purpose was to codify what the fractious and notoriously disunited conglomeration of right-wing extremists and white nationalists stood for. It was meant to do similar kind of work (albeit for diametrically opposite political purposes) as King's statement. The inclusion of the name of the city in the title of Spencer's manifesto would anchor it specifically to what was happening on the ground in the town. Alas for Spencer, the Unite the Right rally did not unfold as he and Kessler may have hoped. "The Charlottesville Statement" sank almost without a trace; Spencer's attempt to make the town's name synonymous with a triumphant, normalized, and newly unified white racist and antisemitic movement did not succeed as he would have wished.[35]

But the Unite the Right rally in Charlottesville was not about a statement any more than it was really about Confederate monuments: in a disconcerting mirror image of the civil rights movement's successful strategies in Birmingham and Selma, the UVA grads Spencer and Kessler chose Charlottesville because they knew there would be (or had every reason to expect) confrontation and violence. They knew they would face opposition by antiracist and antifascist activists. And clashing forces invariably bring media attention.

Months before the Unite the Right rally, it was already crystal clear to Kessler, Spencer, and other rally organizers that Charlottesville had a robust and quick-to-activate antiracist and antifascist community of activists. Twenty-four hours after the alt-right's set of unpermitted and unannounced demonstrations in May 2017, an array of Charlottesville activists, groups, and organizations coordinated to "take back Lee Park" and staged a counter-rally with candles. According to the independent review of protest events in the city (typically referred to as "the Heaphy Report") commissioned in the aftermath of the Summer of Hate: "The May 14 event demonstrated a degree of coordination between various activist groups in Charlottesville and their ability to rapidly mobilize a large-scale response to a perceived threat using social media and interpersonal networks."[36] Charlottesville's organized activist infrastructure would only get more coordinated and sophisticated, particularly in its use of media tools and its outreach to national and international media, as the summer progressed.[37]

The potency of counterprotesters and antiracist activists was on display July 8, 2017. A small contingent of Ku Klux Klan members from North Carolina staged a permitted rally in Charlottesville's renamed Justice Park and faced over a thousand townspeople, clergy, and small groupings of antifa militants.[38] Despite vigorous pleas from both city and University of Virginia officials to stay away and deny the motley group of Klansmen the oxygen of publicity, the protesting community showed up, well organized and angry. They saw the city and state police providing the Klan an escort service to and from the park, thereby protecting the racists while framing the antiracists as a threat. The event culminated in violence as state police tear gassed protesters who didn't disperse quickly enough.

The Klan rally received national media coverage, showcasing Charlottesville as a venue—like Portland, Oregon, and Berkeley, California, before it—for confrontation between white nationalists and activated counterprotesters. Why did alt-right organizers choose Charlottesville as the stage set for their Unite the Right event? Like SNCC's John Lewis—albeit for diametrically opposed outcomes—Kessler, Spencer, and their allies saw Charlottesville as another manifestation of "that cycle of violence and publicity and more violence and more publicity" that fuels ongoing media fascination and can be necessary for movement-building and social change. The point in this case wasn't to change laws but rather to change worldviews, at least among disaffected young white men. The point was to use the inevitable mass media attention as a coming-out party and recruitment drive. And as we'll see in the next chapter, alt-right organizers were savvy about using the media in that endeavor. As a secret directive to all Unite the Right participants released just before the rally instructed: "refrain from being overly edgy for the sake of edginess. There will be no speech police on our side, but realize that we are trying to gain sympathy from whites and the general right wing. Please refrain from roman salutes during the rally and understand that cameras are all over the place at all times."[39] Many participants did not adhere to these general conduct instructions, of course.

The stage was set.

2

BEING MEDIA-SAVVY

The Alt-Right

Twenty-first-century white nationalists and far-right extremists have displayed remarkable facility with new media tools. Beginning around 2015, numerous scholars, journalists, and media outlets began exploring the phenomenon.[1] In the aftermath of Charlottesville's Summer of Hate, sociologist Jesse Daniels, who has studied these groups for two decades, noted how the alt-right were "'innovation opportunists,' finding openings in the latest technologies to spread their message."[2] They did so by commanding discursive space on social media platforms like 4chan and Reddit, organizing via private, invitation-only Discord chat platforms and, perhaps most consequentially, mastering the art of creating and circulating edgy internet memes to lure disaffected young males into a sense of affinity with white supremacy through seemingly innocuous cartoon characters like Pepe the Frog. Alt-right figures also managed to capture mass media attention that came very close to normalizing the burgeoning movement. Local Charlottesville print media, in particular, spilled ample ink disseminating the rhetoric of Jason Kessler in the months leading up to the Unite the Right rally and provided a largely noncontextualized platform for white nationalism. For a brief moment, it appeared that the alt-right could exploit the considerable mass media attention devoted to its activities in Charlottesville, harnessing the visuality of traditional (sometimes now called "legacy") media as organizing tools. And in a most brazen flip-the-script manner, far-right extremists appropriated the media techniques first honed by the civil rights movement. They used new media as organizing and amplification tools in order to undermine and obliterate everything the Black empowerment and antiracist movements of the past half century had achieved.

KKK and New Media in the 1920s

The new media savviness of the contemporary far right may be notable, but it isn't unprecedented. The Ku Klux Klan in the 1920s managed to achieve almost mainstream status largely because of the way it embraced the new media environment of its era: publicity campaigns, tabloid newspapers, film, and radio. Historian Felix Harcourt has shown how the second coming of the Klan succeeded by embracing (albeit ambivalently) the new mass culture. According to Harcourt, "the Klan consolidated and commodified a consumable cultural identity that attempted to brand the organization as an appealing and positive force for white Protestant Americans."[3] The spectacle of cross burnings, parades, hoods, and their attendant pageantry was perfect for "the age of journalistic ballyhoo" and ensured that Klan activity around the country received plenty of press attention.[4] Along with appealing to the new journalistic environment that encouraged sensationalistic stories to boost circulation, the Klan also built its own short-lived national newspaper syndicate and even a nascent radio network. Their foray into national radio broadcasting preceded the 1926 formation of NBC, the first nationwide commercial broadcasting network, which had the economic clout of AT&T behind it.[5] Thus, the 1920s Klan used all the tools of the era's new media technology to boost its image, explode its membership, and ultimately achieve many of its political goals.[6]

The Klan and other assorted white supremacists found themselves in a very different situation in the 1950s and 1960s. The key new media technology then was network television. Martin Luther King and the SCLC developed a keen understanding of the visual and narrative characteristics of the emergent form of journalism that NBC, CBS, and ABC were innovating in the later 1950s and especially into the early 1960s. If the Klan of the 1920s exploited that era's media environment in ways useful for the organization, so too did the civil rights movement in the 1960s in a news environment that required drama, conflict, and powerful images but also, (at least in those early days of TV news) seriousness, "moderatism," and fealty to consensus politics.[7] As I've already discussed, the SCLC launched campaigns that necessitated white supremacist violence to bring the TV cameras. King revealed the usually unacknowledged strategy in a speech he delivered during the Selma campaign: "We are here to say to the white men that we no longer will let them use clubs on us in the dark corners. We're going to make them do it in the glaring light of television."[8] In places like Selma and Birmingham, those white racist men obliged.

Civil Rights–Era New Media

Unlike their predecessors forty years earlier, white supremacists and segregationists in the civil rights era had no facility or successful strategies for dealing with national media like television or other mass media platforms including national news magazines such as *Time* or the photography-oriented *Life*. The ostensibly more "respectable" White Citizens' Councils syndicated both a television talk show modeled on *Meet the Press* as well as a radio program throughout the country, in an attempt to "bring the segregationist message to the rest of the country," as Stephanie R. Rolph details in her history of the organization.[9] Yet Southern white segregationists and white supremacists were never able to frame the national debate about integration and race relations around their states' rights, local customs, and anti-communist talking points.

Alabama Governor George Wallace tried, and using a combative, populist style that made the mass media his target, set the template for future generations of conservatives and their media strategies. During the University of Alabama desegregation crisis, Wallace allowed ABC's team of documentary filmmakers to follow him even as the film crew also gained unprecedented access to JFK, and especially Attorney General Robert Kennedy in the Justice Department, as the two brothers pursued high-stakes decision-making around the crisis. The resulting documentary news special broadcast in October 1963, *Crisis: Behind a Presidential Commitment*, is a cinema verité classic. Kennedy administration officials and especially JFK and RFK understood that they had to ignore the camera crew and go about their business as if the documentarians weren't right there filming.[10] The program ended up burnishing the Attorney General's public image, almost overnight making him into a civil rights hero. Wallace, on the other hand, pointedly addressed the camera crew, a no-no in this form of documentary production. Giving a tour of the Governor's Mansion and pointing out portraits of Civil War generals, Wallace notes the filmmakers' Northern identities and inability to recognize the heroism of the Southern leaders who stood up for principle, as by extension, Wallace was about to do in standing in the schoolhouse door. While the Kennedys came off as natural and unstudied, Wallace grandstanded and speechified before the camera. This was obviously the Kennedys' show and Wallace knew it. While he may have been mostly speaking to his fellow white Alabamians, he nevertheless decided it was worth his time and effort to use this national TV platform to showcase his position of standing up against the "central government" in hopes of appealing to potentially sympathetic Americans outside the segregationist South. He managed to do so in the years ahead with inflammatory populist runs for the presidency, most notably in 1968. Political commentators, along with John Lewis, Barack Obama, and Joe Biden, have argued that Donald Trump echoes Wallace's racist, chest-thumping, grievance-oriented rhetoric.[11]

And a half century before Trump railed against "fake news," Wallace used nationally broadcast news shows like CBS's *Face the Nation* in 1964 to lambast national media for brainwashing audiences: "I think the American people are sick and tired of columnists and TV dudes who get on the national networks and instead of reporting the news as it is . . . slant and distort and malign and brainwashing [sic] this country."[12] David Greenberg has argued that the idea of "the liberal media" as a way to delegitimize national media outlets with broad reach—like the TV news networks, news magazines such as *Time* and *Newsweek*, and newspapers like the *New York Times*—didn't start, as is generally assumed, during the Nixon presidency. He argues that its genesis began among white Southern segregationists during the civil rights movement. "The critique," of national media, Greenberg notes, "cast leading journalists and journalistic institutions as part of a culturally liberal elite that was biased in favor of Black people and other racial minorities and against the values of middle-class whites. Although little heeded in the early 1960s, this idea—and the conservative populism of which it was a part—would prove to be one of the strongest political forces of the last third of the twentieth century."[13]

Richard Nixon, picking up on Wallace's strategy and the segregationists' critique, entrenched the "liberal media" trope within conservative politics. Nixon media consultant and campaign aide Roger Ailes carried the strategy further in establishing Fox News as a right-wing news platform on cable television beginning in the mid-1990s. With the rise of right-wing talk radio in the 1980s, figures like Rush Limbaugh created a media ecosystem for white male grievance and victimization. Susan J. Douglas argues that the world of political talk radio created an imagined community and preserve for a specific type of white male, within which "it became much more permissible to lash out at women, minorities, gays, lesbians, and the poor—the very people who had challenged the authority and privileges of men, of white people, of the rich and powerful, and of heterosexuals in the 1960s and 1970s. Now it was payback time."[14]

For a few years in the late 1950s into the mid-1960s, mass media had provided a selectively and provisionally sympathetic platform for a racial justice movement. For many more years, beginning with the 1987 demise of the

Fairness Doctrine, which had required broadcasters to present opposing views on controversial topics, right-wingers and the progeny of George Wallace and his ilk found much more fertile grounds in national broadcasting and the newer cable TV landscape. Rush Limbaugh would rage against "feminazis" on his radio show, which was broadcast coast to coast. Tucker Carlson, from his Fox News perch, could spout white nationalist talking points while claiming white supremacy was a hoax.[15]

White Hate Goes Online

Radio and television reaching national audiences offered potent and powerful platforms for social change activists and movements when they managed to compel attention from industry gatekeepers. But then along came the internet with its niche-oriented, anonymous, no-gatekeepers characteristics. This media format would prove particularly consequential for extreme-right organizing and movement-building in the new millennium. KKK figures like David Duke and Don Black were early settlers in cyberspace. In 1999 they created the first racist hate website, Stormfront. They also registered the domain name "martinlutherking.org," which Jesse Daniels characterizes as a "cloaked site" disseminating racist propaganda in the guise of basic information. The purpose of the website, which many students and young people would land on in their online searches about King, Daniels argues, "is to call into question the hard won moral, cultural, and political victories of the civil rights movement by undermining Dr. King's personal reputation."[16] The internet became fertile grounds for white supremacists, neo-Nazis, and Klan types, in a way television never would be. Adam Klein, a researcher on how far-right extremists operate online, notes that even when these figures appeared on sensationalistic tabloid talk shows like *The Jerry Springer Show* in the 1990s, they were easily identifiable and cartoonish, and "their bigoted viewpoints were more often mocked than feared by audiences."[17]

The internet made it much easier for white supremacists and far-right extremists to mold their own images and disseminate them globally, exploiting the affordances of these new media platforms to, as Klein, argues, "transmit, but also transform, conceal, and seamlessly merge hate speech into the mainstream of popular online culture."[18] Generally avoiding the use of traditional and easily recognizable racist and fascist images and icons, such as those signifying the Klan or Nazi Germany, many of these newer-generation white supremacist websites have employed more sophisticated and subtle imagery evoking Greco-Roman culture and the European Renaissance. Organizations like Identity Evropa, which created the "you will not replace us" chant, tended to emphasize classical statuary in its posters, flyers, and on its website: heads of Michelangelo's *David* or Nicolas Coustou's blank-eyed, towering *Julius Caesar*, accompanied by slogans like "Protect Your Heritage" and "Serve Your People."[19] The white nationalist website Occidental Dissent featured Renaissance artist Raphael's *School of Athens* painting on its main page. Metapedia, an international racist and multilingual wiki-style online encyclopedia, displays a classical Grecian male bust on its main page.

These signifiers of white European masculinity and heritage could seem almost benign to young web-surfers. But as Klein points out, these hate sites are about recruiting and about linking to other, often increasingly more virulent sites,

Identity Evropa poster.

Masthead of Occidental Dissent, a prominent white nationalist website.

as well as YouTube videos, podcasts, racist rock music, online gaming, and chat communities on 4chan and Reddit. "It is . . . easy to draw a circle around known hate websites," Klein argues, "But it is much more difficult to effectively tackle the burgeoning issue of online fanaticism that has permeated our favorite political forums, social, and video-sharing websites."[20]

Gamergate and the Origins of "You Will Not Replace Us!"

The world of video gaming might not seem like an obvious platform for extremist hate recruiting. A preserve traditionally dominated by young white males, the game world was attracting increasing numbers of female and non-white players and game developers. Some critiqued the violent misogyny and racist stereotyping endemic in many popular games. And then in 2014, a high-profile feminist game developer named Zoë Quinn became the subject of a massive online harassment campaign eventually labeled "#Gamergate." Other feminists and people of color who supported Quinn were similarly doxed, swatted, and inundated with violent threats by mostly young white male gamers. According to Bailey Poland in her book *Haters: Harassment, Abuse, and Violence Online*, these harassers believed that any attempts to open up and diversify gaming served merely to oppress "true" gamers. They disparaged their enemies as "social justice warriors" and "professional victims." When Quinn successfully slapped a restraining order on their main harasser, the misogynist conspiracy theorist and alt-right extremist with a law degree, Mike Cernovich, he threatened Quinn with a lawsuit on First Amendment grounds: this was about stifling men's free speech.[21]

Gamergate trolls insisted that their concern was really about ethics in game-world journalism (Quinn's harassers falsely accused Quinn of trading sex for positive reviews from a video game reviewer). But this was all merely a smoke screen, a way to give the coordinated hate campaign a veneer of legitimacy. The point of #Gamergate as it mushroomed online was to police the world of games as a white male preserve, to generate so much shrill and over-the-top screaming that journalists tended to interpret it all as satirical or juvenile trolling, but then to use the conglomeration of aggrieved young men thus assembled as a rallying point for something bigger. As a Vox journalist observed in 2020 looking back on the phenomenon, "Gamergate was all about disguising a sincere wish for violence and upheaval by dressing it up in hyperbole and irony in order to confuse outsiders and make it all seem less serious."[22] Gamergate turned into a recruiting drive for far-right extremists to bond with young white male gamers and help build a new political movement. Its mantra: "You will not replace us."

There's an almost perfectly direct line from 2014's #Gamergate to 2017's #Charlottesville. From a smoke screen about ethics in games journalism to a smoke screen about protecting Confederate monuments. From an assertion of First Amendment rights for white men in the gaming world to the same assertion of free speech for neo-Nazis and Klansmen in the parks of Charlottesville. From journalists and other observers misunderstanding the inherent violence behind Gamergate activity to the same blindness about Unite the Right organizing. The movement that began coalescing around a set of violent white male grievances initially ignited online by Gamergate would find its apotheosis offline in the streets of Charlottesville.

Meme Magic and Pepe the Frog

Besides Gamergate, the most effective digital media weapon that the alt-right exploited in recruiting to its ranks was the internet meme. Rhetoricians Heather Suzanne Woods and Leslie A. Hahner argue that beginning with the 2016 presidential election, memes have come to the forefront of politics, and the alt-right was particularly innovative in using memes as "tactical propaganda."[23] As with the hate websites Adam Klein examined, memes can also, through irreverent images and humor, serve as gateways to radicalization. Unique to memes as digital material is the requirement that they spread—and do so rapidly. They are also, as Woods and Hahner point out, a shared vernacular for users and thus "the symbolic apparatus from which shared culture is managed."[24] That shared culture can be as innocuous as sharing memes like Grumpy Cat, LOLcats, Distracted Boyfriend, or Most Interesting Man in the World. And, at least initially, memes of Pepe the Frog were just irreverent fun. The cartoon figure, created by comic artist Matt Furie, was initially a "college bro" type unconcerned about social expectations. In one comic panel, an animal pal of Pepe spies him standing at the toilet peeing with his shorts down around his ankles. His unembarrassed, smiling response: "Feels good man."

The character and this catchphrase spread on 4chan for some time before Pepe got appropriated by alt-right meme creators who began loading him up with Nazi imagery.[25] But the semiotic flexibility of internet memes meant it was sometimes hard to determine if the Nazi Pepe memes were merely jokes meant to get a rise out of much-too-serious people and push at cultural boundaries. Pepe was such a silly cartoon character, after all. However, for those willing and prepared to play around with far-right extremist imagery and meanings, Pepe worked as a kind of gateway drug into the alt-right. According to Woods

Matt Furie's original Pepe the Frog and his catchphrase.

Alt-right meme-ing of Pepe the Frog: Joke or signifier of a unified movement?

and Hahner, the figure began to operate as an icon enabling the fractious and nonmonolithic alt-right "to become publicly and collectively marked."[26] The alt-right seemed, at least online, to be a unified movement.

All of this online recruitment, meme-ing, and digital spreading of new age white hate came together in the Unite the Right rally, an attempt to build the alt-right into an "in real life" movement in the streets. We can examine how rally organizers and planners used their new media experience and successes by examining a heavily circulated artifact produced for the rally. While numerous posters and announcements were created for the rally, one dominated as the quasi-official poster. And its aesthetic design hit all the buttons of alt-right appeals.

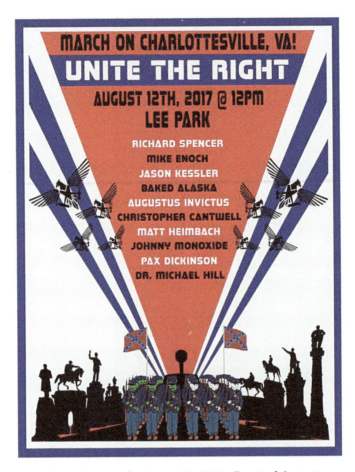

Unite the Right poster for August 12, 2017 rally: Confederate Pepes, monuments, Nazi eagles.

Let's start with the curious set of eagles flying off on either side of the image. Are they representations of the American eagle? Maybe, but the graphic design doesn't really suggest traditional imagery of the US bald eagle. The design more closely evokes the Nazi *Reichsadler* with its vaguely art deco styling, but it's just ambiguous enough for deniability—or joking. Like Richard Spencer at an alt-right gathering right after Trump's inauguration, leading his followers in a "Hail Trump! Hail our people! Hail victory!" chant, and then explaining it as merely irony and exuberance, the Nazified eagles on the Unite the Right poster could be laughed away as ironic fun. Let's melt some liberal snowflakes and create "lulz."[27]

Then there are the silhouetted statues and monuments on the lower sides of the poster. Ostensibly the rally was a protest over the decision by Charlottesville City Council to take down the Robert E. Lee statue. None of the silhouetted statues on the poster resemble Charlottesville's Lee or Stonewall Jackson statues. What we have instead are generic monuments to great white men in classical poses, evoking Greco-Roman statuary or other heroic European monuments to masculine power, just like the handiwork of Identity Evropa. The statues are also there in a gesture to the alt-right's "manosphere" of men's rights activists who celebrate hypermasculinity, who helped orchestrate the Gamergate harassment campaign, and who use Greco-Roman classics and classicism to advocate for an unshackled, muscular white patriarchy that supposedly existed in the ancient world.[28]

And there in front of a silhouette of what may be a World War II tank marches a company of Civil War–outfitted Pepe the Frogs. Next to the Pepes is a company of Wojaks—another online cartoon character also appropriated by the alt-right and often paired with Pepe. These two figures both function as racist alt-right signaling for all the young men who had engaged with Pepe memes online for the past few years on the 4chan message board /pol/ and on the subreddit r/The_Donald: this is your event, here's your subculture. But Pepe and Wojak are also there to continue the joke: you can't take this too seriously, it's all just for fun. Ultimately, the poster serves as a perfect example of what the virulently antisemitic Andrew Anglin of the Daily Stormer called "non-ironic Nazism masquerading as ironic Nazism." As he explained in his useful, if disturbing, "A Normie's Guide to the Alt-Right": "In an age of nihilism, absolute idealism must be couched in irony in order to be taken seriously. This is because anyone who attempts to present himself as serious will immediately be viewed as the opposite through the jaded lens of our post-modern milieu."[29]

This ironic-but-not-ironic poster is one example of the public online organizing around the Unite the Right event. Just as significant, if not more so, however, was the not-publicly available organizing that occurred online, for the most part in secret. In yet another odd example of a reversed mirror image, Unite the Right organizers used a chat platform allowing for anonymous, invitation-only group discussion rooms. As we'll see below, that platform echoed the ways the young activists of SNCC in the civil rights era used a new communication technology to likewise communicate and organize secretly, away from the prying eyes of segregationists and law enforcement.

From WATS Lines to Discord

Organizing and intragroup communication was key for civil rights organizations—and not always something to be done in the open where the communication could be easily monitored by police, white supremacists, or government agencies like the FBI. SNCC, in particular, made use of a now-forgotten telephone technology called WATS lines.[30] Long-distance telephone calling was expensive in the 1960s, and throughout the South, direct dialing (even from one county to an adjacent one in the same state) often necessitated going through a local operator. The Southern employees of "Ma Bell" were all white and likely to be rather hostile to civil rights activity, apt to block or tap calls and alert local sheriffs or white supremacist organizations. WATS lines, a precursor to 1–800 numbers today, provided users access to specific wide-area telephone service for a flat rate and didn't require going through an operator. Introduced by the Bell Telephone Company in 1961, this was the newest of new media and enthusiastically seized upon, particularly by the young activists of SNCC who, as journalist Bijan Stephen described it, used the WATS line infrastructure "to live-tweet what was going on in the streets of the Jim Crow South."[31] More than that, the WATS line allowed activists in the field to alert SNCC offices about racist incidents, the need for assistance, meeting planning, and other issues—and to do so with some degree of cover from hostile prying eyes and ears.

Discord, the chat platform mostly used by gamers, was the alt-right's twenty-first-century version of SNCC's WATS line. In this case white supremacists used it to evade the surveillance and blocking activity of antiracists—another through line from Gamergate to Unite the Right. Jason Kessler, Richard Spencer, Identity Evropa's Eli Mosely, and other Unite the Right organizers set up a private server on Discord labeled "Charlottesville 2.0" for closed, top secret communications among the alt-right inner circle.[32] There were also about forty-three channels set up for specific topics like lodging, transportation, announcements, and so forth. In this secret venue, participants and organizers also discussed, debated, and advocated violence. A channel about gear and attire, for instance, had individuals posting about how to fashion makeshift weapons out of newspapers or poles. Would-be participants uploaded images

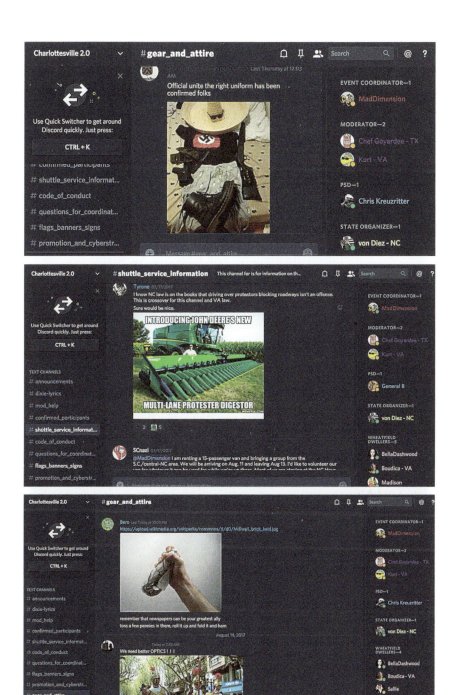

Alt-right Discord chats about upcoming Unite the Right rally: weapons (*top*), using vehicles against protestors (*middle*), violence expected (*bottom*).

of themselves armed or displaying their arsenal.[33] On a channel about shuttle service information, a number of participants posted images of vehicles to be used to plow over protesters.[34] The nonprofit, left-leaning, alternative media collective Unicorn Riot infiltrated the Charlottesville 2.0 Discord server and its channels, dumping its huge cache of screenshots documenting the organizing and discussions among participants leading up to Unite the Right. As Unicorn Riot indicated with its trove of digital evidence, Discord "was used to openly celebrate and incite violence."[35]

Charlottesville Media: "The Kids Are Alt-Right!"

Left-wing media outlets and local Charlottesville antiracist activists (as we'll see in the next chapter) were quite aware that alt-right rally organizers planned and expected violence. They also understood the virulent nature of the movement's racial politics. But readers reliant on Charlottesville's *Daily Progress*, a rather staid 125-year-old newspaper with a generally conservative editorial stance, or the town's hipper, more progressive *C-ville Weekly* would have had a much harder time comprehending just how threatening the forces behind the upcoming Unite the Right rally were. It didn't help those readers that their media provided a frequently uncritical platform for the town's leading white nationalist, who had a canny knack for driving media attention.

Throughout 2017, Jason Kessler became an increasingly visible local figure, identified by both papers typically as a "local blogger" or as a "right-wing blogger." The *Daily Progress* in several instances noted Kessler saying that he didn't identify as a white supremacist or white nationalist; the paper neglected to push back or question that assertion in any way.[36] One month before the Unite the Right rally and mere days after the KKK rally, the *Progress* appeared to perform as little more than a stenographic service for Kessler. An article attributed to "Staff" and helpfully titled "Kessler Discusses KKK, Unite the Right Rallies and His Political Beliefs" gave him space to spout an unchallenged string of easily disputable statements: the leader of the KKK chapter that had just rallied in Justice Park was "paid by 'left-wing groups to discredit legitimate conservatives'"; local groups demonstrating against him have used "violent rhetoric;" no one protected white people; and those coming to America should "see a majority European country."[37]

Kessler, a UVA graduate, was largely normalized and rendered a politically legitimized player, until close to the weekend of the Unite the Right events. But it wasn't evidence from the local antiracists, who had been organizing against him since the beginning of the year, that finally turned the tide.[38] Rather, a couple of his former far-right associates had grown uncomfortable about Kessler's association with "ideologically distasteful" individuals like Richard Spencer and groups like the blatantly neo-Nazi Traditionalist Worker Party.[39] It helped that the Anti-Defamation League released an article the week before (noted by the *Progress*) that included Kessler in a rogues' gallery of alt-right personalities and labeled him a white supremacist.[40]

Local antiracist activists had been ringing alarm bells about Kessler and his associates for months. But, as we will see, those activists never managed—until after August 12—to break out of what media scholar Daniel Hallin has labeled the "sphere of deviance" in news reporting. Hallin, in his groundbreaking analysis of Vietnam war news coverage, developed a useful and influential schema to map how mainstream media presented voices worthy and unworthy of being heard in news coverage of controversial issues. During much of the Vietnam antiwar movement, activists and protesters were not seen as coming from legitimized political viewpoints. In his schema, the two wings of the Democratic and Republican parties demarcated the "sphere of legitimate controversy," and "balanced" reporting focused on contrasting positions within that ideological spectrum of viewpoints. Political perspectives outside that range were deemed deviant. Mass media reports might take account of protesters' and "radical" activists' actions, but not feel bound to present their arguments and positions. Only once newly dovish members of Congress began to embrace aspects of the antiwar movement's positions did some of its activists begin to get respectful mainstream media attention.[41]

Kessler and other alt-right white nationalists like Richard Spencer found themselves included in the sphere of legitimate controversy for a brief but potent period following the Trump election.[42] Their brand of white grievance appeared in line with a segment of the Republican party but most particularly with the new occupant of the Oval Office. The voices opposing and "balancing" Kessler in local Charlottesville media were predictable ones: elected officials like Mayor Mike Signer and other members of City Council; law enforcement leaders like Charlottesville's police chief, Al Thomas; business leaders; and occasionally local clergy. Antiracist activists had a much harder time getting their voices heard.

Even as Kessler's image was slowly becoming more toxic in local reporting, *C-ville Weekly* decided to feature Kessler's face on its August 9–15 cover.

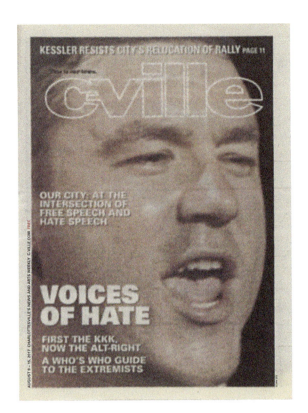

Platforming Kessler: The cover of *C-ville Weekly*, August 9, 2017.

The issue went into distribution all over Charlottesville in the paper's distinctive and ubiquitous blue news boxes scattered throughout downtown and in shopping and public venues around the city. The issue hit the news boxes on Wednesday just as Unite the Right participants were beginning to arrive, along with international media personnel and hundreds and hundreds of counter-protesters. Even with (or perhaps because of) the scare headline "Voices of Hate," Kessler and his white nationalist confederates couldn't have asked for a better media platform. Kessler's image would be unavoidable to anyone spending time in Charlottesville's public spaces over those turbulent days.

If the literal platforming of Kessler wasn't problematic enough, the inside story, a who's-who guide to the major figures headlining the rally, managed to hit all the wrong notes. Consider the cheeky, cutesy title of the article: "The Kids Are Alt-Right." It was a pun on the 1965 song "The Kids Are Alright" by the Who during their British Mod period, evoking a different kind of generational rebellion. *C-ville*'s title suggested that these particular "kids" were more to be made fun of than to be taken seriously as urgent threats. The breezy thumbnail sketches treated the virulent racism and antisemitism of the profiled figures as matters to be ridiculed. Readers learned this about Richard Spencer: "Hates most: Any color except white." About Matthew Heimbach of the Traditionalist Worker Party: "Hates most: Jews."[43] The article quoted copiously from Andrew Anglin's "A Normie's Guide to the Alt-Right," providing yet more oxygen for the Daily Stormer's brand of fascism and Hitler-worship.

The failure of local journalism was only compounded by a major editorial the *Daily Progress* ran concurrently with *C-ville Weekly*'s effort. *C-ville* minimized and eye-rolled at the menace posed by the Unite the Right attendees. The daily paper, however, stern and grim as the weekly was glib and facetious, did see menace. It saw a "conflagration that continues to escalate."[44] But according to this op-ed, it wasn't Kessler or his cronies causing the fire. The fault lay at the feet of the city's African American vice-mayor, Wes Bellamy. In the *Progress*'s view, Bellamy had turned into an "outspoken agitator" with a fistful of matches that he kept dropping into "a gas field" that had erupted into a "raging fire" because of him. In the editorial's hyperventilated prose, Bellamy not only bore responsibility for the town's year-long protests, the Klan rally, and the imminent Unite the Right gathering, he was to blame for Jason Kessler. Kessler's key action in the editorial's narrative was uncovering Bellamy's "racist, sexist and homophobic tweets." Ascribing racism to an African American local leader fighting white supremacy was a surprising move. Kessler was otherwise absent from the *Progress*'s narrative of the escalating conflagration in Charlottesville. Missing also was any acknowledgment of Kessler's role as an organizer of the Unite the Right rally and his responsibility for the spring- and summer-long influx of virulent racists and neo-Nazis into Charlottesville.

The editorial didn't fully lump Bellamy together with the counterprotesters and antiracist activists; journalistic norms would place him, as an elected official, within the sphere of legitimate controversy. However, by labeling him an agitator metaphorically lighting the city on fire (as looters would do), the editorial's impulse was to consign him to the sphere of deviance along with the disruptive and confrontational activists. In fact, the paper overtly mapped out the spectrum of political deviancy: it placed the Ku Klux Klan on one side, and on the other side, Showing Up for Racial Justice (SURJ), the most visible and militant local group organizing the community's opposition to Kessler, the Klan, and the Unite the Right rally. The paper confidently asserted, "We observe that the feelings of a majority of our community lie somewhere between" these "protesters." This equating of antiracist activists with white supremacists and neo-Nazis—presenting both sides as extremist, dangerous, disruptive, and violent—served as a recurring motif in local coverage throughout the spring and summer.

Mass Media Marches

Most attention paid to the alt-right's media savviness has focused on their facility with new social media tools. But in one area of traditional or "old" media, the alt-right harnessed the same skills the Ku Klux Klan of the 1920s mastered: visual media meant for mass audiences. Consider the Klan's 1925 march on Washington. The Klan was at the apex of its revived political strength when it brought thirty thousand white-robed but barefaced members, male and female, to parade down Pennsylvania Avenue. The spectacle was obviously

KKK rally in Washington, D.C.: Orchestrating a march for the camera. (Library of Congress)

meant for the cameras, both those of newspaper photographers and for the new medium of the motion picture newsreel. Newsreels were compilations of nonfiction events or news items of topical interest shown in movie theatres before the feature film. A very loose precursor to television news, newsreel items typically emphasized visually dramatic material. Pathé News, the pioneering newsreel film company, captured the Klan's 1925 march with a title card estimating the numbers at forty thousand and ballyhooing how the marchers "clad in full regalia—make a wonderful spectacle."[45] Striking and spectacular images were precisely what Pathé and other newsreel companies prized.[46] The Klansmen and -women obliged. Choreographed with military precision, one contingent of marchers formed a white cross, but it's only visible from a high perch. A Pathé News camera just happened to capture the marching white cross from atop a building looking down on Pennsylvania Avenue. One might assume that march organizers knew where the cameras might be and constructed a spectacular image accordingly. Other shots provide views of masses of identically clad Klansmen and Klanswomen streaming past Pathé's street-level camera in seemingly endless procession.

The civil rights era provided no comparable spectacular images of white

Klan media savvy: Disciplined, bare-faced marching. (Library of Congress)

supremacist strength and visual power. Rather, it was the civil rights movement that delivered the analogous sets of images, with its own March on Washington. Highly conscious of the TV news cameras and photojournalists who would be covering the march in numbers "exceeding even Presidential inaugurals," according to final organizing material the NAACP sent out to field staff, organizers ensured that marchers would be "camera-ready": most African American participants dressed in Sunday-best dresses and suits with ties, despite the humid late August weather.[47] While in popular memory the 1963 March on Washington for Jobs and Freedom is remembered for Martin Luther King's "I Have a Dream" speech, at the time the news media, the TV coverage in particular, focused mostly on the quarter of a million marchers, their dignity, peacefulness, and good humor. That didn't just happen—it was planned and organized to be that way.

White supremacists and racists, after their 1920s heyday in the mainstream, appeared to have lost any talent for producing powerful, widely circulated, provocative, and arresting visual material consumable by a mass audience. Until August 11, 2017.

Tiki Torches

What happened that evening on the Grounds of the University of Virginia is now generally referred to as the "tiki torch parade." The lighted flames served as the essential prop wielded by alt-right marchers that night. Let's consider the semiotic meanings attached to this object. March attendees were not instructed to make their own torches, even as many made their own shields. Organizer Eli Mosley of Identity Evropa, in a final operation order to all participants, instructed participants to purchase torches, "which can be bought from a local Wal-Mart, Lowes, Home Depot, etc."[48] Tiki torches would be easy to find at those big box stores in the middle of the summer, because the product since the 1950s has been synonymous with summer backyard barbecues, cookouts, and get-togethers with vaguely Polynesian themes. Wholesome, a bit retro, and a tad silly with its bamboo-woven head and snuffer cap bobbing from a string, the tiki torch was an inoffensive signifier of summer outdoor fun.

But now let's consider the meanings attached to massed men marching in unison with lighted torches. Ku Klux Klan gatherings in the 1920s and Nazi rallies in 1930s Germany immediately come to mind. In twentieth-century history, torch parades are inevitably linked semiotically to white supremacy and

Nazi torch rally.

Unite the Right tiki torch parade. (Sanjay Suchak, photographer)

fascism. Obviously, alt-right organizers knew this. They yoked together their coming out into the open demonstration of in-real-life potency with a visually striking image of white power.

But wait. Those are just backyard barbecue tiki torches. Like the Unite the Right poster and Pepe the Frog memes, alt-right adherents could laughingly dismiss it all as "just for fun" games meant to get a rise out of humorless liberals, yet another example of over-the-top histrionics like the Gamergate antics that signal white male potency but also could be dismissed as hyperbolic stunts. On the one hand, we've got an image of fearsome and hateful young white men chanting "You (Jews) will not replace us!" and "Blood and Soil!" as they stream across UVA's iconic Grounds. On the other hand, they hold up a familiar, formerly innocuous item redolent associations with summer parties. So, per Andrew Anglin's point about ironic uses of Nazi symbols, one takeaway might be: don't take this too seriously, they're only playacting torches.

Nevertheless, the images that splashed all over mass media venues in the days, months, and years that followed do not suggest irony and a don't-take-this-too-seriously stance. The visual power—and potential organizing utility—of the tiki torch parade comes from the disciplined demeanor of its subjects. The mostly young men who participated did what they were told to do. Eli Mosley's instructions on "General Conduct" pointed out that "cameras are all over the place at all times" so he counseled against what he disingenuously labeled "roman salutes" or being "overly edgy for the sake of edginess." The point was to "gain sympathy from whites and the general right wing."[49]

Mosley's strategy here echoes the approach employed by the NAACP and other organizers of the 1963 March on Washington. According to an NAACP statement, organizers were "convinced that tens of thousands of people demonstrating with discipline and dignity by their very presence will create great sympathy with our objectives."[50] Disorder and disruptiveness would do the opposite. Nice clothes, disciplined behavior, and a constant awareness that white people would be watching via the massive mass media presence: the March on Washington presented "respectability politics."[51] So too did the alt-right tiki torch rally: most of the participants observed the dress code of polo shirts and khaki pants, a sartorial style connoting middle-class suburban dads. The point was to look "respectable" enough—well ordered and self-controlled enough—to appeal to white conservatives.

The news footage and photographs show mostly younger men (and a very few young women) who, for the most part, heeded the dress code. They chant in unison, with deep voices predominating. They maintain their march formation as they circle around UVA's Central Grounds. The dramatically lit Rotunda forms a spectacular backdrop. It's a useful prop, too, just like the torches. The red brick, white-columned, and white-domed building, modeled by Thomas Jefferson on Rome's Pantheon, does very specific semiotic work for the alt-right. Jalane Schmidt, a UVA faculty member as well as leader of Black Lives Matter Charlottesville, has examined how the alt-right, particularly Identity Evropa, made use of Greco-Roman architecture in its propaganda. Buildings like those that comprise Jefferson's "Academical Village" valorize, glorify, and center whiteness. As Schmidt notes, "UVA's neoclassical design was intended to signal ancient Greco-Roman roots of modern ideals of participatory democracy, citizenship and civic belonging, self-determination and freedom of speech. But the exercise of these values was limited to whites, whose racial subjectivity was the antithesis of the enslaved status assigned to African American people who built UVA's iconic structures. UVA's neoclassical architecture, and the material culture of the Rotunda, a designated UNESCO World Heritage Site, work to racialize the UVA Lawn as 'white' space."[52]

In taking over that space with all its visual grandeur, the alt-right not only claimed and reclaimed it for whiteness ("You will not replace us!") but exploited the affordances of photographic media to amplify the act. By melding lit torches and a lit-up Rotunda, and with not-too-edgy disciplined white men, the alt-right created potentially its most potent instance of white-power propaganda.[53]

The confrontation with a small group of counterprotesters on the plaza dominated by a statue of Thomas Jefferson in front of the Rotunda, which culminated the rally, didn't diminish the propaganda power of the march. It actually enhanced it—at least it appeared to initially. The antiracist group of students with a large cloth banner reading "VA Students Act Against White Supremacy" chanted "Black Lives Matter" but were drowned out by the swarming alt-right marchers. Confrontation ensued. Chris Cantwell (subsequently known as "The Crying Nazi" for a viral video of him sobbing at the prospect of arrest) deployed mace, but also got hit with it himself.[54] Nevertheless, the image that mattered for the alt-right participants was the culmination of the march: the surrounding of Jefferson's statue and the overpowering of "antifa."[55]

A march participant who livestreamed the entire march triumphantly reported to his viewers at the end of the event, "That's what victory looks like in these streets. Antifa was here as a welcoming party. They got thrown out. They gassed themselves. Fuckin' retards." Proclaiming that they took back the statue, he advised everyone watching to come tomorrow: "Total victory tonight."[56]

Perhaps. But alt-right adherents weren't the only ones capable of whipping up some meme magic. Almost as soon as the images of the tiki torch parade began circulating late on August 11, people on social media began ridiculing the marchers specifically for using tiki torches—proclaiming white supremacy while hoisting props redolent of nonwhite Polynesian culture. A photo of marchers in front of the Rotunda became a favorite image to meme in the hours after the parade, before the violence and mayhem of August 12.[57] One well-liked post on Twitter captioned the photo, "Narrator: And that's when the luau went south."

The next day would not be a propaganda victory, of course. August 12 would not provide the kind of media imagery the alt-right needed to boost itself further into a full-fledged in-real-life movement. A12 would do the opposite.

Meme-ing and ridiculing the tiki torch parade on social media until August 12 changes everything.

The Essential Violence of White Supremacy

So, how can we make sense of "Charlottesville" and its attendant violence in comparison to "Selma" and "Birmingham" and the violence associated with those events? What's the thematic through line? The civil rights movement needed media attention, not only to document the injustice of segregation and disenfranchisement but also to display the inevitable and inherent violence of racism and white supremacy. The only way to truly shock the conscience of the nation, discomfort the white "moderates" who were satisfied with the go-slow approaches that Martin Luther King so powerfully critiqued in his "Letter from Birmingham Jail," and motivate action was to orchestrate situations to reveal the viciousness and brutality of white supremacy. When King, during the Selma campaign, talked about making white men use their clubs in front of TV cameras, he wasn't suggesting the civil rights movement could manipulate those white men to do things they otherwise would not do. White supremacy was essentially violent; the trick was to make it visible to all—to broadcast it.

The Unite the Right rally served as a contemporary broadcasting of that essential truth. And like civil rights activists before them, local Charlottesville antiracist activists attempted to publicize that truth—in this case by trying to prevent the rally and its participants from congregating in their town. In a reversal from the Birmingham and Selma situations, activists had no desire for a confrontation with white supremacists, no desire to prove again that white supremacists are always going to be violent. In a letter to City Council a month before the rally, activists pleaded for a rescinding of Kessler's rally permit because of the threats of violence documented with screenshots they'd obtained of both public and private social media messages among alt-right figures.[58] Showcasing white supremacist violence on national TV served a moral and political purpose fifty years earlier; providing a media platform for alt-right violence and intimidation in the streets of Charlottesville in 2017 suggested that the victories that Birmingham and Selma represented not only weren't permanently won but were existentially threatened in the Trump era. The violence of August 11 and 12 might have been avoided had counterprotesters, heeding the pleas of city council officials and University of Virginia administrators, stayed home. But a central tenet of being antiracist is to show up and oppose manifestations of racism. Similarly, antifascists will not allow fascists to claim space. The organizers of Unite the Right knew this.

One of the lessons of Birmingham and Selma was the efficacy of dramatic confrontation between opposing forces to draw television cameras, photojournalists, and reporters. Alt-right organizers knew they would face organized opponents in Charlottesville. That was always the plan: it's clear from the cache of Discord chats. "Charlottesville" ended up telling the same story about white supremacy that Birmingham and Selma did. Its evils were put on display again, as were the forces struggling against that evil. What made the Charlottesville event a reversed mirror image, however, is the fact that the racists and fascists were the instigators—they were organizing and trying to build a movement. Counterprotesters were forced into a reactive position. However, Charlottesville's antiracist activists weren't without powerful resources. In fact, so much attention has been lavished on the media savviness of the alt-right that their actual weakness is often overlooked. The alt-right failed to generate a movement "in real life" in the streets of Charlottesville in part, at least, because their opponents proved to be even more media-savvy.

3

BEING MORE MEDIA-SAVVY

Charlottesville Antiracist Activists

In March 2017 activists dropped banners strategically placed throughout Charlottesville, including a huge one right above police headquarters, demanding: "Where is Sage Smith?" An action on the plight of Black trans women, the point was to put a very public spotlight on the fact that police had done little on the case of a local young trans woman's disappearance. She had been missing since late 2012 and was presumed murdered. In 2014 the disappearance of another young Charlottesville woman, Hannah Graham, an eighteen-year-old white UVA student, generated national headlines, extensive coverage on CNN, and a relatively quick and tragic break in that case. Sage Smith never got CNN coverage.[1] The activists used bold and confrontational tactics to generate media attention in an attempt to bring needed resources to the Sage Smith case.[2]

Charlottesville's local media environment wasn't particularly open or sympathetic to militant antiracist activists. Those activists would need to build their own media platforms, not only to organize but to amplify their own voices and arguments, coordinate with other activist groups, and provide a venue of information and logistics for community members who might want to engage in protest activity. Using confrontational and creative media skills like those mobilized on behalf of Sage Smith, antiracist activists deployed new media tools to organize against the alt-right, subverting and messing with their activities, both online and in the real world. They did whatever they could to push back against white supremacists, who from the North Carolina KKK to a new generation of emboldened white nationalists, were determined to use Charlottesville as a photogenic stage to launch their movement to its next level.[3]

The alt-right appeared to be a movement on the rise, generating lots of media attention, galvanizing apparently large numbers of disaffected young white men online, and enjoying at least tacit support from the new occupant of the White House and some of his associates in the Oval Office.[4] The antiracist movement, most notably represented by the 2014 Black Lives Matter protests in Ferguson, and then sporadically again in the wake of police killings of other Black men in the following two years, generated significant media coverage. However, except for police reform consent decrees in a handful of cities—ones that, like Ferguson, had histories of abusive law enforcement—signed in 2016 but undercut by Trump's Department of Justice two years later, the movement hadn't fundamentally altered public discourse.[5] Trump's election suggested a white backlash. White nationalists had clashed with antiracists and antifascists in the spring of 2017, leading to lots of press coverage of the visual drama and tumult. The UC-Berkeley campus exploded as activists protested a planned appearance by alt-right provocateur and troll Milo Yiannopolous. That spring, Portland, Oregon, also became a flashpoint of clashes between alt-right groups and local antifascists. The loose, leaderless, and decentralized affiliation of activists referred to as "antifa" typically generated scare headlines focused on violence and mayhem.[6]

The movement of emboldened white nationalists and "western chauvinists" seemed to be signaling power and movement capacity as they planned their display to "unite the right" in Charlottesville, which followed on from all these other indications of a growing political phenomenon. Those protesting in opposition didn't appear to have corresponding movement muscle. They certainly weren't getting the media attention lavished on white extremists.

Zeynep Tufekci argues in her 2017 book, *Twitter and Tear Gas: The Power and Fragility of Networked Protest,* that in the twenty-first-century age of digital tools for organizing, movements may be able to scale up very quickly, pulling together large marches and demonstrations that in the pre-internet era would have taken months and years of tedious labor and interpersonal outreach to achieve. Movements could thereby try to signal strength and power by their ability to turn out large numbers of people.[7] Her examples include the 2011 Occupy Wall Street encampments in the US, Egypt's Tahrir Square protests that same year, and the 2013 Gezi Park occupation in Turkey, the latter two expressions of the "Arab Spring" uprisings. The problem with such rapidly built movements is that they may not actually possess the internal capacity of movements that build more slowly. The Occupy protests erupted all over the US—even Charlottesville had a five-week encampment in Lee Park, eventually forcibly removed by police.[8] Once its multitude of encampments was evicted, Occupy, a leaderless phenomenon, found itself unable to develop new protest strategies to keep the movement and its political pressure going in order to push successfully for changes in legislation and the distribution of wealth.

Tufekci uses the civil rights movement as a point of comparison, much as I am doing. That movement, she argues, had to build up a resilient internal culture; it had to foster trust among both activists and movement foot soldiers, as well as create ties with the community, develop decision-making protocols, and cultivate an ability to pivot to new protest tactics in the face of inevitable adversity. Half a century and more on from the 1955 Montgomery Bus Boycott and the 1963 March on Washington that serve as her key case studies, as the Birmingham and Selma campaigns serve as mine, many social change and protest movements around the world still look to and derive inspiration from a Black empowerment movement that continues to loom large in both American and international popular memory and imagination. Tufekci focuses on how the civil rights movement signaled power in three areas she considers crucial for protest movement success: narrative capacity (a movement's ability to frame its story on its own terms), disruptive capacity (a movement's ability to successfully interrupt the regular operations of those with power), and electoral or institutional capacity (a movement's ability to impact elections or force institutional changes).[9] As I'll explore in this chapter, the activist groups who came together in Charlottesville to oppose the alt-right had developed enough internal movement strength to signal all three of these forms of capacity. The alt-right, on the other hand, appeared to collapse, signaling a fundamentally fragile movement on Charlottesville's streets on A12 and thereafter.[10]

While Tufekci's case studies all involve movements that took as their opponent state power, I'll be deploying her analytical tools somewhat differently: what happens when a protest movement takes as its opponent another protest movement? Two social change movements clashed in Charlottesville in 2017. One collapsed, while the other, bringing together antiracist and antifascist activists along with newly activated foot soldiers and community members, prevailed. How did they do so—and signal ongoing movement capacity—using an array of media tools and in the face of almost constant hostility from the local media environment?

SURJ and No-Platforming

In local Charlottesville media, a group with the evocative name "SURJ" garnered sizable amounts of attention. News coverage about Showing Up for Racial Justice tended to paint it as disruptive and violent: the ideologically extremist mirror image of the alt-right. Though not a household name nationally and around the world like Black Lives Matter, SURJ was essential to antiracist organizing in Charlottesville in the spring and summer of 2017.

Composed of people, mostly white, who are interested in being allies to Black-led organizations, SURJ is a national network of chapters and affiliated groups whose mandate is to educate and mobilize white people to engage in antiracist activism. By 2020 SURJ had well over a hundred chapters throughout the United States.[11] Originally founded in 2009, shortly after the election of America's first African American president and the concomitant upwelling in overt racism that Obama's presidency spawned, the organization originally focused mostly on education.[12] One of its founders, Pam McMichael, ran the Highlander Research and Education Center in Tennessee, which in its earlier incarnation as the Highlander Folk School had been a crucial training center during the civil rights years, welcoming Rosa Parks, Martin Luther King, SNCC activists, and others to programming for the development of social change leaders and organizing strategies.[13] In another linkage to the civil rights era, SURJ's website carried a quote from Anne Braden, a key white ally during the Southern movement: "The battle is and has always been a battle for the hearts and minds of white people in this country. The fight against racism is our issue. It's not something that we're called on to help people of color with. We need to become involved with it as if our lives depended on it because really, in truth, they do."[14] In 1963 Martin Luther King, in his "Letter from Birmingham Jail," praised Braden by name for committing herself to the struggle. She nurtured SNCC activists and worked on the staff of the Southern Conference Educational Fund, a white organization that fought against white supremacy and allied itself to civil rights–era Black empowerment organizations.[15]

Fifty years later, SURJ recreated this model for a new generation of white activists wanting to join the struggle against contemporary white supremacy. Following the police killing of unarmed teenager Michael Brown and the rise of the Black Lives Matter movement in the wake of massive protests in Ferguson, Missouri, SURJ adopted a more militant activist stance. The historical rhymes with the civil rights era reverberated.

A Charlottesville chapter of SURJ formed in 2016 in response to yet more police killings of unarmed Black men, specifically Philando Castile and Alton Sterling.[16] Beginning early in 2017, SURJ activists embraced the antifascist strategy of "no platforming." The point is to deny speech rights to fascists, neo-Nazis, and white supremacists, because their views are deemed so toxic and antithetical to liberal democracy that shutting them down and refusing them legitimizing platforms, such as college speaking venues, is necessary since it is the only effective response.[17] Such was the case in Berkeley, California, as activists successfully deplatformed Yiannopolous and also right-wing columnist Ann Coulter in February and April, 2017.[18] As we've seen, Charlottesville media provided a robust and ongoing platform for Jason Kessler. SURJ attempted to intervene in this media environment with a media education lesson for local journalists about how they ought to be covering figures like him and other white nationalists.

In February 2017 Jason Kessler, pursuing his attempt to have Vice-mayor Wes Bellamy removed from office because of his offensive tweets from years before he began his political career, held a press conference to continue bringing more media oxygen and publicity to himself and his white nationalist cause. SURJ members strongly supported Bellamy, but initially the group was torn over whether to actively confront Kessler or ignore his publicity-hound theatrics. It took the intervention of prominent women and femme activists of color, who had been active locally for many years, to convince hesitant SURJ members that Kessler had to be confronted.[19] One way SURJ did so was by trying to undermine his growing local media platform. They refused to participate in the press conference, thus denying local reporters the "both sides" model of balancing Kessler quotes with those of Bellamy supporters, which would thereby legitimize Kessler's views.

Instead, they issued a statement explicitly addressed to journalists in their role as journalists and imparted some media literacy and journalistic education. Noting how few followers Kessler had and how dependent he was on media coverage, SURJ argued that "covering his antics only legitimizes his extremist, fringe views," thus creating an environment for violence against marginalized groups. SURJ also provided local reporters with the Associated Press's guide on how to write about the alt-right, which suggested reporters clarify that the term was "a euphemism for white supremacist or white nationalist movements" and should be identified that way. Local journalists mostly ignored that advice until shortly before the calamitous Unite the Right rally.

SURJ also noted that identifying Kessler merely as a "local blogger" obscured his actual agenda: "Kessler's full background should be explained in any reports: He is a white nationalist. To do otherwise is to normalize his fringe racism."[20] Local media also neglected to follow this advice with any consistency. SURJ's attempt to intervene in the local media environment clearly demonstrated activists' media savviness and ability to deconstruct how the press was framing the story, even if they couldn't quite alter the coverage.

In an odd mirror image to the civil rights era, segregationists manifested a degree of similar media savviness in their own scrutiny of press coverage of civil rights campaigns that had damaged the segregationist cause. During the Selma campaign, for instance, white Alabamians clearly understood Martin Luther King and the SCLC's media strategy and pointed it out to each other repeatedly in local newspapers. The *Selma Times-Journal* featured news photos emphasizing the large number of reporters and photographers in front of marchers and used captions to further point out to local readers the role played by out-of-state media.[21] Letters to the editor and editorials in Alabama papers pointed out repeatedly that King's strategy was to generate publicity by creating a situation of violence that would bring the TV cameras.[22]

Segregationists in 1965 very much wanted to "deplatform" the Black empowerment movement, as they clearly understood how Martin Luther King and his followers were pursuing a media campaign. They just weren't very successful at it, even within their own sectional media outlets. Neither did the Southern white foes of integration and Black voter enfranchisement ever successfully craft media strategies to redirect national media outlets into more sympathetic accounts of the Southern "way of life," nor orchestrate compensating media imagery to contrast the photos and film coming out of the Birmingham and Selma campaigns.

Weaponizing the Civil Rights Movement

It's clear in retrospect that local media did not understand the threat posed by the alt-right, or how white nationalists intended to orchestrate their "coming-out" party in Charlottesville. But Charlottesville's press also tended to mischaracterize the local groups organizing in opposition, comparing antiracist activists in disparaging tones to 1960s civil rights activists. Consider coverage of clashes between SURJ activists and Kessler, who had been meeting with members of the neo-fascist and violent Proud Boys and other alt-right figures at outdoor restaurant terraces on the town's popular downtown pedestrian mall. The men were planning the Unite the Right rally petition, which Kessler submitted on May 30. SURJ members and other antiracists regularly confronted them. In one instance, they encircled Kessler and his cohorts as they dined alfresco, yelling at them to go home, loudly identifying them as Nazis, and demanding restaurants refuse service and seating to fascists. In all these situations, heated confrontations ensued, as did arrests.

C-ville Weekly framed SURJ and its tactics by comparing its members negatively to 1950s and 1960s civil rights protesters. Employing a sanitized popular memory of that era as "African-Americans in their Sunday best peacefully protest[ing]" while facing violence from police and racists, Charlottesville's activists "straddle the line between free speech and criminal behavior."[23] John Whitehead, founder of the Charlottesville-based, free speech–focused Rutherford Institute, compared SURJ activists disapprovingly to those of the civil rights era. Sit-ins "didn't stop someone from free speech," he complained. "You can't block other people's right to move on public property. These people need to grow up and respect other people's rights." Whitehead appeared semantically shy about identifying those "other people": neo-Nazis and white supremacists.[24]

Charlottesville activist Veronica Fitzhugh attempted to use the discourse of the civil rights movement to explain her confrontational actions towards Kessler and his associates in a *Daily Progress* article that ran around the same time as the *C-ville* piece. Asserting that she would not respect the rights of Nazis, Fitzhugh explained her belief "that violating the law in some cases is necessary for righteous movements.... 'that's how civil rights happened.'"[25] Her perspective had no traction, because her quote was buried in an article that focused on the white clergy who were highlighted in the article and framed as presenting a moderate stand against racism and for "peace, love, and justice—something that we can all get behind," in the words of a Methodist minister.

As with the notorious *Daily Progress* editorial printed on the eve of the Unite the Right rally and discussed in the previous chapter, Kessler and his alt-right cronies were rendered as passive; the aggressiveness and violence came from antiracists. The civil rights movement—or at least a very selective image of it—got weaponized to further discredit the antiracists. Even activist Jalane Schmidt, responding to the civil-rights-movement framing, equated Martin Luther King's campaigns with "respectability politics."[26] While that may have been the case in the organizing for the March on Washington, the press did not frame the Birmingham campaign as "respectable" in 1963.

While it may be no surprise to note that local Birmingham media was decidedly hostile to King's direct-action campaigns in the "Magic City," even the Black-owned *Birmingham World* disapproved, editorializing at one point that the demonstrations were "both wasteful and worthless."[27] National media wasn't much more supportive. Historian Richard Lentz has documented how the three major newsweeklies, *Time, Newsweek,* and *U.S. News and World Report,* criticized King and his movement's tactics during the campaign. According to *Time,* King's protest drive "inflamed tensions."[28] When King agreed to send children into the streets, *Newsweek* questioned whether there should be any demonstrating at all considering that Birmingham's (white) voters had elected a more "moderate" administration that waited in the wings.[29] According to Lentz, *U.S. News* "vilified [King] as an intruder inciting racial hatred in Birmingham and prepared to do the same elsewhere."[30] All three magazines castigated the campaign as ill-timed and articulated a "distaste for a confrontation that they [particularly *Time* and *Newsweek*] believed was forced by King."[31]

Majority opinion in the national press changed dramatically in the aftermath of the campaign, when Birmingham officials agreed to the movement's demands and President Kennedy subsequently felt compelled to put forth his landmark civil rights bill. Similarly, Charlottesville's counterprotesters and activists after A12 would be lauded and turned into heroes.[32] It's important to note, however, the headwinds and media disapproval these activists in 1963 and 2017 faced while they were organizing their campaigns against white supremacy.

Torchlight versus Candlelight

The weekend of May 13 changed everything for Charlottesville's activist community. Richard Spencer and his alt-right confederates held an impromptu and unannounced daytime rally in Jackson Park while many Charlottesville residents celebrated cultural diversity a few blocks away in Lee Park at the yearly Festival of Cultures, oblivious to what was happening down the street. Activists found out quickly, however, texting each other and worrying that the white supremacists might endanger the Festival of Cultures.[33] Members of SURJ, students, and other groups descended on Jackson Park as the rally was winding down. They confronted the white, polo-clad men and their Confederate and white nationalist flags with nonstop loud chanting: "All Black lives matter!";

"Fuck the fascists, fuck the KKK!"; "Racists, get outta here!" The antiracist activists trailed the retreating alt-right assemblage as they made their way down East Jefferson Street, right past Charlottesville's synagogue and through the downtown core, eventually to a parking lot at the edge of the town center, where the racists escaped in their waiting vehicles. UVa Students United, an activist organization at the University, livestreamed the entire fifteen-minute confrontation on its Facebook page, garnering upwards of eight thousand views.[34] In marching behind and around their targets, using loud chants to clearly identify their antagonists to nearby community members, and recording the entire event, the activists put into practice the strategy that would guide their approach to the alt-right going forward: confront any gathering of racists and neo-Nazis wherever they appeared in town, attempt to shut them down

No safe space for racists and fascists. May 13, 2017: Antiracist activists confront, loudly and continuously chant at, follow, and livestream alt-right rally-goers as they leave Jackson Park, pass by a synagogue (righthand image; Jason Kessler is at right), and retreat to their vehicles.

through embodied presence and noise, and make that confrontation visible using the new media tool of livestreaming video.

Jason Kessler was also adept at livestreaming. He exploited the technology promiscuously and strategically to boost his profile and stature within the online alt-right movement.[35] He also livestreamed the Jackson Park confrontation, sticking his camera in the face of one of the chanting antiracist protesters, likely choosing this individual because their appearance was gender-nonconforming. Both sides would use livestreaming to galvanize supporters and control their movement's narrative; by the end of the Summer of Hate, one side had prevailed.

That night, Kessler and Spencer staged a photo op in Lee Park with about a hundred neo-Nazis lofting tiki torches around the Robert E. Lee statue and chanting "Russia is our friend," "Blood and soil," and the soon-to-be-(in)famous "You will not replace us." The point was to generate dramatic images. In this endeavor, the white nationalists were quite successful, as they livestreamed and tweeted out torch pictures that garnered national media coverage. But the rally was short; after ten minutes counterprotesters arrived, scuffles ensued, and police broke up the event.[36] The brevity of the rally didn't really matter. What counted were the powerful and provocative media images.

Activists and townspeople responded with their own rally in the park the following evening, galvanized by a text message that circulated among activists and allies Sunday morning. The rally call noted the potency of the media imagery Richard Spencer and his acolytes had created: "Bring all the candles you can find. We will outshine their torches with our love, but we will also be sending a message that they will not come here to intimidate us unchallenged. We will recreate that monstrous photo of them, but our light will radiate with our families and communities standing in solidarity for justice."[37] The May 14 gathering brought together hundreds of local residents in Lee Park, all carrying candles, which generated powerful oppositional imagery. Coverage of the events in national media outlets juxtaposed pictures of the torch rally with film and photos of the candlelight gathering, setting up a powerful semiotic contrast.[38] The activists who hastily organized the event understood the importance of image politics every bit as much as did Richard Spencer, whose tweeted-out selfie with glowing eyes and tiki torch had gone viral. But in an early demonstration of the local antiracist and antifascist movement's disruptive capacity, activists were able to orchestrate a counternarrative of community solidarity and robust opposition to everything Spencer and his band stood for. Spencer may have gotten a mass media platform, but in an exercise of media jujitsu, counterprotesters highjacked his imagery with their own.

Charlottesville activists' successful ability to quickly counter the alt-right visual media campaign from its earliest manifestation compares notably with the inability of Southern segregationists to do so during the civil rights move-

Contrasting alt-right torchlight with antiracist and antifascist candlelight: National media coverage juxtaposed images from Richard Spencer's May 13, 2017 tiki torch rally in Lee Park with Charlottesville's community candlelight gathering the following night.

ment. Consider media coverage of the Selma campaign. George Lewis, a historian of Massive Resistance and Southern segregation, notes that photojournalism of the Selma campaign provided national audiences with very limited and two-dimensional images of segregationist resistance: lines of identical, featureless blue-uniformed law enforcement officers as "machines of the state," never individualized, often positioned away from direct camera view, depicted as faceless automatons without personal agency defending Jim Crow.[39] More generally mass media tended to portray segregationists as young delinquents in ducktail haircuts, sloppy clothing, flipping the middle finger or grabbing their crotch to show disdain towards the photographer. Or, as we will see in the next chapter, segregationists were captured yelling invectives, their mouths black holes of hatred. National media outlets were no more sympathetic to white supremacists in 2017 than they had been in 1965, but because of the affordances of new media tools in the digital age, the alt-right proved more successful in orchestrating coverage that presented a new generation of racists in compelling and captivating ways. It made it that much more important for antiracists to undermine and undercut the alt-right media campaigns.

Solidarity Birmingham 1963 to Solidarity Cville 2017

How does a protest movement ramp up quickly and mobilize a local population? What social media tools are particularly effective? In 1955, those tools included forty thousand bus boycott flyers that Professor Jo Ann Robinson wrote up and that she and her students at Alabama State College mimeographed and distributed to the Black community right after Rosa Parks's arrest. They also included telephone trees as Black female volunteers from Montgomery's Women's Political Council commandeered the phone system to spread the word. Male volunteers canvased the barbershops and pool halls. But the most important social media platform utilized by activists in Montgomery to get out the message urging the community to avoid using the city buses on Monday, December 5, were the local Black churches. One church in particular, Dexter Avenue Baptist Church, pastored by a new-to-town young reverend named Martin Luther King Jr., served as the key social platform for galvanizing the community, explaining the rationale for the boycott, and then as the weeks and months of boycotting unfolded, keeping the community committed, informed, and reenergized.[40]

The Montgomery Bus Boycott set the template for the civil rights movement and the role of Black churches in the struggle. The 16th Street Baptist Church in Birmingham and Brown Chapel AME Church in Selma were crucial to the successes of those two campaigns and in knitting together a community of activists and foot soldiers. But for the Birmingham campaign in particular, a new media platform also proved indispensable: Black radio.

These local stations blossomed in the post–World War II era, with white owners but featuring Black DJs who became local celebrities playing music by Black performers, including gospel and other sacred music as well as popular rhythm and blues.[41] Birmingham had three stations, including WENN, with offices right in the middle of Birmingham's Black neighborhood, two blocks from the 16th Street Baptist Church and one block from Kelly Ingram Park, which would feature so prominently in the iconic photographs of the Children's Crusade. Those radio stations and their popular DJs managed to galvanize and communicate to rank-and-file foot soldiers, especially young ones, more effectively and quickly than any other form of outreach. Considering the hostility to King's campaign of Birmingham's local media environment in 1963, including its Black-owned newsweekly, it was challenging to get word out to the local Black community. The DJs, often resorting to code words and phrases to hide their messages from white owners, managed to reach middle and high schoolers, who were less likely to be regular churchgoers and who weren't already movement activists. And once those youngsters were activated, the Black DJs assisted by broadcasting coded instructions to the hundreds of activists as they spilled into the streets in the midst of the Children's Crusade.[42] According to civil rights historian Brian Ward, Birmingham's Black-oriented radio stations helped foster "the sense of common identity, pride, and purpose" on which the community's civil rights activism was built.[43] Another researcher notes, "The 'foot soldiers' of the local movement credit the Black radio stations in the city with providing an outlet through which listeners could feel part of a cohesive unit."[44] One could call it *Solidarity Birmingham*.

Charlottesville in 2017 also had a rather hostile local media environment when it came to antiracist and antifascist confrontational activism. But in an era of digital media tools and social media platforms, activists could find ways to get the word out. Local groups, such as SURJ and UVa Students United, and high-profile activists like Emily Gorcenski had robust Facebook and Twitter platforms to spread word about rallies and mobilizations. They and other activist groups had been successful in galvanizing hundreds for the candlelight vigil. But in the wake of the May 13 weekend, activists from a range of groups and organizations realized that they would need to work together to confront the growing menace of the alt-right and other white supremacists using Charlottesville as an organizing and media platform. At the same time that Kessler was coordinating with other fascists to assemble his Unite the Right rally, antiracist activists and groups organized themselves into a "spokes council" coalition. They also create a powerful networking, amplification, and organizing platform: *Solidarity Cville*.[45]

Over the course of the summer of 2017, Solidarity Cville evolved beyond being a network connected to local chapters of SURJ, Black Lives Matter, and the newly formed clergy group, Congregate. Most significantly, it was a media outlet. The anonymous members of the collective practiced media relations work, reaching out to journalists, particularly those associated with national and international news platforms. Recognizing the unsympathetic local media ecosystem, Solidarity Cville activists took a leaf from the civil rights movement playbook in prioritizing outreach to and cultivation of nonlocal reporters.[46] These activists realized long before the August 12 weekend that what was happening in Charlottesville with the alt-right and the Klan had national and even global implications. The voices of antiracist activists had to be boosted: Solidarity Cville would be the vehicle for generating much-needed narrative capacity.

As a media platform, Solidarity Cville also dispensed information about, and movement narrative framing of, the movement. With a very basic blog-style website and Twitter account, the collective did the crucial outreach to interested community members, not unlike what Black radio did in Birmingham. Would-be activists and foot soldiers not already in the orbits of Charlottesville's social justice organizations needed to be appealed to, educated, and mobilized.

Media coverage of the candlelight vigil served as the impetus for Solidarity Cville's first statement, which noted that no one had recorded the speeches by the vigil's organizers. And while local Black community leader Don Gathers was interviewed in national media stories, Mayor Mike Signer got more attention, despite having nothing to do with the vigil. Daily Kos, a wide-reaching left-progressive blogging, news, and digital media platform, even implied that Signer was responsible for organizing the event.[47] Activists exploded in outrage. They saw Signer, who voted against removal of the statues, as an adversary, if not an outright enemy. Activists and organizers of the vigil needed to find ways to assert control over the narrative of antiracist organizing in Charlottesville.

Throughout the rest of the summer, Solidarity Cville would serve as a one-stop shop providing press releases, lists of demands to City Council, alternative news reporting, statements from activists, advisories about upcoming events, boosting of local organizing groups and their needs, and perhaps most usefully in the days before August 12, a list of items for community members on how to prepare for direct action to counter the Unite the Right rally.[48] A chronicle about the collective's history noted, "We learned how to craft press releases, how to coordinate with reporters, how to prep community organizers for press interviews, and how to spread our message on social media."[49] A half century earlier, Matin Luther King's SCLC had found itself in the same situation, having to quickly learn how to navigate the new media environment, particularly the affordances of network television. King discovered how to speak in what would come to be called "sound bites." The movement learned to schedule demonstrations to coordinate with network news timetables and ascertained how to spread the civil rights message by staging dramatic and morally clear direct-action campaigns that would be compelling to visual media platforms.[50]

Solidarity Cville and local activists took another leaf from SCLC's playbook by engaging in protest event planning. On July 8, they coordinated a powerful and creative response to an appearance by the Loyal White Knights of the Ku Klux Klan.

#Klanbusters and #BlocKKKparty: Meme-ing the Resistance

Scholars and journalists have heaped plenty of attention on the alt-right's penchant for creating and disseminating cheeky, irreverent, but also outrageous and offensive memes designed to go viral and build their movement, and which perhaps assisted in Trump's election.[51] The concurrent popular assumption has been that "the left can't meme." Dismissed as too "politically correct," earnest, and humorless to be able to counter the gleefully provoking and "triggering" creations of the extreme right, critics have argued that antiracist and antifascist activists were largely unable to counter the alt-right on this digital media terrain.[52]

Charlottesville activists certainly tried. In organizing against the July 8, 2017, Ku Klux Klan rally in Justice (formerly Jackson) Park, they achieved some success. If activists were able to get hundreds to counterprotest the alt-right tiki torch rally in May, only two months later with the formation of Solidarity Cville they turned out at least two thousand, mostly local community members but also some antifa contingents from out of town.[53] On a much larger scale, protesters did what the small May 13 group had done: yell, chant, and make as much noise as possible with drums and air horns to drown out any speeches by the Klan. The activists displayed quite powerful disruptive capacity, not only against the Klan but against a "don't take the bait" narrative dominating local media.

Solidarity Cville promoted it as a "BlocKKKparty." It certainly made for an effective hashtag and a label for the counterdemonstration. Solidarity Cville activists understood that they needed to boost publicity for the event and to push back against the bigger and louder media platforms available to University and city officials. UVA President Teresa Sullivan and Mayor Mike Signer were all over local media encouraging residents to ignore the Klan, avoid confronting the racists, or consider attending University- and city-sanctioned gatherings away from Justice Park and its environs.[54] Local activists had to both counter the "don't take the bait" narrative, circulated in particular by Signer and Police Chief Al Thomas, as well as signal the oppositional movement's own narrative capacity by framing its protest action in cogent, imaginative, creative, and persuasive ways.

A "BlocKKKparty" may have sounded initially like a festive occasion. Some community members objected to the implication that this would be some kind of fun gathering—an actual block party.[55] Organizers did inject a degree of irreverence and pop-culture cheekiness in their organizing materials, including a much-circulated *Ghostbusters* pastiche. Local artist J. Brian McCrory took the 1984 movie's iconic logo and tweaked it slightly, creating a cartoonish, canceled, ghostly Klansman. Charlottesville antiracist organizers saw the meme-worthiness of McCrory's work. The image decorated SURJ Facebook posts, local BLM's Twitter feed in the days leading up to the rally, as well as on posters at a rally a week before the KKK event and most notably in a Medium article by Jalane Schmidt laying out, much like Martin Luther King did with his "Letter from Birmingham Jail," the antiracist case for white moderates to stop valuing their convenience and comfort over the fierce urgency of confronting white supremacy.[56] A caption on the image encouraged people to reproduce it and "send this meme viral!" The organizers' penchant for appropriating childlike cartoon imagery extended even to the *Care Bears*. A poster for the upcoming counterprotest included, along with the Klanbusters image, a not-so-cheery pink Cheer Bear sporting the Klanbusters logo on her tummy rather than the customary rainbow.[57]

CHARLOTTESVILLE ANTIRACIST ACTIVISTS 69

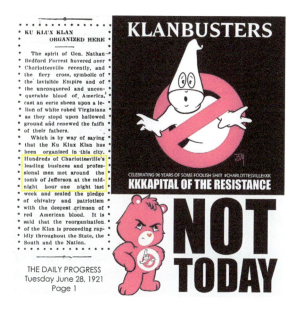

BlocKKKparty poster: From Ghostbusters to Care Bears, using "innocent" pop culture to clap back at the Klan.

In creating these meme-worthy images, Charlottesville antiracist activists were, to some extent, playing on similar social media terrain as the alt-right, with its use of cartoon characters like Pepe the Frog and Wojak. It would, however, be a short-lived strategy. In the organizing and community outreach ahead of the Unite the Right rally, there would be no appropriation of cartoon characters, no pastiches of pop-culture icons, or attempts to create viral memes. Rather than the cleverness of hashtags like #BlocKKKparty, in the run-up to August 12 organizers tweeted out #DefendCville and circulated posters with time-honored and familiar, if perhaps a tad clichéd, mobilization imagery of silhouetted protesters with linked arms. The more sober, nonplayful organizing materials activists distributed to counter the small KKK group's racist event may have been a response to the far greater threat posed by the Unite the Right rally. A motley crew of Klansmen, with no discernable galvanized movement behind it, could be more comfortably ridiculed and mocked than a burgeoning alt-right that was firing up untold numbers of adherents—and that would be bringing hundreds, if not thousands, of them to Charlottesville.

Charlottesville activists would engage alt-right figures on their own social media turf in the run-up to August 12, but meme-warfare would not continue as a weapon of choice. Infiltration of supposedly private alt-right social media

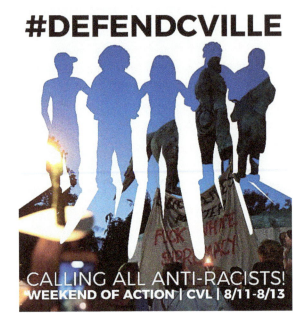

Mobilization poster heavily circulated by Charlottesville antiracist activists in lead-up to Unite the Right rally.

chat rooms and publicizing the violent intentions of Unite the Right attendees would be among the weapons wielded by activists, including a Charlottesville resident named Emily Gorcenski.

Don't Mess with a Data Scientist: Emily Gorcenski

Everything about Emily Gorcenski would make her loathsome to white nationalists. She is a transgender woman. She is non-white. And she is a militant antifascist with prodigious math, engineering, and data science skills. In the summer of 2017 she also commanded a powerful Twitter platform with upwards of 17,000 followers.[58] She was able to infiltrate and publicize planning and communications message boards used to organize the Unite the Right rally. She tweeted prolifically and publicly about her work, thus making her a visible target of alt-right threats. Along with other activists, Gorcenski mobilized the tools of new media to undermine, undercut, expose, and eventually bring to legal justice those who came to Charlottesville to foment far-right violence and mayhem. She also put herself into serious harm's way as a citizen journalist with Solidarity Cville by livestreaming confrontations with both neo-Nazis and police.

Film and photography coverage of the Birmingham and Selma confrontations was crucial to those campaigns' successes, but the civil rights movement had to rely on professional journalists and news organizations to do the documenting and broadcasting. People didn't have cameras and live broadcast distribution technology in their pockets in the mid 1960s. Professional reporters, camera people, and photojournalists would still be indispensable a half century later, but the digital media environment gave activists additional tools to self-document and disseminate their direct-action protest activity. On July 8, Emily Gorcenski would be among the most high-profile activists recording and reporting on the confrontation between protesters and law enforcement at the end of the Klan rally. With the Klansmen safely shepherded away by law enforcement, police turned on protesters by abruptly declared an unlawful assembly and unleashing tear gas on those who remained on the street. Charlottesville police chief Al Thomas, in a subsequent press conference, insisted that aggressive and agitated protesters had dispensed pepper spray on officers first.[59]

Thomas's statement to the press were not unlike those of Birmingham's Bull Connor and Selma's Sheriff Jim Clark who also blamed demonstrators for the police violence meted out to them. Gorcenski, herself overcome by tear gas, livestreamed on the video platform Periscope, reporting and documenting that the counter protesters had been peaceful and that the police hadn't been able "to play with the fun toys they brought out, and so now they're coming out."[60] From her direct vantage point, she and the other activists managed to truth check the police chief's account. It wouldn't be the only time that summer that Gorcenski and local activists would be able to challenge the narratives of police and white nationalists. They had the media evidence.

Unfortunately for Gorcenski and her fellow activists, local Charlottesville media had already framed antiracist activists as the alt-right's flip side. The *Daily Progress* made sense of the simmering tensions around the issue of removing Confederate statues in the wake of the May rallies and confrontations as "public confrontation between ideologues."[61] City Councillor Kathy Gavin (who, along with Mayor Signer, cast the only other vote against moving the Lee and Jackson statues) "warned of potential violence that could result if the political confrontations continue. She said that she has seen 'hate' coming from both sides."[62] A city resident was quoted predicting ominously that SURJ's "irresponsible and dangerous tactics will ultimately result in the serious injury or death of someone." The prediction proved correct about injury and death;

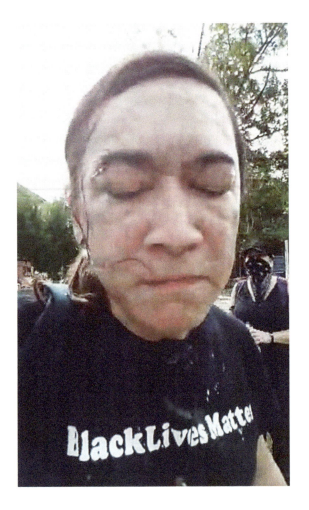

Livestreaming the July 8 confrontation between anti-Klan activists and police: A tear gassed Emily Gorcenski undermines, with video evidence, the police chief's assertion that activists were to blame. (Courtesy of Emily Gorcenski)

it was exactly wrong in forecasting the group responsible for the mayhem. No SURJ member or "left-wing activists" were given space to defend themselves or their tactics.

Along with political leaders like Councillor Gavin, Charlottesville Police Chief Al Thomas also received privileged space in local media to paint a negative portrait of the activists. A few weeks before the KKK rally, *C-ville Weekly* highlighted Thomas's "candid" concern that the Klan wasn't his main worry: "It's being in a situation where local citizens make poor choices and we have to step in."[63] While infantilizing activists, Thomas presented his police officers as the grown-ups in the room.

In the aftermath of the KKK rally, SURJ activists suddenly began receiving more media attention, with its activists quoted more fully. However, in a major *Daily Progress* piece on the controversy about the police response that Gorcenski and other activists had documented, Thomas still received the most space to present law enforcement's perspective. Activists including Gorcenski got quotes in about the tear gas being excessive, the police protecting the Klan and viewing the protesters as the real threat, and refuting Thomas's assertion that his officers had been pepper-sprayed by protesters.[64] Nevertheless, the SURJ activists' quotes were all reactive, defensive responses to Thomas's framing of the event. Ultimately there were two sides: on the one side, peaceful community members who came together in unity,—"good people," as Chief Thomas put it, showing "support and unity in our community"; on the other side were the violent, confrontational anti-Klan protesters who turned on the police. But Gorcenski had social media evidence that told a different story.

In the weeks leading up to the Unite the Right rally, Gorcenski amassed other forms of media evidence as well. Using social media proof, she and other activists were able to document that the white nationalists coming to Charlottesville weren't expecting to gather peacefully and protest the removal of Confederate statues. They were coming to instigate violence. Solidarity Cville compiled a dossier of materials from Gorcenski that included private Messenger chat logs from a Kessler associate threatening violence on city council members and on antifa, but also against Richard Spencer. Rounding out the dossier were myriad other declarations of violent intent from social media posts on Mountaineers Against Antifa's Facebook site and from the Daily Stormer.[65]

Citing the clear and present danger to public safety posed by the Unite the Right rally, Solidarity Cville and other activists tried to persuade city officials not to grant Kessler's permit request. The city's response: nothing in the dossier rose to the level of a "credible threat": there was no "*specific* statement advocating, or planning, a *specific and imminent* act of violence."[66]

The activists couldn't get the city to stop the rally; they also couldn't get the local newspaper to headline the threat evident in Gorcenski's dossier on the violent intent of Unite the Right participants. In a comprehensive 2,300-word article two weeks before the rally and largely organized around free speech and First Amendment questions, the *Daily Progress* briefly noted—but thoroughly buried—the evidence that Solidarity Cville had revealed. In one sentence deep in the long piece, the *Progress* reported that "posts on social media and far-right blogs in which supporters of Unite the Right rally seemed to revel in the possibility of violence and call on others to prepare for a fight."[67] There was no further elaboration. The article quoted Kessler's attorney, Kyle Bristow, who has been identified by the Southern Poverty Law Center as the alt-right's "charismatic legal consigliere," as warning that if Charlottesville police didn't protect alt-right participants from "leftist thugs . . . it would not be farfetched to postulate that the alt-right rally participants will stand up for their rights by effectuating citizen's arrests or by engaging in acts of self-defense."[68] A police spokesperson countered that "at no time was Mr. Kessler informed officers would not take action against those that attempted or committed violence towards another."[69]

Solidarity Cville, Gorcenski, and the antiracist activists were entirely correct in their urgent warning and their pleas to City Council to revoke Kessler's rally permit, because its participants were, in fact, planning violence. Had the *Progress*'s reporter chosen to make the logical connection between Solidarity Cville's evidence and Bristow's threat rather than frame his reporting around free speech issues, Charlottesville's newspaper might have presented the stakes about the upcoming rally more helpfully. Also, in retrospect, it was clear that the Charlottesville police spokesperson's quoted comments would prove to be wholly inaccurate: local police and Virginia State Police did stand down and passively look on while Unite the Right participants and counterprotesters fought each other in Charlottesville's streets.[70]

While unsuccessful with local media, Gorcenski continued to use her skills to mess with Unite the Right organizers, especially Richard Spencer and Jason Kessler. On July 23, she tweeted out a post addressed to @RichardSpencer alerting the alt-right leader that Kessler had been "thoroughly infiltrated by antifa. Probably residue from his Occupy days. This the ship you're tied to?" In another set of tweets, she informed Spencer that his security detail had been penetrated and that she had "insight on org structure" and knew all about an exposed disagreement. On August 10, she declared, "We have infiltrated @RichardSpencer's communication and his security team. He's safe because we choose non-violence."

Gorcenski's deep web–sleuthing and fascist-exposure work during 2017 was part of a larger movement to fight far-right extremism online and publicly expose ("dox") individual Nazis. That work would go into overdrive following the Unite the Right violence, with skilled investigators like Antifash Gordon leading workshops for novice antifascists wanting to do similar work, especially as US federal intelligence and investigatory organizations like the FBI and Homeland Security under the Trump administration began stepping away from rigorous monitoring of the extreme right.[71] Even as Gorcenski was penetrating, exposing, and messing with Spencer and Kessler, so was the left-wing media collective Unicorn Riot, as we saw in chapter 2. With Unicorn Riot's exposé, the "credible threat" of specific and imminent violence became much clearer.[72]

The dossier would serve as the impetus for a far-reaching lawsuit, *Sines v. Kessler*, which would attempt to prove that the organizers of the rally conspired to commit violence against minority groups, acts not protected by the First Amendment.[73] Solidarity Cville had argued the same thing with its dossier in July 2017. In October 2021, the high-profile attorney Roberta A. Kaplan led the case in a Charlottesville federal courtroom. Kaplan had previously argued the landmark Supreme Court case that brought down the Defense of Marriage Act (*United States v. Windsor*) clearing the way for subsequent legalizing of gay marriage. The *Sines v. Kessler* plaintiffs were all counterprotesters who had sustained various forms of injury from the tiki torch parade of August 11, the clashes around Emancipation Park on August 12, and the terrorist car attack that injured dozens and killed Heather Heyer. The lawsuit succeeded. In November 2021, a Charlottesville jury in a federal court building, steps away from where the mayhem of the Unite the Right rally had occurred, found for the plaintiffs. The guilty defendants included, along with Jason Kessler, alt-right poster boy Richard Spencer, "Crying Nazi" Chris Cantwell, the Traditionalist Worker Party's Matthew Heimbach, Identity Evropa's Elliot Kline (AKA Eli Mosley), car attack perpetrator James Fields, and the Daily Stormer's Andrew Anglin and Robert "Azzmador" Ray, along with other Klan and white nationalist leaders and groups. They were found liable under Virginia law for conspiracy to commit violence and for perpetrating racial, religious, and ethnic harassment. Jurors handed down almost $26 million dollars to the plaintiffs in punitive and compensatory damages.[74]

The ease by which the alt-right got infiltrated was an indication of the movement's fundamental weakness and fragility. As Antifash Gordon explained to a journalist, "They don't accept accountability, and they don't care for each other. If one of us [antifascists] got doxed, we'd offer safe houses and material support. For them, it's 'You were weak and stupid.' And when someone doesn't get support, they get pissed and come snitching to us."[75] Gorcenski suggested that because right-wing white males didn't have a history of trouble from the police, they never developed defensive protocols, as those on the left had to.

"We've been targeted by law enforcement forever, so there's a security culture," she argued.

Community care and mutual aid were key concerns for activists as they organized the response to Unite the Right: from street medics, to movement lawyers and legal witnesses, to "care bears" dispensing water and energy bars, to safe spaces in a designated church and in parks, to the production of leaflets with crucial instructions and phone numbers, and even pointers for activists about how to be media-savvy.

Charlottesville activists understood that media from around the world would be on their streets on August 12. So did those planning to participate in the Unite the Right rally. Gorcenski, knowing that UTR organizers were following her tweets, had some media-savvy advice for them and their followers. In a July 22 post, she warned: "We will have so many cameras, so many microphones, so many streams watching every cheer for calls to white nationalism." She continued: "It will follow you. Your coworkers, your kids, your future dates will all know that you chose to stand with kkk 2.0."[76] Consequences for Unite the Right participation would indeed follow for many who took part. Gorcenski, using her social media sleuthing skills, unmasked UTR organizer "Tyrone," who repeatedly posted calls for violence on Discord (see images in chapter 2). Tyrone's real identity was US Marine Michael Chesny.[77] He was quickly booted from the service.

Gorcenski's tweets signaled her movement's capacity and muscle. Charlottesville activists' media savvy—both in the online digital realm as well as on the streets, in what would be a battlefield full of activists' recording apparatuses supplemented with that of mainstream media outlets—would control the narrative, not only on the August 12 weekend but into the future. Three years later, Joe Biden in his successful presidential campaign would adopt Gorcenski's and Solidarity Cville's narrative of standing up to neo-Nazis. That narrative was at the heart of his campaign plea for the soul of the nation, as we'll discuss further in chapter 7. The counternarrative provided by the city of Charlottesville and its police, along with University officials' "don't take the bait" warnings, ended up in history's dustbin as Joe Biden asked Americans over and over again in the summer of 2020 to remember "those spreading hate and those with the courage to stand against it."[78]

They would stand up on the night of August 11 in part because of the infiltration work of Gorcenski and other antifascist activists. They knew that

How to Oppose White Supremacists Safely and Effectively

The White Supremacists want
- to make themselves look like victims in the media
- to gain acceptance as legitimate public protesters

How they'll try to provoke us
- THEY WILL get in our faces
- THEY WILL shout things like "get out of my country" or "we're in control now"
- THEY WILL touch or hold their guns

What you SHOULDN'T do
- DON'T bother talking to them or trying to persuade them
- DON'T engage in any physical or verbal violence
- DON'T direct any action or anger towards the police
- DON'T resist arrest

What you SHOULD do
- DO stay calm and upbeat
- DO think about how the media will present your actions
- DO stay cogent and respectful, if you are interviewed by media
- DO have prepared sound-bytes that cannot be taken out of context.
- DO obey police instructions and commands

remember:
**YOUR ACTIONS MAKE A DIFFERENCE
DON'T PLAY INTO THEIR HANDS!**

*Furnished by Charlottesville Center for Peace and Justice
www.charlottesvillepeace.org*

Community care and media savviness among Charlottesville activists: Flyer from Charlottesville Center for Peace and Justice. (University of Virginia Albert and Shirley Small Special Collections Library) another tiki torch rally was coming. Law enforcement had some inkling as well, but no definite intelligence on where.[79] Activists, having penetrated the Discord planning chats, knew everything. Early that evening, Gorcenski, retweeting from the anarchist news collective It's Going Down, broadcast news about a torchlight rally coming to UVA that night to all her Twitter followers—who included, of course, Richard Spencer and Eli Mosley. In other tweets she also taunted the two about all the leaks from their supposedly secret communication channels.

The alt-right had planned a grand, visually stunning media event that would surpass in semiotic richness and movement-building splendor their May 13 coming-out party. It would be disrupted.

August 11: Tiki Torch Disruption

Almost a thousand Charlottesville residents filled St. Paul's Episcopal Church for an interfaith service the night before Saturday's Unite the Right rally. Located almost directly across the street from UVA's Rotunda, with its statue of Thomas Jefferson in front on an expansive red-bricked plaza, the church welcomed famed Princeton scholar-activist Cornel West, Rev. Traci Blackmon, known for her leadership during the Ferguson uprisings, and Rev. Osagyefu Sekou. The latter, a noted militant nonviolent civil disobedience trainer, had been tutored by James Lawson. In the early 1960s, Lawson had conducted pivotal workshops on nonviolence for students in Nashville who would go on to engage in lunch counter sit-ins and lead the Freedom Rides as well as other key civil rights–era campaigns—students like Diane Nash, Bernard Lafayette, and John Lewis. All three would be indispensable in the Selma campaign.[80] Rev. Sekou, who had been in Charlottesville for weeks conducting trainings, led a final one for about a hundred people in St. Paul's on the afternoon of August 11.[81] A group of students who would face torch-wielding neo-Nazis also received nonviolent training, and it would prove essential for them as they stood up at the Jefferson statue that night.

At 7:43 p.m., It's Going Down tweeted out that neo-Nazis would be converging at the Thomas Jefferson statue at 9:00 p.m. A small band of students carrying a banner made from a white sheet with the words "VA Students Act Against White Supremacy" arrived at the statue and encircled it with linked arms, singing and chanting as they awaited what was to come. When the alt-right marchers swarmed over the Rotunda steps onto the plaza and surrounded the students, the neo-Nazis thought they'd quickly vanquished the enemy and added to their image of power and virility. But the alt-right livestreamer who proclaimed to his followers "total victory tonight" made his declaration prematurely.

Charlottesville antiracist activists were also livestreaming. UVa Students United posted a thirty-minute recording of the entire confrontation on its Facebook page and declared: "We are here to oppose the Neo Nazis and white supremacists who are trying to poison our community #DefendCville."[82] Charlottesville activists used that hashtag, along with #NoNewKKK and others on both Facebook and Twitter as well as the video streaming platform Periscope, to do exactly what Emily Gorcenski predicted: flood the internet with myriad activist-produced cell phone videos of what was happening in Charlottesville that weekend, especially how the community was standing up to confront the alt-right invasion.

UVa Students United's post was shared hundreds of times. The livestream didn't capture the violence at the statue, but Emily Gorcenski did, as did professional journalists. The pictures and videos of nonviolent, militant resistance to the alt-right quickly became counterimages to disrupt, undercut, and subvert the "total victory" narrative that the tiki torch march's organizers and participants thought they were creating. Gorcenski's livestreamed images would be amplified by a ProPublica and PBS *Frontline* documentary, *Documenting Hate*, which won an Emmy in 2018. The documentary privileged Gorcenski's retelling of what happened that night, supplementing her blurry, shaky cell phone images with professional-grade footage. In her cell phone livestreaming of the torch-wielding marchers converging, she narrates, "We are penned in. We are surrounded on all sides by hundreds of Nazis. We have no way out." The *Frontline* documentary supplies footage of what Gorcenski and her comrades encountered: neo-Nazis making Hitler salutes, screaming "White lives matter" into the camera, and then punching and attacking counterprotesters, creating violent mayhem. Over dramatic music, Gorcenski recounts being punched, kicked, and hit, perhaps by a torch: "I thought I was going to die. The thing I was thinking as the melee was happening is: I need to keep the camera going. That was the only thing I could do."[83]

Documenting in the moment—and then recounting afterwards: that was how antiracists prevailed. The images were indelible. They were also familiar, echoing images of other students standing up (or in some cases sitting down) against white supremacy. At the statue, the students holding the banner kept

UVa Students United Facebook post reporting on the tiki torch confrontation: Student protesters in nonviolent stance. Emily Gorcenski is at right livestreaming.

their heads down, strategically and consciously, during much of the confrontation. They also remained at the statue as the neo-Nazis swarmed towards them.

Consider the disproportionality of forces: hundreds of alt-right marchers versus, at most, thirty counterprotesters; one side armed with flames; the other only with their bodies. UVa Students United blasted out a social media post about what happened, using a photo that would be recirculated over and over that clearly showed how the students were surrounded and menaced. The Facebook post, with over 20,000 views and 289 shares, garnered close to 200 comments including one from renowned civil rights movement historian Barbara Ransby, who connected the Virginia students to the students of SNCC, noting: "You did the right thing even if temporarily outnumbered. In the spirit of SNCC and other brave young freedom fighters of the past."[84]

Civil rights-era white supremacists surrounding student protesters who face away from their attackers and remain nonviolent. The disproportionality of forces and methods of assault were echoed at the tiki torch confrontation August 11, 2017. (Fred Blackwell, photographer/Wisconsin Historical Society)

Students like John Lewis, Diane Nash, and Bernard Lafayette, all trained by Rev. James Lawson, had also encountered disproportionate force. Similarly, they avoided facing or looking at their attackers. They also were often surrounded and then pummeled. The young white men who in 1960 and 1961 punched students sitting-in at those lunch counters, pouring sugar over their heads and putting out their lighted cigarettes on the activists' skin, likely thought they were achieving victory for the Southern segregationist way of life. Their alt-right progeny thought so as well.

The students had, however, derailed the alt-right victory parade by showing up—even the fact that their numbers were small added to their disruptive and narrative power. They were brave because there were so few of them. From Barbara Ransby's comment on August 12, to retrospective documentaries like the ProPublica/PBS effort, to the speeches of then presidential candidate Joe Biden, the narrative that became dominant was the one that SURJ and Solidarity Cville and Emily Gorcenski and UVa Students United had been insisting on since the very beginning of Charlottesville's Summer of Hate. Only by showing up and fighting back against racism and fascism could the alt-right be defeated.

Aftermath

On March 5, 2018, Richard Spencer canceled his university speaking tour after violence broke out at his Michigan State appearance. Taking to YouTube, he conceded that "antifa is winning."[85] He admitted he hadn't taken them seriously before. In previous college talks in 2016 (whose purpose was to organize and recruit), he went on to say, the "hostiles" didn't "go overboard," and Spencer claimed he was able to engage with "curious students—and that's exactly what I wanted." But since Charlottesville, antifa had grown and were much more willing to escalate, be violent, and "do things to scare people away." Spencer bemoaned the media's acceptance of the "antifa narrative" that he inspired violence. The alt-right leader thus suspended his movement's only "in real life" organizing, along with its hopes to become politically tangible beyond digital spaces. Counterprotesters' relentless deplatforming had achieved its goals.

Charlottesville antiracist activists' response to Unite the Right helped solidify the playbook. White nationalists had faced significant opposition elsewhere before A11 and A12, particularly in Portland and Berkeley, but the scale, magnitude, and sheer media spectacle were much greater in Charlottesville. Other communities repeated what Charlottesville activists had modeled by refusing to concede any space ever to neo-Nazis. One week after the Unite the Right debacle, the Boston community did just that, turning out over forty thousand to drown out a neo-Nazi "free speech rally" originally slated to include speakers connected to UTR. Only about fifty neo-Nazis showed up.[86] Michigan State University activists also took a leaf from the book written by Charlottesville activists, effectively shutting down Spencer.

The Charlottesville activist community displayed the disruptive and narrative capacity that Zeynep Tufekci discusses as crucial for effective and sustained social change movements. Spencer admitted as much in his concession speech to his followers. But what about electoral and institutional capacity? For Tufekci, all the disruptive and narrative power activists can wield ultimately doesn't amount to much if it doesn't lead to demonstrable change. The Birmingham and Selma campaigns led directly to the passage of the Civil Rights and Voting Rights Acts. Both had profound sociopolitical impacts, even if the legislative victories on their own weren't enough to eradicate racism and discrimination from the American body politic.

The political impact of the counterprotesters in Charlottesville came quickly. Nikuyah Walker, an African American independent candidate for city council ran an initially long-shot campaign in 2017 with the slogan "Unmasking the Illusion," referring to the city's self-satisfied image as a bastion of progressiveness oblivious to its long history of entrenched racism.[87] With the Summer of Hate bolstering her argument, she won and subsequently replaced Mike Signer as mayor, centering racial justice issues and an "uncivil" discursive style that had long since characterized the local antiracist movement's public mode. Then two years later, Democrats assumed control over both houses of the Virginia General Assembly for the first time in two decades and successfully passed legislation allowing cities in the Commonwealth to remove Confederate monuments.[88]

As the law went into effect in the summer of 2020, Albemarle County, the seat for the city of Charlottesville, took down a monument. Ironically it was neither the Robert E. Lee nor Stonewall Jackson statues at the heart of the Summer of Hate whose removal was still tied up in a lawsuit. Rather, first to go was the "At Ready," or more popularly named "Johnny Reb," statue flanked by battle cannons and placed in front of the county courthouse in 1909 by the United Daughters of the Confederacy. The statue of a soldier wielding a rifle stood right next to the former Jackson, former Justice, and currently named Court Square Park, the scene of the KKK rally in July 2017. Elsewhere in Virginia, Confederate monuments also began to meet their demise, especially in Richmond, former capital of the Confederacy. A statue of Robert E. Lee in the state capitol building got evicted, and the city began the arduous task of grappling with its many grand and opulent memorials to the racist Lost Cause on Monument Avenue.

And then George Floyd was murdered by a white Minneapolis police officer pressing his knee into the Black man's neck for eight minutes and forty-six seconds as cell phone video documented his horrifying and heart-rending last moments. The racial justice movement exploded back into the streets with unprecedented numbers and geographical reach, despite a raging pandemic. The protests brought together a remarkable coalition of activists and protesters across racial categories, including many activated individuals new to protesting. Charlottesville had its share of demonstrations, with Richmond a

2020 Black Lives Matter protests in Richmond: It's still about Confederate statues. Activists decorate Robert E. Lee's giant monument with graffiti and a projected image of George Floyd.

higher-profile center of antiracist activism over the summer of 2020. But the Confederate statues remained a galvanizing issue.

Over the summer, activists spray-painted and decorated Richmond's Confederate monuments, toppling some and turning the plaza around the humongous Robert E. Lee statue into an activist cultural center. Photos of the repurposed and remodeled Lee statue quickly became iconic images of the 2020 Black Lives Matter movement, along with news coverage of the Lee statue with George Floyd's face superimposed on it.[89] Those images communicated antiracists claiming space, asserting their power, demanding to be heard.

Why were the protests so powerful and so wide-ranging? Deva Woodly, a scholar of Black Lives Matter and social change movements, was quoted in the *New York Times* noting the crucial role of organizations like BLM: "While the group isn't necessarily directing each protest, it provides materials, guidance and a framework for new activists . . . Those activists are taking to social media to quickly share protest details to a wide audience."[90] Solidarity Cville was doing much the same during the spring and summer of 2017.

The activism in Charlottesville wasn't isolated; it was an iconic moment of the new civil rights movement that started with anguished responses to the killing of a young boy named Trayvon Martin and the not-guilty verdict of his killer in 2013, then burst into prolonged street protest in Ferguson during the summer of 2014, and then again in the following years with the deaths of more Black people at the hands of police. The 2020 protests merged outrage at police brutality with demands that the United States face its history of racism, including by grappling with the symbolic celebration of that history in the built environment.

4

A12

Iconic Images

Why did the Birmingham and Selma campaigns become worldwide media events that continue to resonate down to the present moment? Because of the pictures. Violent clashes, brutalized bodies, the viciousness of unrestrained white supremacy—all got put on searing display. Photojournalism and the new medium of network television news brought the drama and the political conflict into stark relief for national as well as global audiences. In Birmingham it was news film and photographs of Bull Connor's high-powered fire hoses and police dogs unleashed on nonviolent civil rights demonstrators. In Selma it was the news film of Governor George Wallace's state troopers advancing on, plowing over, beating up, and tear-gassing nonviolent voting rights marchers. Those pictures are now iconic. August 11 and 12, 2017, in Charlottesville produced searing pictures of violent clashes and brutalized bodies, as well as unrestrained white supremacy. That's one of the reasons #Charlottesville became a worldwide media event, consuming large amounts of media bandwidth for weeks, and why it remains a defining moment of the Trump era—and potentially as consequential to the twenty-first-century renewed struggle against white supremacy and for democratic access, as those two civil rights–era events were to the struggles of the latter half of the twentieth century.

What makes a media image iconic? Robert Hariman and John Louis Lucaites define such images as "widely recognized and remembered . . . understood to be representations of historically significant events" that "activate strong emotional identification or response, and are reproduced across a range of media, genres, or topics."[1] Most news photos and film footage are highly disposable, meant to engage viewers in the present and then disappear from collective memory, deposited in the ash heap of quickly discarded media ephemera. But some media images stick. They end up shaping a society's understanding of an event and, to a certain extent, they may even *become* the event.[2] The iconic image of an historical moment appears to exemplify it, seems to "say it all" (in visual form), and manages to crystallize key issues, problems, and conflicts that animate the event, as David Perlmutter has argued in his influential characterization of what makes for iconic media images.[3] These highly visual artifacts also function as "collective mnemonic devices" about the past for subsequent generations. Akiba Cohen, Sandrine Boudana, and Paul Frosh posit that they supply "a formal blueprint for other images made in later periods which echo or deliberately imitate it." They provide "a symbolic template for the creation of transgenerational and transnational symbolic forms and meanings and for memory 'echoes' from one event, period or group to another."[4]

Specific images and news film of the civil rights era have entered into a pantheon of iconic images. They illustrate history textbooks, get used over and over again in documentary films, grace book covers, get recreated in Hollywood movies about the era, and even form source material for statues and monuments.[5] And as I want to explore in this chapter, media imagery from August 12, 2017, in Charlottesville graphically and thematically echoes famous images from Birmingham and Selma, suggesting a continuity of representational tropes about how mass media presents racial conflict and confrontation, Black bodies and their suffering, and the forces of white supremacy.

Selma/Charlottesville: Television Covers the Confrontations

The day in Charlottesville started with unmistakable echoes of the Selma images: an interracial line of clergy with linked arms prepared to confront a menacing force of white supremacists. Congregate C'ville, the activist clergy group in Charlottesville, had sent out an appeal to a thousand faith leaders from around the country to come and stand in prayerful opposition to the alt-right. A couple hundred answered the call.[6]

Fifty years earlier, in the immediate aftermath of "Bloody Sunday," Dr. King had sent out a similar plea to clergy from around the country to come to Selma and stand with the brutalized marchers. Hundreds came, including a white Unitarian minister, Rev. James Reeb, who would be beaten to death by white racists. His murder followed an aborted march across the Pettus Bridge, dubbed "Turnaround Tuesday" by disgruntled SNCC activists angered that

Selma-to-Montgomery march: Media attention to presence of numerous clergy marching with MLK and John Lewis.

King decided to turn the march back rather than disregard a federal judge's order against the march. Before the retreat, the marchers, at King's direction, knelt and engaged in an act of "performative prayer" meant to elicit media attention, which it did.[7] *Life* magazine in its expansive and front-cover coverage featured a powerful photo of kneeling clergy pictured in the center middleground of the frame, while looming in the foreground side of the image is the blue-uniformed leg of an Alabama trooper, his billy club positioned menacingly over the heads of the praying clergy arrayed before him.[8] Here was another example of segregationist power represented by a faceless, in this case visually amputated, automaton. The photo, spread over two pages, emphasized the whiteness of the prayerful line of marchers.

Two weeks later, the now federally permitted march from Selma to Montgomery went ahead with the presence of clergy—Black and white ministers, priests, rabbis, and nuns—highly visible in the resulting news coverage. Otherwise religiously observant Alabama segregationists disparaged and ridiculed the priests and nuns. For mainstream media, however, the members of the clergy—especially the white ones—served to legitimize the protest and provide it dignity and moral weight. King knew what he was doing in sending out that call. The cameras would be there to document the newsworthiness of white allyship.[9]

Photos and film of the clergy's action on the morning of August 12, 2017, however, never became iconic images, even though Congregate's local leaders, Rev. Seth Wispelwey and Brittany Caine-Conley, a minister in training, achieved high media visibility in the days following the violence. With Dr. Cornel West and Ferguson's Rev. Traci Blackmon in attendance, the clergy's action had enough star power to elicit media attention. Congregate's press release displayed plenty of media savvy by foregrounding and highlighting their expected presence. Linking arms, singing civil rights–era freedom songs, wearing clerical vestments, and standing in a nonviolent gauntlet at the south entrance into Emancipation Park, where alt-right marchers were supposed to enter for their rally, and also engaging in performative prayer, the faith leaders' actions had undeniable echoes and historical rhymes to the Selma campaign. But, as was the case in Selma and Birmingham before it, it was images of horrifying white racist violence that dominated media coverage and ended up producing the iconic images that would define the events as moments of historic import.

The violent images from Selma, broadcast Sunday night, March 7, 1965, on television screens around the nation and then splashed onto newspaper front

Charlottesville clergy confront alt-right forces on the morning of August 12, 2017: Echoes of the Selma campaign. (Anthony Crider, photography/Creative Commons)

pages the next day, galvanized clergy to descend on the Alabama town. The pictures also spurred ordinary people all over the country to make the journey south, including a Detroit mother of five, Viola Liuzzo. But why those images? What was it about the Bloody Sunday coverage—especially the film broadcast on television—that proved so potent in generating outrage, but also driving protest activity?

It was the images' visual and moral clarity. The footage provided a clear delineation of evil menacing good: violent perpetrators vanquishing innocent victims. The images, like other iconic civil rights–era photos and film, displayed those victims' suffering in graphic detail. The Pettus Bridge film told a story deeply sedimented in the American popular imagination, dating back at least to Harriet Beecher Stowe's *Uncle Tom's Cabin*. Film scholar Linda Williams has argued that the "mode of melodrama," exemplified by Stowe's novel and the explosion of hugely popular theatrical "Tom" shows that followed it, provides a way of understanding the dominant (and inevitably, albeit unconscious, white supremacist) narrative about American race relations that relies on hyperbolic Black suffering.[10] Melodrama, as literary scholars like Peter Brooks have argued, is a narrative mode of the West's modern era, requiring crystal-clear delineations of good versus evil—victims versus victimizers—enacted in an often over-the-top, exaggerated manner. The ultimate point of melodrama is to provide moral clarity in a secular world no longer undergirded by the primacy of the church.[11] The melodramatic mode isn't limited only to literary, stage, and screen fictional stories, but can also be found in media events. Williams argues that they all "move us to sympathy for the sufferings of the virtuous."[12] And in American democracy, the influence of melodramatic modes structuring race relations helps "explain why it is that in a democracy ruled by rights, we do not gain the moral upper hand by saying simply that rights have been infringed. We say, instead, much more powerfully: 'I have been victimized; I have suffered, therefore give me rights.'"[13] In order to produce melodrama's moral legibility, our heroes' (and heroines') suffering need to be egregious and emotionally resonant for audiences; the affective register needs to be almost "too much."[14]

In the Pettus Bridge news film, viewers see white segregationist law enforcement officers clearly arrayed against Black marchers. They're outfitted with billy clubs and gas masks. The voting rights marchers, with John Lewis and MLK stand-in Hosea Williams in the lead, have only their vulnerable bodies, some carrying bundles for the anticipated long trek to Montgomery. They stand

Selma "Bloody Sunday" news film of Alabama State troopers plowing over nonviolent marchers.

in a nonthreatening and dignified line in front of the massed troopers. The sides are visually and graphically clear and easy for viewers to discern. The violence, when it comes, is obviously perpetrated only by the troopers and Sheriff Clark's posse; the Black marchers' brutalization is initially visually clear and fully observable as marchers fall, run, and get trampled. Once plumes of tear gas begin to obstruct the view that news cameramen can capture, it's still obvious that Black bodies are being beaten and chased as we see marchers succumbing to the ground, coughing and hacking, flung around, beaten by groups of troopers behind squad cars, carted off by other marchers, and attempting to retreat back across the bridge. The violence is obviously one-sided and brutal; the suffering of the victims undeniable.

The initial television news footage coming out of Charlottesville showing clashes between the alt-right and counterprotesters on August 12 had none of the visual clarity or melodramatic moral power of Selma's Bloody Sunday film. It was often difficult to distinguish one side from the other, and both appeared to be behaving violently. The Charlottesville counterprotesters were a notably diverse movement, with white people tending to dominate the front lines. They were diverse also in protest tactics, from locals who trained rigorously for nonviolent direct action, to others, local and not, practicing more aggressive street-fighting tactics. It made for chaotic media imagery. Who were the victims of neo-Nazi violence? This was not imagery in a melodramatic mode.

CNN and other national TV news outlets did not lead their early "breaking news" coverage that Saturday with the clergy protest, instead beginning live coverage after neo-Nazis had pushed through the faith leaders' nonviolent obstructive line at the park. Hundreds of local residents had also been instructed in the nonviolent direct-action strategies honed during the civil rights era, but little of that activity or those local counterprotesters got captured in media coverage on August 12.[15] In the early hours of TV news reporting, the images viewers saw emphasized "antifa" activists clashing with white nationalists, the antiracist activists aggressively confronting and fighting against their neo-Nazi antagonists. CNN looped a piece of film over and over again showing an apparently very strong counterprotester lifting and lobbing a *C-ville Weekly* blue news box at a group of white supremacists at the entrance of Emancipation (formerly Lee) Park. As powerful, dramatic, and alarming as these images were, they had none of the moral legibility of iconic civil rights imagery. Had this been how A12 continued, "Charlottesville" may have been a major news story, but it probably would not have become an iconic moment, a defining event, a symbol of the threat to the "soul of the nation" that galvanized a successful presidential campaign three years later.[16]

CNN early coverage of confrontation between alt-right and counter-protesters: Difficulty in discerning the two sides.

Car Attack: Charlottesville's "Bloody Saturday"

Two contingents of counterprotesters, numbering several hundred, were marching just south of the downtown pedestrian mall, responding to rumors that armed militia groups scattered throughout the city core might be threatening a low-income, largely African American housing complex nearby. Following prolonged mayhem and violence around Emancipation Park unchecked by law enforcement, Virginia State Police finally stepped in, declaring an unlawful assembly. But all that did was flush Unite the Right participants away from Emancipation Park and throughout the downtown area. Discovering that the militia members were retreating from the area, the now jubilant marchers began heading back towards the designated safe parks and other destinations. Walking up narrow 4th Street at 1:41 p.m., they faced the horror of a Dodge Challenger muscle car bearing down on them at high speed. The antiracist marchers were about to become the innocent and grievously suffering victims of a neo-Nazi perpetrating a terrorist attack.

Before the awful weekend, activist Emily Gorcenski, as noted in the previous chapter, had alerted the alt-right leaders she knew were reading her Twitter posts: "We will have so many cameras, so many microphones, so many streams watching every cheer for calls to white nationalism." One of those cameras belonged to local resident and activist, Brennan Gilmore, who had joined

First appearance of footage documenting terrorist car attack: Brennan Gilmore's original tweet.

the marchers and used his phone to document their celebratory mood from his vantage point on the pedestrian mall, looking down 4th Street. He heard the car and managed to record the attack.[17] Within half an hour, he'd uploaded his video to Twitter, alerted news outlets that they could freely use it, and by early evening his and other cell phone and aerial recordings were available to the TV networks and cable news channels.[18]

While it took time to identify the driver as a neo-Nazi participant in the Unite the Right rally, the clarity of the footage showing the perpetrator deliberately using his vehicle as a weapon—a tactic heretofore associated with Islamic State (ISIS) extremists—was unassailable.[19] Network and cable TV news outlets showed the footage numerous times, with ABC looping Gilmore's footage over and over again in its initial breaking coverage.[20] Once it was clear that the driver, James Fields, was not only a Unite the Right participant but an ardent admirer of Adolf Hitler, the Charlottesville story had its own version of the Edmund Pettus Bridge film: the car speeding down the side street, plowing towards the jumble of people; the sudden wave of bodies trying to escape; the screams; the indistinct contact between car and bodies in the deep background of the image; the cell phone camera momentarily losing its view, only to pick up the car barreling in reverse back across the bricked pedestrian mall as a large red athletic shoe improbably bounces from the horribly mangled front of the car, coming to rest on the mall as the car disappears from view.

The film graphically displays the white supremacist violence against defenseless and nonviolent demonstrators but also obscures that violence. We don't clearly see the deadly and injurious action of Fields's car, just as the beatings on the Pettus Bridge are mostly hidden by tear gas. But as with horror films, what viewers don't see is often more terrifying than what is plainly shown. Also, like the faceless automatons of civil rights–era iconic images, Gilmore's footage gives us a faceless, remorseless, inhuman machine of racist murder. It makes the distinction between villainous perpetrator and unwitting and utterly defenseless victims all the more stark and emotionally heartrending.

In both segments, the worst of the white supremacist violence occurs deep in the background of the frame. In analyzing the Pettus Bridge film, media studies scholar Sasha Torres has argued that by the professional standards of television news, which prized clarity and visual legibility, this was not good footage. However, the Selma news film was, she argues, an exemplary case of "crisis coverage." This kind of film "is marked visually by long static shots of nothing much happening, replaced suddenly by frenzied, oddly-framed or

Selma and Charlottesville footage: obscured violence deep in background of the film heightening the horror of the images.

blurry images once the crisis begins to unfold. These visual markers, which often add up to one or another kind of illegibility, are in fact the formal markers of the political process that is unraveling before our eyes: the loss of the camera's control of the image is one of the things that tells the audiences that political control, too, is up for grabs."[21] Brennan Gilmore's footage is quintessential "crisis coverage." It's horrifying in part because he loses camera control, shooting the ground, whipping around in a way disorienting to viewers.

Television news outlets have eagerly made use of nonprofessional visual recordings produced by bystanders, beginning most notably with the 1991 camcorder video documenting the vicious police beating of motorist Rodney King. It continues to our current moment of cell phone recordings and livestreaming of disasters, tragedies, and other calamitous events as they happen. The 2020 footage of George Floyd's horrifying death under the knee of a Minneapolis police officer, which led to a sustained worldwide Black Lives Matter uprising, is the quintessential example of the potential power this kind of visual document can generate.

One way to understand such media is as "militant evidence." Media scholar Ryan Watson notes that in a "cameras everywhere" environment, where cell phone and police body cam video flood social media channels and occasionally television news with images of violent death and brutality to Black and Brown bodies, viewers can become anesthetized, especially in the face of judicial indifference. It's difficult for this kind of video evidence to have any staying power. Nevertheless, wielding a camera can be a "productive tool of rebellion" providing affective and effective evidence for a variety of oppositional and social justice purposes. "Militant evidence," he argues, "does not consist of texts to be read and interpreted. Rather, it is the accumulated evidence of individual and collective traumas that are to be forcefully felt, to awaken and move others into new frames of reference, rebellion, and collective activism and toward justice."[22]

In 1955 when Mamie Bradley had *Jet* magazine photograph the grotesquely pulverized face of her fourteen-year-old son, who was murdered by racists in Mississippi, she was providing militant evidence. Her act catalyzed the civil rights movement. A decade later during the Selma campaign, when Martin Luther King told a photographer to keep taking pictures rather than put down his camera and assist youngsters being brutalized by Sheriff Clark's racist forces, he was using that *Life* magazine photographer to gather militant evidence.[23] In the Black Lives Matter era, with activists' easy access to media documentation tools, ubiquity becomes a problem. But some militant evidence breaks through, can start to accumulate, can create a movement—can lead to a media event. As I've argued, in a fractured and fragmented media environment, the media event is what cuts through and demands sustained national (and even international) attention. The George Floyd video did so, coming in the wake of so many other videos of Black death at police hands. Why did that particular video break through? It fit the melodramatic mode so poignantly, the depiction of the suffering victim who called out for his mother with his dying breaths being almost too much for any viewer to bear. The through line to Emmett Till was an easy one to draw.

Gilmore's cell phone footage also broke through, went viral, and developed staying power, as have some of the other videos of the car attack. They've been appropriated by filmmakers like Spike Lee and recording artists like Will.i.am, and shown in the numerous documentaries about #Charlottesville that have appeared in the years since the summer of 2017.[24] Spike Lee, recognizing the melodramatic poignancy of the footage, tacks it on to the end of *BlacKkKlansman*, his 2018 semifictionalized film about a Black police officer in the 1970s infiltrating the Ku Klux Klan and endearing himself to David Duke. Heightening the moral legibility of the film's coda, Lee interspersed a clip of the real David Duke in Charlottesville pumping up Unite the Right marchers by declaring, "This is the first step to taking America back." Lee edited that together with Trump's now infamous declaration about "very fine people."[25] Lee makes it appear that Trump is identifying Duke directly in his praise. Those clips provide visual evidence about who the white supremacist villains are, just before Lee shows viewers the car attack video in all its varied horror—Gilmore's cell phone recording and the aerial drone video, images from the very midst of the carnage with swelling orchestral music to intensify the audience's emotional response. Imagery like this does not really need musical cues, but the "melos" in melodrama requires it. And then to fully render the Manichaean moral distinctions between villains and victims, Lee included footage of a young Black woman screaming in piercing tones as the music swells and a Black man, emotionally overcome, yells that there are bodies lying on the ground. The sequence ends with a photo that would also become iconic: Heather Heyer. The melodramatic merges with the tragic.

Birmingham/Charlottesville: The Iconic Photo

Charlottesville *Daily Progress* photographer Ryan Kelly was working his last day at his job for the newspaper. He would win a Pulitzer Prize for his photo of Fields's car plowing into the crowd of counterdemonstrators. In the days following the attack, TV news outlets began to privilege the photo over the videos, a seemingly odd decision for a journalistic medium grounded on moving rather than still images.

It's a chaotic image and, initially at least, almost impossible to decipher. The

Ryan Kelly's Pulitzer Prize-winning photo: an American "Guernica"? (Ryan Kelly, photographer/Daily Progress/AP)

jumble of bodies and parts of bodies don't make sense in their configuration. Columbia University literature professor Jennifer Wenzel tried to grasp the image's visceral power. The photo, she argues, is "an American 'Guernica.'" She compares the car attack photo to the Cubist fragmentation and disassembly of the Picasso masterpiece protesting the inhumanity and terror of a war on civilians. Like a Cubist painting, Kelly's picture also gives us fragments of bodies, objects, signs. Wenzel argues that the photo echoes the *Guernica* painting because it presents a fragmented collage. It requires the viewer to "do the work of reassembling what has been rendered apart," even as one can never make sense of the destruction represented in both these representations of fascistic carnage.[26] The *Washington Post*, however, tried to do just that with Kelly's photo. In an online interactive article at the event's one-year anniversary, the *Post* zoomed in on various sections of the photo and supplied descriptive and analytical text in an attempt to grapple with the complexity of the chaotic image and put the fragments of the photo together in some meaningful way. Noting how hard it still was to look at his photo, Ryan Kelly is quoted noting, "So much is contained in that moment."[27]

That's one reason it's an iconic image, according to David D. Perlmutter in his influential compendium of iconic photos' characteristics. Kelly's picture gives us a striking composition of a "decisive moment" in which "all the elements (including lighting, angle, and the subject position, action and expression) are 'right.'"[28] It gives us an instance of visual conflict, with revealing juxtapositions. However, Perlmutter suggests that such images also tend to be spare in their composition (consider the 1989 image during China's brief democracy protest movement of a lone young man in Tiananmen Square facing a line of tanks).[29] Robert Hariman and John Louis Lucaites, according to their taxonomy of iconic images, would probably deny iconic status to Kelly's photo despite its ubiquity on mass media platforms and its Pulitzer Prize. It isn't "structured by familiar patterns of artistic design," doesn't conform to conventions of representational realism such as balanced composition, and stays "within the realm of everyday experience and common sense."[30] The image is fundamentally uncanny, strange, profoundly unsettling; it defies common sense. Like Picasso's protest painting, the photo's defying of conventional realism is precisely why it's so powerful. Capturing the exact moment of horrific violence and injury, apparently the split second before the car slams into Heather Heyer, the photo gives viewers a sense, in visual form, of what it felt like to be in the midst of a terrorist attack.

There is one element of the photo, however, that is not fragmented, chaotic, or difficult to decipher. It's the Black, male body at the very center of the image. The man is frozen horizontally in midair, just above the car's clearly visible Ohio license plate, his left leg bent in an improbable angle. What makes the image remarkable, and is another of its unsettling qualities, is the impassive expression on the young man's face. That expression provides a remarkable echo to one of the most circulated, iconic photos of the civil rights movement. It's the very same expression we see on the face of another young Black man frozen in a moment of white supremacist violence in the streets of Birmingham during the Children's Crusade.

Associated Press (AP) photographer Bill Hudson captured a photo of a police officer with a German shepherd straining at the leash, seeming to bite at the midriff of a Black male youth, Walter Gadsden, who appears to be leaning right into the canine attack. Along with the actions of the dog, the grimacing policeman, whose eyes are shielded by sunglasses, is grabbing at the youth's sweater. In the foreground, another leashed dog with open jaws appears ready to strike. Yet in the midst of this attack, the youth's facial features are utterly impassive and calm. In both the Charlottesville and Birmingham photos, the

Iconic image from 1963 Birmingham "Children's Crusade." (Bill Hudson, photographer/AP)

photographers have snapped their images at the moment a young Black man is displayed helplessly submitting to brutalization.

Here is the melodramatic mode in full operation. Both photos provide a graphic representation of the suffering victim. Kelly's photo doesn't have quite the visual clarity of the famous Birmingham photo, but we still have a stark delineation of a violent force (the police officers' dogs in the Birmingham photo; the Nazi's car in the Charlottesville image). We also have a nonviolent, horrifically assaulted young Black man as victim at the center of both images.[31]

Martin A. Berger, in his influential book on the photography of the civil rights movement, argues that it's no accident that images like this became iconic. While his analytical work doesn't overtly embrace theories of the melodramatic narrative form, he comes to similar conclusions as Linda Williams about this mode being essential to understanding how white Americans understand and make meaning of race and racial struggle. Berger suggests that the most circulated and well-known civil rights photos followed a specific narrative: abject, disempowered, victimized Black people as hapless objects of activated and powerful (albeit villainous) white people. By favoring images of unthreatening, passive Black bodies suffering the vicissitudes of segregationist violence, the assumption (conscious or not) by white mass media news editors was that white sympathy would be the result, potentially nudging white audiences to favor legislative action on segregation and voting rights issues.[32]

Birmingham/Charlottesville: Active Black Bodies

The civil rights era generated a plethora of images, some that showed African Americans as activated, not as beleaguered victims but as forceful agents in their own freedom struggles. However, these images tended not to get the most distribution and did not become the iconic photos that, fifty years on, continue to be reproduced and now function as our collective memory of that period. The Birmingham image of the young man appealed because of what the AP editor at the time deemed his "saintly calm."[33] Who wouldn't be outraged and want to assist this young man, or the young people crouched helplessly on the ground getting bombarded by high-powered water hoses? (That image ran as a two-page spread in *Life* magazine, along with photos of dogs shredding the clothes of an older Black man.)[34] Similarly, who wouldn't want to assist, or at least sympathize with, the Selma marchers knocked down and brutalized on the Pettus Bridge as they offered no resistance at all? As morally legible images suggesting a narrative of dramatic confrontation of good versus evil, with the good enduring obvious bodily suffering, viewers activating the melodramatic imagination would be encouraged to respond to the poignancy represented: the evil on display here cannot be allowed to prevail, the victimized innocents must receive justice.

Birmingham offered other images, of course. One that Berger highlights shows a Black man with a small knife fighting back against a police officer and his dog. While this photo and others of more "active" Black subjects appeared in some newspapers, they quickly dropped from view "and have effectively vanished from present-day photographic histories of civil rights."[35]

Charlottesville also produced some powerful photographs of activated Black bodies, such as the AP's Steve Helber's photo of twenty-three-year-old Corey Long, who made an improvised flamethrower out of an aerosol can, pointing the impressive flame at a white nationalist, who uses his Confederate flag as a weapon against the flame. The image is dense with meanings: consider the flower in the foreground directing our gaze to Long's bare and powerfully muscled arm, the chalked word "love" visible between the splayed feet of the white nationalist lunging his wrapped Confederate pole against Long, and the small, cowering white man behind Long, whom he might have been trying to

Birmingham 1963: Non-iconic image of Black man fighting back, gripping a small knife. (Bill Hudson, photographer/AP)

Charlottesville 2017: Corey Long with improvised flamethrower fights back against white nationalists. (Steve Helber, photographer/AP)

protect. The image had wide circulation in media coverage at the time and after, as Long faced significant jail time for his act of self-defense. However, this photograph has not achieved iconic status.[36] It's not used as a go-to image to illustrate any story referencing "Charlottesville" as is the case with Ryan Kelly's photo. Helber did not win the Pulitzer Prize. An image of a Black man fighting back, even in justifiable self-defense—in Long's case, a white supremacist had pointed a gun at him and then discharged it towards Long's feet—did not fit the evolving narrative of Charlottesville that would be solidified by the car attack. The images of violent scuffles between alt-right white nationalists and counterprotesters have not disappeared from media circulation, but they are not the predominant images typically seen in retrospective media coverage in the years that have followed.

These photos don't fit the melodramatic frame of the suffering Black body, a trope that extends back to Uncle Tom bearing the whippings of the evil slave master, Simon Legree. Less morally legible, at least for many white people, the Black male figure fighting back evokes another set of tropes from the American cultural repertoire: "the brutal black buck" entrenched most enduringly by D. W. Griffith in his 1915 cinematic masterpiece of racism and Ku Klux Klan glorification, *The Birth of a Nation*.[37] Out to raise havoc, these figures rampage in black rage, assaulting white men with impunity, according to Donald Bogle in his classic study of Black stereotypes in American cinema.[38] Linda Williams, building on Bogle's foundational work, proffers a label for these images of "negrophobia": "anti-Toms." In the civil rights era, images signifying Black "violence"—such as the now iconic photos of Black Panthers toting long guns—began to displace images emphasizing white brutality and Black nonviolent suffering.

Active White Racists

Along with the Ryan Kelly photo, the other image that has become iconic and is often used to illustrate media coverage about the Unite the Right rally in Charlottesville is an image from the August 11 tiki torch parade through the University of Virginia's Central Grounds. It features one white polo shirt–wearing marcher, Peter Cytanovic, his mouth stretched wide open in his chant, his eyes fervent, his hair in a Hitler Youth haircut.

Why this photo? Within the context of Berger's argument about civil rights–era photography and the emphasis on hapless victimized Black people and

August 11, 2017 tiki torch rally: Peter Cytanovic, the face of racist hate. (Samuel Corum, photographer/Getty)

empowered, active white people, we can see a similar narrative theme playing out. The neo-Nazis in Charlottesville were as much the villains in 2017 as Southern white segregationists were in the 1950s and 1960s. As we've seen, however, many of the most reproduced civil rights images tend to present segregationists not as individuals but as faceless, depersonalized brute forces. There are, however, some frequently used images that present white racists in a different manner. The image of Cytanovic provides a remarkable echo to an iconic early civil rights era photo. Consider the round, black hole of the young neo-Nazi's mouth spewing racist invective. It's just like the image of young Hazel Massery yelling at Elizabeth Eckford, one of the Little Rock Nine, in the midst of the 1957 school integration battle in Arkansas.[39] One familiar image of emboldened white supremacy provided the visual template for another a half century later.

In both cases we have racists caught in the act of being verbally vicious. They were active villains: bad white people doing and saying awful things and making bad things happen. Other white people, repulsed by what they saw, could conversely feel empowered by actively distinguishing themselves from these disgusting white racists and potentially making good things happen by

Little Rock school integration crisis, 1957: White mob menacing Elizabeth Eckford, Hazel Massery as the face of racist hate. (Will Counts, photographer/Getty)

disavowing them. According to Berger, the problem is that the power dynamic doesn't change: the naturalization of white people as the ones with power isn't disturbed, merely which groups of white people. Black people and other people of color remain powerless, needing the intervention, sympathy, and ameliorative actions of nonracist white people. The photo of Elizabeth Eckford resonates because she appears so vulnerable, alone, and obviously in need of rescue from the racist mob that surrounds her.

But notice a key feature of the Eckford photo: she's surrounded by a white supremacist mob composed entirely of white women. There are a few hard-to-see men in the background, but it's the women who are fully activated and thoroughly visible. There's another frequently circulated civil rights photo that often illustrates segregationists as individualized and active, and it also features only white women. Echoing the Hazel Massery image, this photo also includes a white woman with her mouth wide open, presumably yelling some racial epithet.

Media representations of segregation's automatons and faceless forces were typically all-male. But here we have activated Southern white women. Within patriarchal notions of proper (always white) femininity, women are not active agents, not to be aggressively making things happen or brazenly displaying strong emotion. Men do; women appear. And in visual media, that appearance had traditionally been coded for the pleasures of the (always white) male gaze.[40] These Southern white women aren't behaving properly; they are deviant. Certainly their whiteness bestowed on them the privilege of being subjects rather than objects of visual and narrative attention. However, within male supremacist discourses that were still largely unquestioned in the 1950s and 1960s, their femininity meant their ability to act was highly constrained. These particular photos achieved such visibility as icons of white supremacy by using white women as signifiers of segregation, which suggests the ideological power of signaling the evils of that system by presenting white women behaving in a gender-inappropriate way.[41]

Imaging segregationists as white women: 1960 school integration protest in Louisiana. (Bettmann Archives/Getty)

The Cytanovic tiki torch photo flips the script of gender deviance. However, in alt-right gender ideology, the picture presented an image of empowered and homosocial masculinity that the movement argued needed to be reasserted. Alexandra Minna Stern in her book *Proud Boys and the White Ethnostate* interrogates this ideology, according to which feminism, social justice leftism, and multiculturalism have left white men depressed, marginalized, and feeling dispossessed, largely because they had never before had to acknowledge how the deck had heretofore been stacked in their favor.[42] The response, Stern notes: assert a rigid male/female biological binary, gender difference, and natural hierarchies. The Proud Boys in particular emphasize the importance of male bonding rituals and hypermasculinity. It's important that there are no women in the tiki torch picture and that the enraged men are engaging in ritualistic activity. Cytanovic is likely chanting, "You (or Jews) will not replace us." Minna Stern links that chant directly to "Great Replacement" ideology and its gender implications: feminists being the archenemy and impediment to the restoration of the White Republic.[43] A half century before, the women protesting school integration in Little Rock and New Orleans upheld traditional notions of women as domestic protectors of children, while also undercutting that notion through their visual representation in the public (masculine) sphere as grotesque figures acting out in unfeminine ways. The tiki torch photo also gives us an image of active men being both traditionally masculine and grotesquely and hyperbolically manly. This is deviant, out-of-control, frightening white masculinity.

Brutalized Black Bodies

The inevitable violence of that form of masculinity was on display over and over again on August 12. A Black twenty-year-old special education teacher's aide became the victim of that violence after the Unite the Right rally was declared an unlawful assembly and alt-right participants swarmed throughout the downtown core. They found DeAndre Harris at the entrance of a parking garage next door to Charlottesville police headquarters. Harris and other counterprotesters had verbally and physically confronted the group, which was made up of white supremacist League of the South and neo-Nazi Traditionalist Worker Party members.[44] Harris ended up isolated inside the garage and prone on the ground, surrounded on all sides by pole-wielding white supremacists, who beat him as he desperately tried to raise himself from the

DeAndre Harris beaten by white racists in parking garage, August 12, 2017: Prone on the ground and helpless.

ground.[45] The brutal images went viral. They did so at least in part because they were so familiar. They fit the enduring beating-of-Uncle-Tom narrative that Linda Williams argues is so deeply engrained in the (white) American racial imagination. The Harris images also echo well-known civil rights–era iconic images. Consider the photo of John Lewis being beaten on the Edmund Pettus Bridge. Martin Berger notes the prevalence of images depicting Black bodies in similar visual arrangements: prone, sprawled out, felled, overrun, flattened onto the pavement. The narrative of emboldened, racist white power prevailing upright over victimized Black bodies prostrate on the ground is a painfully familiar visual trope.[46]

The power of the DeAndre Harris photo and video was in its appeal to conscience-stricken viewers to react and possibly do something. In Berger's argument about widely circulated civil rights–era photographs, he emphasizes the presumed appeal to appalled white people of these kinds of images. He suggests that white liberals, from unexamined positions of privilege, would want to disassociate themselves from these violent white people and intervene somehow. Engagement with these kinds of images, he argues, "encouraged white sympathy for blacks, and hence more support for legislative action. By placing blacks in the timeworn position of victim and supplicant, the photographs presented story lines that allowed magnanimous and sympathetic

John Lewis beaten by Alabama state trooper, Selma March 7, 1965. (AP)

whites to imagine themselves bestowing rights on blacks given that the dignified and suffering blacks of the photographic record appeared in no position to take anything from white America."[47] But the response to the DeAndre Harris imagery didn't quite play out as Berger's argument suggests. Rather than motivating tut-tutting white liberals to feel badly and perhaps donate money to an appropriate cause, the Harris images ended up as militant evidence. The activists wielding it managed to achieve justice in the courts, a result so seldom the case with cell phone video involving racist police. The racists in the DeAndre Harris images weren't protected by law enforcement badges.

Shaun King, a somewhat controversial Black Lives Matter activist, led a campaign to identify the culprits.[48] Crowd-sharing the images, King's social media followers managed to do what police did not: identify most of the racist attackers, all of whom ended up with lengthy prison sentences.[49] The people who came together to identify the culprits were part of a movement. In line with Watson's definition of militant evidence, the accumulation of these images moved people "into practices of resistance and militant action," as well as "into new frames of reference, and collective activism."[50] So while the images, on the one hand, conform to Berger's argument about iconic pictures of racism not fundamentally troubling race hierarchies and distributions of power, on the

Activists fight back: Using social media to identify the racist attackers of DeAndre Harris.

other hand the circulation of the Harris imagery provides yet another example of how antiracist and antifascist activists used the tools of new media to fight back against white supremacists and prevail over them.

A template for the DeAndre Harris image is the 1965 picture of John Lewis's beating on the Edmund Pettus Bridge. With his passing in July 2020, that photo became ubiquitous in the voluminous media coverage providing tributes to Lewis's life. Shortly after it was taken, the media images of his beating and of the Alabama state troopers billy-clubbing, gassing, and whipping hundreds of marchers on the Edmund Pettus Bridge sparked such national uproar and protests that landmark voting rights legislation got voted into law with dizzying speed. Those images supplied the civil rights movement with some of its most potent militant evidence.

Lewis died in the midst of another national uproar and widespread protest movement about racial justice. The 2020 uprisings were sparked, again, by media images of a Black man's brutalization—in this case, George Floyd's death agonies under the knee of white police officer Derek Chauvin. Since the beginnings of the Black Lives Matter movement in 2014 with the sustained street protests in response to the police killing of unarmed teenager Michael Brown in Ferguson, Missouri, protests have often followed the dissemination of images of Black men being killed at the hands of police. Both the death of Eric Garner, whose 2014 choke-hold killing was distressingly similar to Floyd's, as both men gasped over and over again, "I can't breathe," and the death of Philando Castile during a traffic stop two years later were, like Floyd's death, caught on cell phone video that quickly went viral. All were examples of militant evidence.

These images appear to tell the same story of white power and Black victimhood. But the circulation of the media images of Garner, Castile, and Floyd weren't due to the editorial decision-making of white newspaper, magazine, and TV news professionals who assumed they were reaching a largely white audience. Witnesses, bystanders, and in Castile's case, his girlfriend in the car seat next to him, provided the videos that got boosted on the internet by social media users and then boosted further by antiracist activists. Unlike the civil rights era's top-down process of media selection and circulation, we have a much more bottom-up dynamic in the Black Lives Matter era. The images may tell the same story of white racist violence against Black bodies, but the identities of those who create, disseminate, and frame the meanings of those images have changed, putting far more control into the hands of Black and antiracist groups.

And while large numbers of white protesters were a much-remarked-upon feature of the massive uprisings all across the United States in the summer of 2020, from large cities to small towns, appealing to white opinion and stirring the consciences of white people wasn't a key motivating factor in the movement. The uprisings of 2020 looked a lot like the local movement against the alt-right in Charlottesville in 2017. White people came out as antiracist allies in a sustained mobilization that was notable for its interracial solidarity. In Ryan Kelly's car attack photo, Marcus Martin, the Black man, may be the most fully visible victim, but we see bits and pieces of other victims' bodies, many of them white fellow protesters.

And there in the deep background is the partially obscured face of a white woman seeming to register the fact of the speeding car. Ryan Kelly caught the final moments of Heather Heyer.

5

VIOLA/HEATHER AND ANNIE/VERONICA

Two men and one woman died violently during the Selma campaign; numerous activists were badly injured. The Unite the Right rally in Charlottesville, in an odd symmetry, also resulted in the deaths of two men and one woman and injuries among dozens of activists. And in both cases, the female victim, a thirtysomething-year-old white woman, got the majority of the media's attention. In 1965, the white female victim was further victimized by a campaign of virulently misogynistic commentary from white supremacists that managed to seep into mainstream media coverage. In 2017, similar misogyny from alt-right figures on social media spewed forth, but the mainstream media response was very different. How did mainstream media frame these two white women as martyrs who died in the cause of opposing white supremacy?[1]

Fifty years and a transformative liberal feminist movement separate Viola Liuzzo from Heather Heyer. How and why were they treated as they were in media coverage? How and why did white supremacist media discourse manage to further victimize Liuzzo but not Heyer? In the wake of intersectional feminism and the Black Lives Matter movement separating Liuzzo's era from Heyer's, we'll consider as well the ways mass media has continued to elevate the white female victim while marginalizing the violence done to Black women activists.

Selma and Viola

When Viola Liuzzo, a thirty-nine-year-old wife, mother of five, and part-time student from Detroit, saw the news film of Bloody Sunday on the Edmund

Viola Glegg Liuzzo and Heather Heyer in CBS News coverage

Pettus Bridge, she made a decision to get into her car, leaving her husband and family behind. During her days in Selma, she worked with the local activists and participated in the culmination of the Selma campaign: the triumphant and now legendary five-day Selma-to-Montgomery march, with thousands assembling in front of the state capitol to hear Dr. King deliver one of his greatest speeches. Liuzzo spent the immediate aftermath ferrying marchers in her car back to Selma from Montgomery. On a final run and accompanied by a nineteen-year-old Black male fellow activist, Leroy Moton, Liuzzo was ambushed and murdered on Highway 80. The now dark and lonely highway had only recently been peopled with hundreds of singing and American flag–holding voting rights marchers, clergy, students, and many, many reporters. A car filled with Klansmen—one an FBI informant—sidled up next to her car after Liuzzo had fruitlessly tried to outrace them. A shotgun blast killed her almost instantly. Moton, spattered with her blood, pretended to be dead.[2]

Liuzzo was the third activist to be murdered during the campaign. A white clergyman, Rev. James Reeb, heeding Martin Luther King's call for clergy around the country to come to Selma following Bloody Sunday, had been beaten to death by white racists on the streets of Selma. And before Reeb, Jimmie Lee Jackson, a Black activist from nearby Marion, Alabama, participating in a nighttime voting rights march, had been shot by a state trooper as Jackson tried to shield his mother and his eighty-two-year-old grandfather from troopers' blows. Jackson's death served as the impetus for the march that was so viciously halted on the Pettus Bridge, but the martyred Black activist received only a small amount of coverage in the mainstream media. Reeb received far more, including interviews with his wife and condolences from President Johnson. Jackson's family received none of that kind of attention. Liuzzo, however, received by far the most media coverage, perhaps because her death came at the end of the campaign and what would have likely been the end of that particular news-event cycle, but mostly because she was white and female.[3]

Charlottesville and Heather

Heather Heyer's killing, like Liuzzo's, involved a car whose driver was propelled by aggrieved masculinist and white supremacist hatred. Heyer was a thirty-two-year-old paralegal from Charlottesville. Like Liuzzo, Heyer could be described as "blue-collar."[4] As Liuzzo had done, Heather Heyer made an impromptu decision to join counterprotesters on August 12 after seeing footage of white supremacist violence. Her friend, Courtney Commander, had been livestreaming the tiki torch march on UVA grounds. Appalled at what she saw, Heyer decided to join Commander and another African American friend and colleague, Melissa Blair, at the protest, texting a friend, "I feel compelled to go, to show solidarity."[5] She was marching with hundreds of antiracist counterprotesters who were celebrating what seemed to be the end of the Unite the Right rally. Then, suddenly, a neo-Nazi accelerated his car across the pedestrian downtown mall, deliberately smashing into the crowd, and then, throwing the car into reverse and injuring more people, retreated back and away. Heyer was killed almost instantly by blunt force trauma; dozens more were injured, some grievously.[6]

The two men killed during the Charlottesville Unite the Right debacle were not activists, as had been the case in Selma. Lt. H. Jay Cullen and Berke M. M. Bates were state police pilots who had spent the day in their helicopter above the scenes of confrontation in downtown Charlottesville providing video to

Virginia State Police of the melee below them.[7] Their helicopter went down, apparently because of a technical failure, exactly three hours after the car attack, killing the two pilots instantly. Cullen and Bates's deaths received mostly local coverage.

Mediating Viola: From Brave Heroine to Race Traitor

Media coverage of Viola Liuzzo initially extolled her bravery and her status as a loving wife and mother. News coverage played up the pathos of her grieving husband and now motherless children. CBS's *Evening News with Walter Cronkite* broadcast a story inside the Liuzzo home documenting the family's grief. The wire service UPI provided a similar story illustrated with photos of the Liuzzo family.[8] Politicians described her as brave and courageous, and her motivations were framed as the actions of one "who spent much of her life fighting for the rights of others."[9] Predictably, white supremacists pushed back at this way of understanding Mrs. Liuzzo. Imperial Wizard of the Ku Klux Klan Robert Shelton told reporters that Liuzzo was "set up to become a martyr and another rallying point for the Civil Rights Movement. If this woman was at home with the children where she belonged she wouldn't have been in jeopardy."[10]

Liuzzo was thus responsible for her own murder, according to the KKK. In white supremacist gender politics, white women's fundamental duty was to bear white children—and Liuzzo accomplished that task. But they were also supposed to accept and subordinate themselves to white male patriarchs. And Liuzzo failed at that requirement, having left her home and family, refusing to submit herself to her husband's wishes and putting the rights and concerns of Black people above those of her white family. She was, by this logic, a race traitor.[11]

This kind of misogyny and victim-blaming could have stayed sequestered in white supremacist publications. It did not. As Mary Stanton, Liuzzo's biographer, has detailed, Selma's Sheriff, Jim Clark, contacted a police commissioner that he knew from Liuzzo's home state of Michigan, requesting a file on the murdered civil rights activist. The resulting report full of personal details quickly found its way into the hands of the Klan, and then not only into the segregationist press but into national media as well. Liuzzo's reputation deteriorated as newspapers like the *New York Times* circulated details from the report.

In a story initially framed around the question of how the information about Mrs. Liuzzo had become available, the *Times*'s piece delved into details from the report about the murdered woman's private life. The formerly brave and courageous civil rights crusader extolled for jumping into her car and driving alone to Selma after seeing the violent news film from the Edmund Pettus Bridge was now, in the pages of the "newspaper of record," described rather differently. Drawing from the report, the *Times* noted a period in 1964 when Liuzzo, reported missing by her husband, drove alone through the state of New York and into Canada. With quotes directly from the report, readers learned that Mr. Liuzzo received despondent letters from his errant wife: "One letter was written by Viola while she was in a cemetery. She was giving births and deaths of various people and concluded the letter with her own birth and death date."[12] The unstated implication: this woman was possibly suicidal, with a penchant for impulsively jumping into her car for long-distance trips that had less to do with social justice aims and more to do with mental illness.[13]

In July 1965 the *Ladies' Home Journal* ran a poll of women's responses to Liuzzo's actions in leaving her home and children to support the voting rights movement in Selma. Of the women polled, 55 percent responded that she should have stayed home; only 26 percent thought she had a right to go.[14] Selma's other white martyr, Rev. James Reeb, also left behind a large family of children and a spouse when he traveled to Selma, but as Gary May notes in his book on the Liuzzo case, Rev. Reeb was not castigated for his actions: "Liuzzo's rejection of traditional gender roles and expectations played a significant role in robbing her of her martyrdom."[15] *Newsweek* magazine now dismissed and diminished her as "a plumpish, perky blonde, belatedly a sophomore at Wayne State University who liked a cause."[16]

Segregationist and white supremacist media responses became far more brutal. Because Viola Liuzzo was a race traitor, it only made sense that she must also have been involved in interracial sexual relations. A Klan-produced magazine, *Night Riders: The Inside Story of the Liuzzo Killing*, featured crime-scene photos of her dead body on the cover and, inside the volume, claimed that she was "hopped up" on dope and insinuated a sexual relationship between her and her teenage Black companion, Leroy Moton. They were seen "holding hands in public and walking around with their arms locked about each others' waists."[17] In fact, the two barely knew each other.[18] But to racists and segregationists, any images of white females and Black males in close proximity had to suggest sexual intimacy. The publication featured a photo of Liuzzo marching in bare feet, holding her shoes, and wearing a determined

Night Riders: KKK obsession with the mixing of Black males and white females during Selma-to-Montgomery march. Viola Liuzzo at far left.

expression. A tall Black man in the photo, partially obscured, may have been Moton. Numerous other pictures of Selma-to-Montgomery marchers were highlighted with circles around every white female seen next to a Black male. One such photo included the helpful caption: "Choose your partner. Throughout the march, white girls found Negro men irresistible."[19]

Because Liuzzo had violated racial and gender boundaries, Grand Wizard Shelton, during the trial of the Klan defendants, lashed out to reporters: "They portrayed her as being the mother of five lovely children and a community worker. The fact is she was a fat slob with crud that looked like rust all over her body [and] she was braless."[20] The Klan lawyer representing the defendants in his cross-examination of the doctor who performed Liuzzo's autopsy wanted to know whether she'd worn underpants and had had sexual relations (she had not). What were the conditions of her clothes and body—clean or unclean? Because she had been marching all day, sometimes taking off her shoes, probably to relieve swollen feet, the doctor testified that she hadn't been very clean.

This trope about the unclean white female body fits within white supremacist gender and race ideology. The non-white body was diseased, unclean, and inferior. Interracial contact between non-white and white people, especially white females, infected the white body, threatening to make white people dirty as well.[21] The insinuation that Liuzzo must have been sexually intimate with a Black male meant her body was now polluted and disgusting.

Mediating Heather: White Supremacist Misogyny Redux

Fifty-two years later, the mainstream media covering the death of Heather Heyer described her in ways quite similar to initial press coverage of Viola Liuzzo. Heyer was "a strong woman who stood up against discrimination" according to a *New York Times* headline. The story focused on friends who "described her as a passionate advocate for the disenfranchised."[22] Politicians extolled her bravery, tweeting out that Heyer "died standing up against hate & bigotry. Her bravery should inspire all to come together."[23]

But just like their predecessors a half century earlier, alt-right leaders and influencers pushed back with misogyny. Unite the Right rally organizer Jason Kessler sent out a tweet calling Heyer "a fat, disgusting Communist."[24] Other alt-right white supremacists and racists piled on more fat-shaming in social media posts. Viola Liuzzo had been similarly discounted for being fat. In both cases, this criticism of their bodies was another means to mark these women as not properly white and female. In white supremacist thinking beginning in the nineteenth and early twentieth century, fatness became tied to signs of ethnic and racial inferiority, according to Amy Farrell in her book *Fat Shame: Stigma and the Fat Body in American Culture*. "Primitive" peoples and all women had proclivities to fatness, which, according to this school of thought, proved that they were lower on the evolutionary scale. British and American white women were urged to avoid becoming fat, because to do so meant they "had moved down—had degraded—on the scale of civilization."[25] Heyer and Liuzzo, because their bodies did not conform to ideals of white femininity and because they actively engaged with racial "others," were cast out of whiteness. Labelling their bodies as fat and disgusting did the job.

And just as white supremacists deemed Liuzzo responsible for her own death by being out of place and not under the proper protection of her white husband, so Heyer was also blamed for her own death. In her case it was because she was fat, which caused a heart attack. (Heyer actually died of blunt force trauma.)[26] Hunter Wallace, a prominent white nationalist on the alt-right blog *Occidental Dissent*, appears to have started this bogus theory based on a confused initial media quote of Heather's traumatized mother, Susan Bro; it got amplified by others in various white racist social media hubs where Heyer was further fat-shamed.[27] Some of these 2017 social media venues, like the Klan's *Night Riders* publication in the 1960s, also had no qualms about publishing photos of the dead woman's murdered body. In both Liuzzo and Heyer's cases, the photos displayed their bodies but not their faces, further dehumanizing and degrading them.

The most notorious debasement of Heather Heyer occurred on the Daily Stormer a mere day after her murder. Written by neo-Nazi Andrew Anglin, the piece also blamed Heyer for her own death, in this case claiming that her fatness made her too slow to get out of the way of an admirably fast car. But Anglin seemed particularly interested in the one significant way that Heyer differed from Liuzzo: Heyer had no children. Anglin pointed out her age and her childless state. He went on to make loathsome comments about what that meant about her value, burden to society, and neglect of her fundamental maternal duty.[28] His comments were vile enough to get the Daily Stormer booted off the internet, at least for a while, with one service provider after another refusing to host the site.

There wasn't anything terribly surprising or novel about his comments, however. They were at the heart of modern white supremacy and its "Fourteen Words" mantra: "We must secure the existence of our people and a future for white children."[29] Heyer had, by this logic, neglected to secure that existence by not giving birth to white children. Kathleen Belew, writing about the white power movement in the post-Vietnam era, points out how white power activists believed that "the future of the white race . . . rest[ed] with the mothers of white children." Every white woman was required to bear them. She quotes one neo-Nazi newspaper declaring over a photo of a white woman: "If this woman doesn't have three or more children during her lifetime she is helping to speed her Race along the road to extinction."[30] By not being married (to a white man) and childless, Heather Heyer was another race traitor hastening "the Great Replacement;" she was therefore disgusting.

While some of the white supremacist misogyny that swirled around Viola Liuzzo found its way into mainstream media coverage, undermining and tarnishing her status as a civil rights martyr, nothing similar happened with Heather Heyer. In fact, Heyer has become the name and face of resistance to the Summer of Hate in Charlottesville. The narrow side street off the city's downtown pedestrian mall where the car attack happened has been officially renamed by the city "Heather Heyer Way." For well over a year after the attacks, shops and businesses around town displayed decals with her name and a heart, always in violet, known among many Charlottesvillians to be her favorite color. A foundation in her name would provide scholarships to students pursuing degrees or certifications in fields dedicated to social change and unity.[31]

Heather Heyer Way in Charlottesville with chalk and craft decorations by locals. (Aniko Bodroghkozy, photographer)

Honors and respect for Liuzzo would come only many decades after her death, as her children struggled to rehabilitate her legacy.[32]

Why were white supremacists so successful in turning the mainstream media against a white female antiracist activist in 1965, whereas their alt-right successors in 2017, though using similar tropes, were not only unsuccessful in raising questions about Heyer's status as a woman, as well as about her appearance and activities, but were, in the case of Anglin, literally chased off the internet? Mary Stanton, in her 1998 biography, ponders the question of why Liuzzo never became a civil rights movement symbol and why the sullying of her reputation went unchallenged. She suggests that Liuzzo had "no organized constituency to defend her." Because Liuzzo went to Selma on her own, she had no coordinated group to speak or vouch for her. Her husband, a member of the Teamsters union, which was under scrutiny at the time for its strong-arm tactics, was himself being smeared publicly. He didn't have the emotional strength to become her champion in front of the media.[33]

And to make the situation more daunting, J. Edgar Hoover personally launched the smear campaign against Liuzzo to divert any attention to the role played by FBI informant, Gary Thomas Rowe, one of the four men in the car that ran her down, a violent man implicated in other seminal moments of civil rights–era violence.[34] Of course, Hoover also ran a years-long campaign to smear Martin Luther King, wiretapping his motels and trying to get the press to run stories about the civil rights leader's extramarital affairs. Hoover's attempts to discredit King never went anywhere. King had a movement behind him, with many powerful allies, friends, and political officials in his corner. His image also conformed to dominant ideals of respectability and middle-classness, with a highly formal self-presentation that made him "media-ready." King thus had resources to marshal against the power of Hoover and the FBI. Viola Liuzzo and her family did not. She had no powerful allies to vouch for her on an ongoing basis, and she didn't fit dominant ideals of proper feminine respectability and middle-classness. Viola Liuzzo had no one to be her spokesperson and media advocate when it mattered most. It would take decades before her grown children could effectively step into that role, eventually securing powerful media platforms to broadcast their accounts of what the KKK and the FBI had done to their mother's posthumous reputation and to their own brutalized family.[35]

Susan Bro's Media Platform: Magnifying Heather

Heather Heyer, on the other hand, did have a powerful advocate: her mother, Susan Bro. Heyer's status as the martyr of the Unite the Right violence would be solidified four days after her murder, at her memorial at the thousand-seat Paramount Theater, two short blocks from where she had been killed. National and international media covered the memorial and made a diminutive woman with long, white-grey hair and a schoolteacher's demeanor a sudden media phenomenon. Susan Bro, from the depths of grief and anguish, was somehow able to speak memorable sound bites: "They tried to kill my child to shut her up. But guess what? You just magnified her"; "I'd rather have my child, but by golly, if I have to give her up, make it count."[36]

Without preparation or any media training, Mrs. Bro was blessed with natural on-camera communication skills. One CBS reporter covering the memorial remarked that she was "incredibly articulate—and emotional." He noted that while Heyer's mother didn't like talking on camera, she was ready to do it for her daughter.[37] And she did, over and over again. Susan Bro became a frequent media presence, whether on cable news or at the MTV Video Music Awards, where she announced the formation of the Heather Heyer Foundation. She was a go-to interviewee when alt-right violence perpetrators were

Susan Bro speaking at the memorial for her daughter broadcast by national media: "Guess what? You just magnified her."

arrested, charged, and put on trial. Media outlets went to her for comments on the first anniversary of the Summer of Hate; when the neo-Nazi who killed her daughter was tried and convicted, first on state charges and later federally; when Joe Biden announced his candidacy for the presidency in 2019 by invoking "Charlottesville" in a campaign video; at a Congressional oversight committee on white supremacy; and at President Biden's signing of the Jabara-Heyer No Hate Act in 2021.

Susan Bro had a powerful and continuing media platform. She spoke calmly, with deliberation, but never appeared coached or scripted. Her grandmotherly and folksy demeanor made her approachable. Channeling her daughter's antiracist cause, Susan Bro was adept at making antiracist politics legible and acceptable to white viewers, and perhaps more palatable to those in the white working class since Bro self-identified as working-class. Unlike Viola Liuzzo's Teamster husband, Susan Bro was unassailable. While she was inevitably fat-shamed like her daughter in the dank corners of the white nationalist web, in mainstream media she controlled her message and beginning at her daughter's memorial almost single-handedly ensured Heather Heyer's status as a martyr to white nationalist hate.

Another reason the same misogyny that circulated against Viola Liuzzo in the 1960s did not spread successfully outside the dark web of the alt-right in 2017 is the impact of feminism in the decades since her death. Mary Stanton suggests that "for feminists, [Liuzzo's] blue collar lifestyle made her uninteresting."[38] This explanation doesn't seem quite adequate. The organized second-wave women's movement was only in its early days in the mid-1960s. The National Organization for Women would not come into being until a year after Liuzzo's murder. Betty Friedan's *The Feminine Mystique*, a best seller that attempted to diagnose the dissatisfaction and lack of fulfillment that marriage and stay-at-home motherhood provided for middle-class white women, appeared in 1963. Liuzzo's biography seemed a textbook case of a woman responding admirably to what Friedan called "the problem that has no name."[39]

But at the time of Liuzzo's death, feminism as a political movement had not quite asserted itself into the national consciousness, let alone garnered the mass media attention it would by the late 1960s and 1970s.[40] White supremacist gender politics were fundamentally not very different from what predominated in post–World War II America when it came to naturalized understandings of appropriate roles for white women and men. Klan members and white supremacists may have stated those politics in more crude and hateful terms, but the underlying arguments wouldn't have been all that shocking, as polling by the *Ladies' Home Journal* suggested: the majority of white women polled agreed with the Klan's Grand Wizard about Viola Liuzzo's proper place.

By 2017 a newly energized fourth-wave feminist movement, from the 2017 Women's March to #TimesUp and #MeToo, ensured that alt-right misogyny, bearing little difference from its predecessors, would have much less of a chance to gain any purchase in mainstream media.[41] Alexandra Minna Stern's arguments about the alt-right's timescape, wherein 1965 looms large, are instructive here. It was during this annus horribilis that the White Republic and its attendant male dominance was lost. After 1965, women like Heyer could no longer be controlled in life or death as Liuzzo had been in death. Second-wave liberal feminism, enabled in many ways by the passage of the Civil Rights Act, has successfully and enduringly protected the reputations of some women, as attested by the rapid and aggressive shutting down of Andrew Anglin. What happened to Viola Liuzzo in 1965 would have been much less likely in 2017.

Mediating the Black Female Activist Victim: Annie Lee Cooper, 1965 / Veronica Fitzhugh, 2017

But what if Heyer had been Black? What if Liuzzo had been Black? The title of the foundational volume that helped give birth to the scholarly field of

Black women's studies and that inspired legal scholar Kimberlé Crenshaw in her seminal work on intersectional feminism remains salient here: "All the men were black, all the women were white, but some of us were brave."[42] The mass media saw Black men as civil rights leaders and white supremacy's victims; the media also took note of white women. Black women, for the most part, were largely invisible, both during the coverage of the Selma campaign and in the media's treatment of the Summer of Hate in Charlottesville. The press during and immediately following August 12, 2017, tended to privilege the city's male white mayor and Black vice-mayor, along with a white clergyman, Seth Wispelwey, who was involved with a local activist clergy group. Black women organizers and leaders remained largely invisible, with the exception of Dr. Jalane Schmidt, a UVA religious studies professor and key activist and organizer with Charlottesville's Black Lives Matter, who received some national and international media attention in the aftermath of the crisis.[43]

The situation fifty years earlier in Selma hadn't been all that different. For instance, the SCLC and SNCC's Diane Nash and the Dallas County Voters League's Amelia Boynton were key leaders and organizers of the Selma campaign. Boynton achieved media visibility only briefly. On one occasion early in the campaign, she was manhandled by Sheriff Clark during a march on the county courthouse and dragged by her coat in front of news photographers; the dramatic photo appeared in both the *New York Times* and the *Washington Post*.[44] During the Edmund Pettus Bridge assault, a photo of Boynton crumpled on the ground, unconscious from the blows of a state trooper, also circulated widely.

Activist Annie Lee Cooper also received fleeting media attention when, foregoing movement leaders' admonitions to remain nonviolent, she slugged Sheriff Clark after he shoved and insulted fellow would-be registrants waiting in line at the courthouse. With photographers and TV news cameras recording, Clark and a few of his deputies threw Cooper violently to the ground. A photo of Clark on top of Cooper with his billy club poised as the deputies forcefully pinned her down appeared in newspapers around the country.[45]

None of these instances of white supremacist violence against African American women resulted in ongoing media attention to them. Like Boynton, Cooper was not quoted in national media coverage; only her brutalized body spoke. Annie Lee Cooper would likely have remained unknown to everyone but historians of the Selma campaign had it not been for filmmaker Ava DuVernay and Oprah Winfrey, who highlighted Cooper in DuVernay's acclaimed and

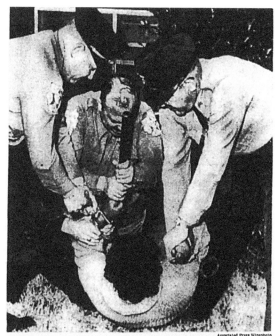

VIOLENCE IN ALABAMA: Sheriff James G. Clark, center, and two deputies struggle with Negro woman who stepped out of voter registration line in Selma and hit the sheriff.

Annie Lee Cooper fighting back against white supremacy on the front page of the *New York Times*.

successful 2015 Hollywood film *Selma*.[46] By taking the role of Cooper, Winfrey ensured this civil rights activist would no longer be unheard and invisible.[47]

The beating of Black civil rights female activists by law enforcement may not have been as newsworthy as the cold-blooded murder of a white female activist by Klan members, but for the mass media even the most inconsequential appearance of a white woman during the Selma campaign could get boosted into a significant news event. *Life* magazine ran a multipage cover story on the aftermath of the Edmund Pettus Bridge violence and found it worthwhile to devote an entire page, featuring two color photos, to Illinois Senator Paul Douglas's wife, who had traveled to Selma along with so many others. Mrs. Paul Douglas was in no way a significant political figure, but *Life* magazine's decision to highlight a large color image of her maternally placing a white-gloved hand on Martin Luther King's shoulder in a gesture of support suggested that she mattered.[48] What mattered was her whiteness.

The media treatment of Selma's Annie Lee Cooper maps surprisingly closely onto that of Charlottesville's Veronica Fitzhugh in 2017. Fitzhugh, a queer femme Black activist, was known for her community defense work and for her creative and eye-catching sartorial presentation. Like Annie Lee Cooper, Fitzhugh was physically large; in her 2017 protest activity, she took up space and was confrontational. Cooper and Fitzhugh could both be defined as "unruly women," a concept first deployed by the historian of early modern Europe, Natalie Zemon Davis and then adopted by media studies scholar Kathleen K. Rowe who defined as unruly "whenever women, especially women's bodies, are considered excessive—too fat, too mouthy, too old, too dirty, too pregnant, too sexual (or not sexual enough) for the norms of conventional gender representation . . . . Through body and speech, the unruly woman violates the unspoken feminine sanction against 'making a spectacle' of herself."[49]

In the case of Cooper, a CBS News story emphasized her excessiveness and represented her protest action as an unruly spectacle. She was portrayed as odd: tracking down a line at the courthouse of mostly well-dressed Black women would-be registrants, CBS's news camera paused on a shoe-less Cooper, zooming in on her stockinged feet and panning over to her shoes placed on another step. She was then shown in close-up appearing shifty-eyed. During the confrontation with Clark and his deputies, CBS managed to get a disconcertingly extreme close-up of Cooper either grimacing or smiling strangely, and then in a longer shot being roughly rolled over and hauled up, still shoeless, by the law officers.[50] Everything about Cooper was depicted as "too much": her bodily presentation, her refusal to appear properly dignified, her resistance.

Veronica Fitzhugh was similarly depicted in local media accounts as unruly and excessive. She was arrested a number of times during the Summer of Hate on dubious charges for challenging white supremacists in the run-up to the Unite the Right rally on August 12. She forcefully confronted Jason Kessler and was charged with disorderly conduct and assault: she apparently shook the chair he was sitting in on a patio with Proud Boys on Charlottesville pedestrian downtown mall. Her action was part of a community-defense antiracist effort to confront the white supremacists who were increasingly congregating publicly in the months leading up to the Unite the Right rally, as discussed in chapter 3. More visibly, during the Ku Klux Klan rally on July 8, 2017, Fitzhugh, in an act of civil disobedience, tried to block the path of a motley crew of Klansmen into Justice Park as Virginia state troopers and local police protected them, rather than the thousand-plus anti-Klan protesters. Fitzhugh was aggressively arrested and charged with obstruction. A photo of her arrest, prone on the ground with police over her, echoed the more famous photo of Annie Lee Cooper.[51]

Just as media coverage of Cooper had silenced her and focused on her visual excessiveness, local media in Charlottesville did the same with Fitzhugh. The University of Virginia English graduate and poet was seldom given voice to explain her activism or her self-presentation. News coverage emphasized what they deemed her strangeness. An article on her not-guilty verdict in *C-ville Weekly* opened with this lede: "Wearing a hot pink wig and carrying the head of Donald Trump as a purse...." The article went on to quote both her attorney and the Commonwealth Attorney who prosecuted her case. The latter opined that she may have been arrested for "admirable reasons" but that "she simply took it too far." Framed as an unruly Black woman in her refusal to stay within proper bounds, she confronted the fact that the Klan had not only been invited to rally in a city park but received a police escort and protection in order to do so. The article ended with the reporter observing: "The activist, known for her outlandish wardrobe, will go on trial for the assault and disorderly conduct charges [her actions against Kessler] November 20. What will she wear next?"[52] Fitzhugh's self-presentation was obviously a component of her message, but local media's disinclination to quote her inevitably silenced and marginalized her.

It matters whose lives, voices, bodies, and experiences are given a media platform. In dying for racial justice, two white women mattered. But what does one do with that fact? Susan Bro, speaking before a House committee examining white supremacist violence, chose to be self-reflexive about the platform she had continued to be given in the years following the Unite the Right mayhem. "Heather was killed primarily because Mr. Fields was aiming to kill someone who he thought was Black," she told Congress, noting that the neo-Nazi ploughed into a crowd of Black Lives Matter supporters. "I've been given a huge platform because I'm white, and many black parents lose their children, many Muslim parents lose their children, Jewish parents lose their children, and nobody pays attention. And because we have this myth of the sacredness of the white female, I've been given a platform, so I'm going to use that platform to keep drawing attention back to where the issues are."[53]

White women as a slice of the population are certainly imperiled by the rise of right-wing extremism and white supremacy, considering how their life choices would be constrained by the *Handmaid's Tale*-style patriarchy that the alt-right envisions. However, as Bro noted, other groups with less immediate access to news media microphones are far more vulnerable and more clearly in the crosshairs of this movement. Recent mass murder events—at a mosque in Christchurch, New Zealand, in 2019, killing fifty-one Muslims; a Walmart in El Paso, Texas, that same year, targeting Latinos and murdering twenty-two; a synagogue in Pittsburgh in 2018, massacring nine Jews; a Tops food market in a predominantly Black Buffalo neighborhood in 2022, killing ten—are all examples of white supremacist extremism, with all the shooters in these cases leaving online manifestos parroting the ideology of the alt-right.[54] As it was in 1965 when the death of a white woman motivated the nation—and its president, who involved himself personally in Liuzzo's case—to get voting rights legislation passed, so it was in 2017 when the death of another white woman concentrated the nation's attention on the palpable threat of alt-right extremism. If these two martyrs to the antiracist cause had been Black women or Latina women, it is possible that "Selma" and "Charlottesville" would never have elicited the sustained national outrage that made both these Southern towns into symbols of the struggle against white supremacy.

6

"THIS IS WHAT COMMUNITY LOOKS LIKE!"

It all comes back to monuments. How do communities use their built environments to make sense of, interpret, and communicate their histories, both distant and more recent? Whose stories get told, and whose are ignored? In 2017, Charlottesville became an international media event as it struggled with right-wing extremists over these questions. In the aftermath of the Summer of Hate, Charlottesville residents continued to grapple with the question of how to use public space to communicate something meaningful about the community, in the wake of what had happened in its streets and parks when alt-right racists, KKK, and neo-Nazis came to town.

In the summer of 2019 on the second anniversary of the Summer of Hate, a group of Charlottesville activists came together to create a temporary public installation telling a local story about racial and social justice activism. It was an attempt to push back against the entrenched media narrative about "Charlottesville," which emphasized alt-right violence, hatred, and the martyrdom of Heather Heyer. A giant photography mural wheat-pasted on an expansive wall by the town's downtown pedestrian mall and just a few blocks from the street where the terrorist car attack happened, it was called "Inside Out Charlottesville: This Is What Community Looks Like."[1]

In this chapter I want to explore the theme of mass media narratives, local counternarratives, and lessons from civil rights movement venues—Birmingham in particular—by examining how communities that became symbols (then) or hashtags (now) can create new monuments. What kind of work do these public-facing installations perform? Who are they for? How do they engage the public in thinking about (or rethinking) iconic, dramatic, and seminal events that seem familiar because their media images have seeped so deeply into the American cultural imagination?

Birmingham's Kelly Ingram Park: Civil Rights Movement Monuments

Let's begin by visiting Kelly Ingram Park. This four-acre-square green space in downtown Birmingham resembles the smaller Emancipation (former Lee, currently Market Street) Park in Charlottesville. Both city parks served as the major battlegrounds that turned their towns into international, headline-making media news stories and pivot points in American racial politics.

On Thursday, May 3, 1963, Martin Luther King's SCLC was in the second day of its "Children's Crusade," flooding the area around the park with Black schoolchildren, truant from their schools and ready to be arrested and sent to jail in place of the dwindling number of adults willing or able to put themselves at such risk. On that day, Public Safety Commissioner Bull Connor made the fateful decision to send in not just police officers but also the fire department and the police K-9 corps to repel and terrify the hundreds of young people who streamed out, wave after wave, from the 16th Street Baptist Church, the movement's staging ground, which was by the northwest corner of the park. On the scene were photojournalists and network news cameramen, capturing the iconic images that half a century later continue to signify the evils of segregation and white supremacy.

One of the most enduring of the photos to come out of the civil rights era was one we've already encountered in chapter 4: Bill Hudson's picture of fifteen-year-old Walter Gadsden being attacked by a police dog and displaying a seemingly "saintly calm" (see p. 100). But is that what was really going on? Along with being one of the most famous civil rights movement images, it's also notably deceptive. Young Gadsden wasn't a participant in the Children's Crusade; he was a bystander. He wasn't a particularly sympathetic one, at that. His family owned the *Birmingham World* newspaper, which was quite disapproving of Martin Luther King and his direct-action protests. According to Diane McWhorter in her comprehensive history of the Birmingham movement, "Walter shared his class's resentment of King's intervention."[2]

Go back and look carefully at that photograph. Walter's left hand is grabbing the wrist of the policeman, Dick Middleton. Walter's left leg is up, in an attempt to kick away the dog (whose name was Leo). Middleton, despite the grimacing mouth and hostile-looking dark shades, is pulling Leo away from the young man.[3] The reality is more complex and nuanced than the story told by the still image. Nevertheless, there's a valid reason the photo is iconic: it documents the system of white supremacist violence and hatred. That Middleton as an individual may not have been personally racist, and that Walter Gadsden as an individual was not a nonviolent civil rights activist, doesn't ultimately matter.[4] The power of the photo lies in the larger truth it illustrates.

Thirty years later, Birmingham elected its first African American mayor, Richard Arrington Jr., and unveiled a plan for building a "civil rights district" for heritage tourism in the city. 1992 saw the opening of the Civil Rights Institute, a museum and research center facing Kelly Ingram Park and close by the 16th Street Baptist Church. The park also got a makeover, using landscape design and statuary to memorialize and monumentalize the story of the Children's Crusade. The park is chock-full of statues. One design set titled *Freedom Walk* brings the park's visitors into direct engagement with sculptures that evoke some of the famous photographs, such as a statue of young people cowering against a wall with water cannons pointed at them.

As visitors continue along the paved walkway through the park, they

Kelly Ingram Park "Freedom Walk" statues evoking iconic photographs: Young people menaced by high powered fire hoses. (Alan Spears, photographer; National Parks Conservation Association/Creative Commons)

suddenly find themselves passing through a sculpture of vicious dogs lunging at them from both sides. The *Freedom Walk* sculptural designs encourage visitors to place themselves in the position of the civil rights activists who braved the high-powered hoses and the snarling police dogs. What did it feel like to have a water cannon pointed at you? What was it like finding yourself surrounded by snapping German shepherds? The design encourages not the distanced, somewhat removed sympathy elicited by the iconic photos they reinterpret but rather an embodied, active empathy: you are a besieged African American activist, not an onlooker.

Who's missing from this assemblage of statues? We've got water cannons, but no firefighters; dogs, but no K-9 police officers. The *Freedom Walk* monuments give us the tools of segregationist violence, but not the white human antagonists who perpetrated it. Another sculptural element of the grouping presents two Black children, who represent the youngest among those who spilled out of the 16th Street Baptist Church right into buses to be carted off to jail on the first day of the Children's Crusade on May 2, 1963. Connor wouldn't bring

Kelly Ingram Park "Freedom Walk" statues: You are threatened by Bull Connor's dogs. (Wikicommons)

Kelly Ingram Park "Freedom Walk" statues: School children carted off to jail during the "Children's Crusade." (Aniko Bodroghkozy, photographer)

out the dogs and fire hoses until the next day. In this sculpture, the children are presented on one side of the walkway, standing on a platform with the words "I ain't afraid of your jail" carved under their feet. On the opposite side of the walkway is a sculpture of prison bars. If you walk around that structure, you see the youngsters behind bars. A jail, but no jailers. Scholar R. Bruce Brasell has noted the omission of white antagonists from the *Freedom Walk* assemblage. He argues that for white people engaging with the sculptures, there's no bothering of their consciences with how their whiteness is implicated in these historic acts of racism.[5]

Perhaps. But on the other hand, the sculptural representation of white racism's tools of violence may be enough to suggest the systemic nature of the oppression these monuments are asking us to remember. Martin Berger, whose exploration of civil rights photography I discussed in chapter 4, critiqued the iconic civil rights photographs for centering white people as the active agents making things happen while the Black civil rights marchers and activists are rendered as passive, piteous objects acted upon. The *Freedom Walk* monuments evoke the photographs but are not telling the same story. By taking the white bodies out of the representation, visitors can focus their engagement and their emotional response on the Black demonstrators as the human agents who mattered. White supremacy, rather than a group of bad individuals, is a system and structure wielding violence.

Foot Soldier: Re-narrating the Walter Gadsden Photo

Continue along the pathway, and you come to *Foot Soldier.* It looks very familiar—but also not. While the *Freedom Walk* statues were all created by James Drake, a white sculptor, this one is the work of African American artist Ronald McDowell. Even more than Drake's pieces, McDowell's statue is an obvious evocation of the Children's Crusade's most iconic photo: the Walter Gadsden picture. It's not a recreation, however, and the statue's departures from its source material are crucial to the different story it tells. There's none of the ambiguity of Bill Hudson's photo. Consider how McDowell represents the young boy. He looks much younger and smaller than Gadsden, more a child than a high schooler. His arms and hands are flung out behind him, his legs straight as his torso tilts away from both the dog and the policeman. The boy is neither submitting to the attack (as most people casually looking at the photo would surmise) nor engaging in self-defense (as Gadsden was actually doing). He also looks straight at the police officer—his eyes are not cast down in the "saintly calm" that *Life* magazine's photo editor attributed to Gadsden. The boy is in a nonviolent but also a confrontational stance toward the white police officer: "I'm looking at you." In the Jim Crow south, Black looks, or what bell hooks has called "the oppositional gaze," got Black people lynched.[6]

Now look at the dog. It's not actually a German shepherd: McDowell has transformed it into a wolf.[7] In the Hudson photo, Leo's jaws are in full contact with Gadsden's midriff; in McDowell's sculpture, the wolf jaws are fully visible at the center of the sculptural design. Then there's the police officer. This is the only statue of a white person in Kelly Ingram Park. He doesn't look much like Dick Middleton. This younger-looking figure is standing ramrod-straight and tall with a strong, muscled physique and is not pulling back on the wolf's leash. The chain hangs loose. The face isn't grimacing either, as Middleton's was. Rather, McDowell sculpted a resolute and determined line to the mouth. Like Middleton, the sculpted figure has on a police hat and sunglasses. But there's something odd about those shades. Are they just a bit too big for the face?

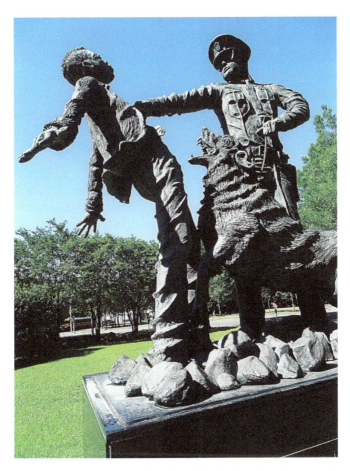

Kelly Ingram Park, "Foot Soldier": Evoking Walter Gadsden but telling a different story. (Adam Jones, photographer/Wikicommons)

McDowell shared a message here too: the policeman is blind.[8] This is what white supremacy looks like: powerful, violent, and unable to see the viciousness it perpetuates.

The well-known writer Malcolm Gladwell in an episode about this statue in his popular podcast, *Revisionist History,* focuses a lot of attention on how both the photograph and the statue mess around with truth. He unearths interviews with Middleton's wife and a friend, as well as finding an obscure interview the Civil Rights Institute did with Gadsden when *Foot Soldier* was unveiled in the mid-1990s. In conversation with McDowell during the episode, Gladwell suggests repeatedly, albeit with sympathy, that the artist was engaged in "mischief" in the ways he recreated the famous photo. McDowell was messing subversively with "history." In Gladwell's definition, history comes down to this: "Each side writes their own story, and the winner's story is the one we call the truth. You don't think white people told their share of whoppers over the years in the South? You don't think that there's a statue in a Southern town somewhere of a champion of the Confederacy that makes a hero of someone who was actually a villain? White people got to do that in the South for centuries. *Foot Soldier* is just what happens when the people on the bottom finally get the power to tell the story their way."[9]

Gladwell comes uncomfortably close to drawing a moral equivalence between the work done by Confederate monuments and by these newer civil rights movement statues. But let's consider the actual power dynamics at work here. Charlottesville's statues to Generals Stonewall Jackson and Robert E. Lee provide a useful and representative example. The monuments went up, respectively, in 1921 and 1924, the years of the Ku Klux Klan's greatest power and the full entrenchment of segregationist Jim Crow politics in the South. The park that would display the Jackson monument had previously been an African American neighborhood known as McKee Row. It was filled with tenements, many owned by a well-to-do Black landlord, John West, who was among the largest property-owners in the county. All the buildings were expropriated, the Black residents thrown out and their homes demolished, initially to make way for a white school but ultimately to create a whites-only park.[10] The Jackson statue that looms over the whitened space—like Lee Park with its heroic man on horseback, which was created a few years later—marked the forced removal of African Americans from the center of the city as well as from any property rights or political power. Jackson and Lee, who had never set foot in Charlottesville or Albemarle County during the Civil War, inspired statues whose purpose wasn't ultimately about telling one group's "whopper" of a story, as Gladwell suggests, making heroes out of traitors. Those statues, as public historian and director of Charlottesville's African American Heritage Center Andrea Douglas has argued, did political work in marking a power dynamic: African Americans were not welcome in downtown Charlottesville; they would have no control, no rights. The statues concretized the forced removal of Black people from the area's body politic.[11] The built environment memorialized that act. Needless to say, Confederate monuments in other Southern towns and cities did similar political work.

Compare that to the work done by the statues in Kelly Ingram Park. They aren't marking and asserting the rights and physical presence of one group over and against another. If the statues are telling a story of Birmingham's Black community, it isn't as part of a larger scheme to disenfranchise and displace others. The point of the Birmingham statues is to memorialize and monumentalize the efforts of ordinary people (even as there is also a statue of Martin Luther King in the park), especially the most vulnerable and youngest of historical actors: children. The truth these statues tell is that anyone can make history and that their actions matter.[12]

It took thirty years and more, but Birmingham found a way to tell the story of how it confronted racism; it found a means to memorialize its civil rights movement activists. Permanent monuments to historically significant events generally take time. Solidifying historical incidents' meanings and significance is a long process, especially if they are politically or ideologically contested.[13] It may still be too soon to understand the long-term historical significance for the United States of Charlottesville's Summer of Hate. That it will serve as a seminal moment of the Trump era seems certain. But what it ultimately signifies about American racism, antisemitism, rising fascism and white nationalism, and the struggles against them remains to be seen. As a media event, #Charlottesville brought all these issues into maximum discursive visibility, signaling the precariousness of the civil rights–era victories and the necessity for antiracist and antifascist activists to mobilize.

Nevertheless, even in the near term, two years after the events, Charlottesvillians wanted to intervene in the solidifying narrative about "#Charlottesville." It started with "Unity Days." In February 2019, City Council authorized a series of community events to span the entire summer, reserving space in all the downtown parks to supersede any other potential requests. By commandeering the parks, the city ensured that it wouldn't have to grapple with Jason Kessler or any other alt-right extremists requesting a park permit and hoping for a replay of Unite the Right 2017. Unity Days was also a response to the city's problematic decision-making for the first anniversary in August 2018. Fearing a possible return of those extremists, the city had cordoned off much of downtown with roadblocks and brought in a very heavy police presence, with checkpoints, militarized riot squads, and an oppressive approach by law enforcement towards antiracist activists wanting to mark the one-year anniversary with marches and a large gathering at the site of the car attack.

Place as Memorial: Heather Heyer Way and Edmund Pettus Bridge

To the extent that Charlottesville has a memorial to A12, it is at Heather Heyer Way, the portion of 4th Street just south of the downtown pedestrian mall where the car attack occurred and officially renamed by the city in Heyer's honor. While the naming of the street was an official act of memorialization, the chalked messages on the brick wall near the site of the carnage, along with the flowers, knitted sleeves, and purple ribbons attached to nearby poles, function as much more informal kinds of memorialization work (see p. 120). Whether the space evolves into a more permanent shrine and gathering venue for future acts of collective memory and solidarity remains to be seen.[14] Consider what happened with the Edmund Pettus Bridge.

As was the case in 1965, the bridge remains the main route out of downtown Selma onto Highway 80, taking drivers to destinations like Craig Airforce Base due south of town or off to the state capital, Montgomery, fifty miles east. But the bridge spanning the Alabama River is also a shrine and memorial. Every Spring in March, hundreds and thousands come to walk ceremonially over the bridge. It started on the tenth anniversary of Bloody Sunday in 1975, with Coretta Scott King leading thousands in a march commemorating the event but also emphasizing the work that still needed to be done.[15] On the fiftieth anniversary, President Obama, his family, and Selma campaign veterans marched across the bridge, and Obama delivered one of his signature speeches at the spot where attendees, including John Lewis and the now 104-year-old Amelia Boynton, had been beaten and gassed. The commemoration received wall-to-wall media coverage. In July 2020, mass media returned to cover the ceremonial return to Selma of John Lewis's body, as his flag-draped coffin on a horse-drawn carriage retraced his 1965 path, from Brown Chapel to the bridge and triumphantly across it, one last time. A nonprofit called "Selma Bridge Crossing Jubilee" plans yearly festivities in early March at the bridge and every five years hosts marches all the way down Highway 80 to Montgomery.[16] Rather than build a monument to the voting rights activists, the iconic structure, so visible in news film and photojournalism of Bloody Sunday and the triumphant beginning of the Selma-to-Montgomery march, became itself the monument.

It's impossible to predict why certain sites of trauma and violence become places of pilgrimage and commemoration. In the short number of years since

John Lewis's final crossing over the Edmund Pettus Bridge, July 26, 2020. The bridge as monument to the movement for voting rights.

the Unite the Right mayhem, the car attack site has served in that capacity. Frequented by locals, it does also appear to attract the attention of tourists. I've been asked a number of times while on the downtown mall to point visitors to the place where the attack happened.

For the first anniversary, in 2018, this "from the bottom-up" public memorial space served as the venue for a large rally to remember the dead and injured. Unfortunately, lines of riot police with shields along with armored vehicles did little to comfort the activists.[17] There was, of course, a significant media presence and much attention on Susan Bro, who appeared briefly at the memorial. If the criticism of city and state officials in August 2017 was too little police action and in August 2018 too much police action, what would happen in 2019? There was unlikely to be the great amount of national media attention on the two-year anniversary as there had been in 2018. The first-year anniversary of a major media event is almost inevitably newsworthy. After that, the fifth year will sometimes provide a news peg, but more frequently news organizations wait a decade to descend again for stories meditating on what's changed and what hasn't, whether the community has healed, and what it all means for the nation.

Re-narrating "Charlottesville":
The Inside Out Photography Installation

The second-year anniversary would be a mostly local affair, with "Unity Days" an opportunity for the community to reflect on what "#Charlottesville" meant two years on from the Unite the Right cataclysm. The impulse to push back against entrenched media narratives was clear. One of the key city officials behind the organizing of Unity Days, Charlene Green, Director of Charlottesville's Office of Human Rights, said this to local press: "People feel like the loss of the influence or control of the narrative happened back in 2017 about what Charlottesville is all about." Suggesting that local people needed to be involved and engaged, she went on to ask: "And so, how do we as a community affect that narrative?"[18] Each month was to have a specific theme, with August devoted to remembrance, education, and inspiration.

Lisa Draine, the former manager of Charlottesville's LOOK3 Festival of the Photograph and parent of an activist daughter seriously injured in the terrorist car attack, responded to the call for projects. She proposed a public art installation inspired by the work of renowned French street photographer JR. To create "Inside Out: The People's Art Project," the anonymous artist-visionary known for his fedora and dark sunglasses had used a million-dollar TED Prize he'd received after delivering an inspiring TED Talk. Based on the huge street portraits of ordinary, often disadvantaged people that JR had been installing in unauthorized guerrilla-style wheat-pastings around the world, the Inside Out Project encouraged local communities and groups to partner with JR's organization to "share their portraits and make a statement for what they stand for" and "share their untold stories," transforming them into works of art.[19] Draine's idea was to recognize and honor those who stood up to the white supremacists in 2017, as well as acknowledge other social justice activists, in a photography installation on the expansive brick wall of the Violet Crown motion picture theatre at the west end of the downtown pedestrian mall.

The idea generated immediate enthusiasm from community members and activists who had volunteered to work on Unity Days projects. But would such a public display of individuals involved in antiracist and social justice work endanger their safety? Would the installation inevitably get defaced? The Heather Heyer memorial had recently been vandalized by neo-Nazi and Unite the Right attendee Dustin Dudley, who posted his actions on Instagram.[20]

Racist destruction of memorials is nothing new for those honoring martyrs of the civil rights movement. Viola Liuzzo's monument on Highway 80 was so frequently vandalized that the Women of the SCLC who commissioned it built a tall, metal fence around it. More famously, the marker memorializing where Emmett Till's body was found has been so frequently defaced, stolen, or shot at that in 2019, with significant media attention, it was replaced with a bulletproof one.[21]

Initially it wasn't clear whether A11 and A12 survivors would want to be visually presented in public, considering how vulnerable that could make them in a political environment characterized by emboldened racist hatred and far-right animus. And then among those willing to expose their faces and names, how to decide who should be honored? What about those less visible activists who supported those in the streets? What about local social justice activists who chose not to participate in any way directly? Why focus the installation around the Unite the Right mayhem at all—wouldn't that just feed into the dominant media narrative about Charlottesville? If the point was to tell a different story about those doing the hard work of racial, social, and economic justice in this community, why center it around that event?

A small steering committee, of which I was a member, came together in May to bring the project to life, grapple with those questions, and somehow get everything installed by August.[22] It seemed a gargantuan job. A nominating committee pulled together 150 names of individuals who would be invited to have their portrait made. As expected, not everyone contacted felt comfortable having their image displayed in public, but, surprisingly perhaps, most said yes. A single silhouetted portrait would serve to honor both activists who chose not to participate as well as those the committee neglected to identify. Should the framing rationale be the Summer of Hate? Not only was it the motivation for the project and for Unity Days more generally, but because we were partnering with JR's Inside Out Project and our action would be archived on its website, we needed to articulate why we were doing this.[23] Even as we expected mostly to address the local community and summer visitors, through the exposure we would get with Inside Out we'd also be reaching a larger global audience that knows "Charlottesville" as a set of media images of neo-Nazis with tiki torches. We planned to use visual media as well, but in a bottom-up way to tell a more empowering and affirming narrative. Like the statues in Kelly Ingram Park, we'd elevate and make visible our own foot soldiers, some who had been visible in the mass media coverage, but many more who had not.

Inside Out Charlottesville Project, August 2019: Honoring Charlottesville social justice activists with a large scale photographic installation near the site of Unite the Right violence. (Sanjay Suchak, photographer)

Our public statement, drafted by Lisa Draine and me, led with the dominant media narrative:

> CHARLOTTESVILLE, VIRGINIA: In 2017—"The Summer of Hate"— the Ku Klux Klan came out of the shadows and rallied in a downtown park in July. Then on August 11 & 12, white nationalists and Neo-Nazis paraded with tiki-torches, shields, and weapons on the grounds of the University of Virginia and in downtown streets protesting the proposed removal of Confederate statues. After a domestic terrorist drove his car into a group of peaceful protesters, killing one woman and wounding dozens of others, our town became a hashtag for modern-day racism and antisemitism.[24]

But then we pivoted to the different story our project would tell:

> ... one that shows what it looks like when a community fights back against the destructive forces of white supremacy, hatred, and systemic racism.
>
> These are people who speak truth to power, and who work quietly behind the scenes. They raise their voices, their pens, their paint brushes for affordable housing, educational excellence for all children, access to healthy food, immigrant rights, legal rights, LGBTQ+ rights,

and against environmental racism. With many other life obligations, they still find time to devote themselves to this work.

They are activists, historians, lawyers, rabbis, ministers, educators, students, chefs, gardeners, actors, and artists. They bring forgotten stories to life and confront systemic racism from both inside and outside institutions. Sometimes they resist racial injustice just by surviving. . . .

To the individuals represented on this wall, and those unable to be pictured, we say, "You make our community stronger. We thank you. We honor you. We *see* you. Now the world will too."

Representing Local Activists: Being Subjects

How would we represent these activists; how would we see them? How did they want to be seen? Two local photographers, Ézé Amos and Kristen Finn, activists in their own right, were asked to make the portraits.[25] They would have been familiar to many of the participants. Per Inside Out guidelines, the photos would have to emphasize faces. Nevertheless, many of the participants found ways to speak their political and social justice allegiances in this static and nonverbal medium. Black Lives Matter tee shirts adorned numerous bodies, and that theme functioned as a recurring motif throughout the project. Some wore tee shirts with the slogan in its standardized graphic layout. Others donned variations on the theme. African American historian and preservationist Niya Bates sported a "Black History Matters" shirt, and

Inside Out Charlottesville photography installation: "Black Lives Matter" and its variations as a recurring motif. Use of gestures to communicate political commitments. Pictured: Zyahna Bryant, Niya Bates, Katrina Turner, Gloria Beard. (Ézé Amos and Kristen Finn, photographers)

another community activist, leader of the Charlottesville Civilian Police Review Board Katrina Turner, wore one declaring: "Black Lives Built Charlottesville." Gloria Beard, with her hand raised in a fist, wore a shirt illustrated with the faces of renowned Black women from Ida B. Wells to Oprah Winfrey and Michelle Obama. Other activists used hand gestures, mostly raised fists, to articulate their commitments. Some used props. Food justice activist Jeanette Abi-Nader held a pristine tomato. Ridge Schuyler, who worked in community self-sufficiency and workforce development, cradled a book about Robert F. Kennedy, signaling how RFK inspires his activism.

Consider the portrait of Don Gathers, a prominent community activist and former member of Charlottesville's Blue Ribbon Commission on Race, Memorials, and Public Spaces, which advised City Council on removing the Lee and Jackson statues. Gathers's arm assumes a now familiar "Black Power" salute. It may remind some viewers of the iconic photo of the two African American athletes at the 1968 Olympic Games on the medals platform raising their arms in clenched fists as the national anthem played. However, I find another resonance: between Gathers's portrait and a prominent photo made by Danny Lyon, SNCC's first staff photographer. As Martin Berger and UC Berkeley scholar of African American studies Leigh Raiford have noted, Lyon captured civil rights activists quite differently from photographers who were not movement-affiliated.[26]

Berger argues that Lyon captures Black bodies in empowered and activated stances, not as victimized and brutalized objects of pity. The photo, used by SNCC for its recruiting posters, emphasizes the young man's long, upraised arm and is graphically similar to the Gathers portrait. Lyon, as an insider, was able to use his photography to narrate very different stories about SNCC activists. Amos and Finn were doing something comparable with their Inside Out Charlottesville portraits: the individuals they captured with their lenses are subjects, actively engaged in communicating truths about themselves.

Some of the individuals included in the project had garnered mass media attention. The project gave them an opportunity, within the confines of a head-to-waist photograph, to construct their own image of themselves. Susan Bro is pictured without the long, flowing grey hair TV viewers would have been familiar with. Sporting a short bob that may have made her less readily recognizable, Bro wears a tee shirt with the quote "If you're not outraged, you're not paying attention." Because Heather Heyer's story was so familiar, a fair number

146 MAKING #CHARLOTTESVILLE

Inside Out Charlottesville: Don Gathers portrait (Ézé Amos, photographer). SNCC photographer's image of activists used in a recruiting poster: Empowered stances.

of people seeing this picture would know that the quote was connected to Bro's daughter—the last message she left on her Facebook feed.

Rev. Seth Wispelwey also achieved a significant degree of media exposure as one of the faith leaders who confronted alt-right forces on A12. Clergy were a crucial component of the resistance to the KKK and the alt-right throughout the Summer of Hate. Wispelwey and Brittany Caine-Conley, as we saw in chapter 3, garnered a lot of media attention in the immediate aftermath of the event—perhaps because they were particularly visible among the clergy nonviolently facing off against the alt-right. They had donned their full, white clerical robes and stoles as they stood in the middle of a line of clergy locking arms and attempted to prevent alt-right marchers from entering Emancipation Park. News footage and photographs of the clergy action, while not the most heavily circulated images from the weekend, provided powerful pictures and clear echoes to the civil rights era. Conley's and Wispelwey's whiteness also inevitably gave them an added platform for media attention, Wispelwey in particular as a white man. In his portrait for the Inside Out Charlottesville project,

"THIS IS WHAT COMMUNITY LOOKS LIKE!" 147

Inside Out Charlottesville: Susan Bro's portrait: communicating her daughter's message. (Kristen Finn, photographer)

however, he decenters his whiteness. He's got his clerical collar on but pairs that religious signifier with a tee shirt bearing the slogan "Trust Black Women." And unlike any other portrait in the project, his includes another person: a young Black girl—his daughter—to whom he points.

The project featured some survivors of the terrorist car attack, the most familiar being Marcus Martin, who was captured in the Pulitzer Prize–winning photo suspended in midair after tumbling over the car, having just pushed his fiancée, a friend of Heather Heyer, out of the way. Photographed by Ézé Amos, Martin's stance is quite different from many of the other individuals pictured. He does not look directly at the camera, nor does he smile. There's a pensiveness and vulnerability to his expression. Martin suffered not only physical injury, but mental health issues in the aftermath of the attack. Amos's photo captures that fragility, even as the photo also displays Martin's physical strength.

Inside Out Charlottesville: Rev. Seth Wispelwey, decentering whiteness. (Kristen Finn, photographer)

Marcus Martin's portrait tells a story of survival, but also of ongoing trauma and struggle. In Ryan Kelly's iconic photo, Martin functions as the only fully visible body brutally acted upon, as if he is the object of James Fields's racist hatred. Here for Inside Out Charlottesville, Martin is a subject: he's in control of how he shows himself.

Choosing and photographing the individuals is only one part of an Inside Out action. The acts of installing the photos and documenting how the community responds to the project are also key components of what these worldwide photography installations encompass. Just as the statues in Kelly Ingram Park are meant to be participatory—one engages physically with the sculptures—so too did people interact with the Charlottesville installation. Wheat-pasting the pictures, statement, and list of names onto the wall and using a large, motorized hydraulic lift over a number of weekend days in late July 2019 made for

Inside Out Charlottesville: Marcus Martin as subject—survival, trauma, pensiveness. (Ézé Amos, photographer)

a very visible action. The downtown pedestrian mall is a magnet for locals and visitors during the summer, and the west end of the mall is particularly heavily trafficked. The side street we used is—along with 4th Street / Heather Heyer Way—the only cross street that allow vehicles to traverse the pedestrian mall. Lots of people stopped to watch the installation, many asking questions about it. Over and over, passersby expressed gratitude for the project. African Americans walking by or driving down the street, in particular, tended to stop, look, and engage with the installation. Many took pictures. In fact, picture-taking in front of the project became a significant way that community members engaged with the installation.

Among the many individuals who posed in front of the wall, one provides a powerful coda to the Inside Out Charlottesville project. Corey Long was the A12 counterdemonstrator who fashioned a makeshift flamethrower to protect himself and others from neo-Nazis, resulting in a heavily circulated news photo discussed in chapter 4 (see p. 102). We invited him to be part of the Inside Out project. Long's post-A12 situation had been particularly trying and high-profile. He'd been convicted of disorderly conduct and sentenced to 360 days in prison with a hundred hours of community service. Throughout his extended ordeal with the criminal justice system, local activists protested the charges against him, as well as his conviction.[27] The jail term was mostly suspended, but he ended up serving ten days over five weekends for what he and Charlottesville activists (who created a slogan, "Corey Long did nothing wrong," and a hashtag, "#dropemcville") insisted was justifiable self-defense.[28] Our nomination committee invited Long to be photographed for Inside Out Charlottesville, but scheduling posed insurmountable challenges. However, after the installation was complete, Long happened to come by the project with his two young children. Kristen Finn took a cell phone photo that presents a visual narrative every bit as powerful as the more famous "flamethrower" picture.[29]

Here is a very different Corey Long. In the "flamethrower" photo we can't see his face, which is masked; nor can we see his eyes, as his face is turned away from the camera. The image emphasizes his body and powerful bare arm. And because this anonymous Black man is engaged in aggressive activity, the photo perpetuates a familiar narrative about Black masculinity and violence, even as the photo can also be read as self-defense and protection of the cowering elderly man standing behind. In Kristen Finn's photo, on the other hand, he faces the camera smiling: he's a person, not a body. The two children on either side of him further humanize, individualize, and soften him: he's a dad.

But notice how all three emulate the raised fists in the portraits above them. It's particularly significant that the Long family had placed themselves under the pictures of two local matriarchs, Rosia Parker and Katrina Turner, well known in the community for their activism. The photos-within-a-photo composition creates a visual transmission of Black pride and power through repetition of the raised fists, with the elders above providing a form of protection and generational benediction to the young family below. Also visible above Long and the children is Maxine Holland, an esteemed educator, holding a sign with a quote from the early twentieth-century African American scholar Carter G. Woodson: "We must tell our own story to the world." As a teacher of African American youth, Holland focused on how to impart Black history,

Inside Out Charlottesville: Corey Long telling a different story. Mirroring the gestures of community's activist matriarchs, Rosia Parker and Katrina Turner. (Kristen Finn, photographer)

so the quote speaks to her own work in the community. But within the context of Inside Out Charlottesville, Woodson's words reiterate the rationale for the project. Positioning Holland's image here within the picture of Corey Long and his children, the quote assumes yet another significance. While Long was interviewed a number of times in major media outlets giving his account of what was happening in the "flamethrower" photo, the ambiguity of the image meant he could never be in control of its meanings.[30] The photo carried too many signifiers of the long-standing and tenacious racist stereotype of the "brutal black buck."[31] He'd always have to push back against that image, not just in media appearances but, with real consequences, in court.

Ironically, the Walter Gadsden photo was also ambiguous and an image of Black self-defense, but because that photo's ambiguity got read as a Black male body behaving nonviolently and submitting to white violence, Gadsden's few attempts to clarify the photo gained no real hearing. And when Ronald McDowell decided to re-narrate the photo in his sculpture for Kelly Ingram Park, he chose not to tell Gadsden's story.

Corey Long's portrait in front of the Inside Out Charlottesville project tells a story of Black pride and power, but those fists are rendered unthreatening, as the two children—the boy standing tall and serious and the girl smiling shyly and twisting away from the camera—present endearing images. Cory Long, in the middle, may have fisted hands, but he uses them to encircle the children.

The use of public space to tell a story about a community that faced violence and trauma and found itself under the mass media microscope can be therapeutic. It can be nurturing. It can be somewhat healing—both for those on the wall and for the community, like the people who posed for pictures in front of it or who merely engaged in conversation about it. But unlike the statues in Kelly Ingram Park, the Charlottesville project would be ephemeral, lasting little over a month before being removed. Statues are meant to last a long time; wheat-pasted posters, by their very nature, degrade quickly and disappear. The Inside Out Charlottesville project lives on only digitally at JR's website. Birmingham's monuments give enduring honor to the mostly anonymous foot soldiers of the civil rights movement. Charlottesville did something similar in a more fleeting way for its antiracist foot soldiers. Perhaps this chapter provides a bit more longevity to that act of memorialization.

7

FOUR PRESIDENTS

Activists take to the streets, protesting, marching, engaging in confrontations. They use public acts of protest to push for social and political change. If they get national and even international media coverage, they've achieved some measure of initial success. If they then get their nation's leader to take to the bully pulpit to engage with the activists and support their protests, that's an even bigger gauge of effectiveness, even if some of the activists remain dubious about their head of state's embrace of their cause. In the civil rights era, President John F. Kennedy and his successor, Lyndon B. Johnson, both felt compelled to address the nation in response to the protest actions in Birmingham and Selma. With eloquent and rhetorical power, both presidents threw their support to the racial justice activists and their movement, forcefully condemning white supremacy and racist hatred. In 2020, Joe Biden, in what would turn out to be a successful campaign for the presidency, echoed his Democratic predecessors by addressing protest actions in Charlottesville and the issues of white supremacy and racial hatred. All three of these Democratic leaders took on the mantle of their era's racial justice movement and promised change.

In the immediate aftermath of the Unite the Right rally, Donald Trump addressed the nation about the protests but did not embrace the cause of the antiracist activists. His response was entirely different. He did not even unequivocally condemn white supremacy. If Charlottesville's Summer of Hate is a defining moment of the post-Obama era, then Trump's televised responses (he provided three) further define Trumpism and the politics of white racial grievance that animated the alt-right and Trump's fervent base of supporters.

Just as the highly visible campaigns against white supremacy in the civil rights era became crucibles for that era's chief executives, so too did "Charlottesville" for a most norm-defying president and for his challenger to that office. In all four cases, they signalled something important about the nation's embrace of diversity and democratic norms.

JFK/Birmingham

On June 11, 1963, President John F. Kennedy requested airtime from all three television networks for a major speech at 8:00 p.m. As the first true "television president," JFK exploited the new medium quite successfully with frequent live broadcasts of his press conferences, interviews, and news documentaries, bringing him; his brother, the Attorney General; and his glamorous wife, Jacqueline, into Americans' living rooms on a regular basis.[1] But live, prime-time presidential addresses, outside of State of the Union speeches, were unusual occurrences. The last time President Kennedy had requested evening airtime from the TV networks was on October 22, 1962, to deliver perhaps the most frightening speech any American president had ever given: the Soviet Union was placing nuclear weapons in Cuba, and Kennedy used his televised address to give Soviet Premier Khrushchev an ultimatum to remove them. Nuclear war seemed imminent.

Eight months later, JFK again went before the television cameras in prime time and addressed the nation about American race relations, bigotry, and what the country needed to do about it. By taking to television, the president signaled that the issue was of monumental importance, requiring a platform only network television provided. But JFK had waited more than a month following the searing images of Bull Connor's dogs and fire hoses that were broadcast around the globe. He used as immediate impetus for his televised address yet another civil rights crisis in Alabama: Governor George Wallace's threat to "stand in the schoolhouse door" to prevent the admittance of two African American students to the University of Alabama.

Kennedy's speech was remarkable because he finally embraced what the civil rights movement had been pushing for since he entered the White House. Beginning in 1961 with the Freedom Riders, with students sitting-in at lunch counters, and with SNCC kids venturing into the dark heart of Mississippi to begin the deadly dangerous work of encouraging Black citizens to register to vote, activists had been pressuring the Kennedy administration from its earliest days. They used both mass actions and grassroots organizing to address white supremacy, Jim Crow statutes, and Black voter disenfranchisement. It took the images from Birmingham to finally break through and create an international media event that finally moved the White House. When JFK ultimately made the decision to take on Black civil rights, he did it by framing the issue of desegregation and racial equality as the civil rights activists did: it was a moral crusade. In the most quoted line from the speech, Kennedy affirmed: "We are confronted primarily with a moral issue. It is as old as the Scriptures and as clear as the American Constitution."[2] Before this moment, Kennedy and his brother, Attorney General Robert F. Kennedy, had tended to fall back on dispassionate legalisms rather than ethical principles and appeals to conscience about what was right.[3] JFK used the prime-time speech to introduce sweeping civil rights legislation that became, a year later, the landmark Civil Rights Act.

LBJ/Selma

On March 15, 1965, at 9:00 p.m., President Lyndon Johnson stood before a special joint session of Congress to speak to house representatives and senators as well as to the nation in a prime-time televised address about the ongoing crisis in Selma, Alabama. Comparing it to Lexington, Concord, and Appomattox as a time and place that signaled "a turning point in man's unending search for freedom," Johnson used stirring words to present to Congress a sweeping voting rights bill. It was the first time in twenty years that a president had come before Congress to personally request passage of legislation.[4] It was also the first time that network TV cameras brought the event to living rooms around the country. Achieving heights of eloquence and rhetorical power, this typically uneloquent president borrowed the very phrasings of the civil rights movement: "Their cause must be our cause too. Because it is not just Negroes, but really it is all of us, who must overcome the crippling legacy of bigotry and injustice. And we *shall* overcome."[5] Like Kennedy before him, LBJ embraced the movement's own framing of the cause. By using the words of the ubiquitous anthem of the movement, LBJ verbally aligned himself directly with the Selma marchers. They were the heroes, he proclaimed: "[The Negro's] actions and protests, his courage to risk safety and even to risk his life, have awakened the conscience of this Nation. His demonstrations have been designed to call attention to injustice, designed to provoke change, designed to stir reform."

Martin Luther King, watching the televised speech, wept recognizing the significance of what LBJ had just done.[6]

There was a right side and a wrong side in the struggles in Selma, and LBJ put the full force of the presidency on the side of African American civil and voting rights activists. The movement had pushed him to submit voting rights legislation; it had not been his plan to do so this quickly following passage of the Civil Rights Act.[7] When it became clear that the perpetrators of Viola Liuzzo's murder were Klansmen, Johnson took an unusual step for a president: going back before the television cameras to announce their arrests and to condemn the Klan in highly personal terms: "My father fought them in Texas. I have fought them all my life because I believe them to threaten the peace of every community where they exist. I shall continue to fight them because I know their loyalty is not to the United States but to a hooded society of bigots."[8]

With the Birmingham and Selma campaigns, the movement created dramatic media events bringing the struggle against white supremacy to such heightened visibility that it forced two presidents to pay attention and put forth significant legislation. Just as significantly, the activists succeeded in compelling JFK and LBJ to adopt the movement's definitions of the crisis, its language, its framing of the stakes.

Trump/Charlottesville

There have been numerous instances since the mid-1960s when presidents have come before the TV cameras in the wake of national crises to speak to the American people about what had happened, what it meant to the nation, how to respond, and what actions the federal government might take. When Donald Trump went before the TV cameras on August 12, 2017, less than two hours after the terrorist car attack, to address the situation in Charlottesville, he did not echo the eloquence and moral clarity of JFK, nor the unambiguousness about which side was right and which was wrong that LBJ asserted. Speaking from his golf course in New Jersey, Trump delivered some hastily prepared remarks: "We condemn in the strongest possible terms this egregious display of hatred, bigotry and violence," he declared, reading from a text. "On many sides—on many sides," he added, seemingly going off-script.

The resulting criticism of Trump, even from within Republican party ranks, for not calling out neo-Nazis and white supremacists was withering. Senators like Orrin Hatch, Marco Rubio, and Cory Gardner took to Twitter, not only to condemn the neo-Nazis in Charlottesville but to criticize Trump for not clearly doing so himself. Hatch was particularly quotable in tweeting, "My brother didn't give his life fighting Hitler for Nazi ideas to go unchallenged here at home."[9] Rubio posted a less quotable, but nevertheless pointed, instruction to the president: "Very important for the nation to hear @potus describe events in #Charlottesville for what they are, a terror attack by #whitesupremacists." In a hasty do-over two days later at the White House, Trump, obviously reading verbatim from a teleprompter, recited his "egregious display" line without the "many sides" addendum. He even signaled: "the KKK, neo-Nazis, white supremacists, and other hate groups that are repugnant to everything we hold dear as Americans." He never went off-script this time.

Richard Spencer along with fellow white nationalist and Identity Evropa founder Nathan Damigo, interviewed by the *Atlantic*, weren't particularly perturbed. Spencer dismissed Trump's new words as "kumbaya nonsense" and not a repudiation of the alt-right.[10] As far as they were concerned, Trump was on their side. They wouldn't have to wait long for Trump to go off-script again and validate Spencer and Damigo's assertions. During a combative press conference at Trump Tower on August 15, Trump not only doubled down on his "many sides" position but decided to emphasize the violence of what he referred to as the "alt-left," which, he declared, "came charging in without a permit—and they were very, very violent." Rhetorically asking about their guilt, he yelled at the scrum of reporters, "What about the fact that they came charging—they came charging with clubs in their hands, swinging clubs?" As reporters pushed back, trying to get a handle on what he meant, Trump asserted that there were "very fine people" among those protesting the taking down of the Lee statue. And then, perhaps to appear evenhanded, he added: "on both sides." However, he directed his animus toward the people he considered not so fine among the counterprotesters. Jousting with the reporters, he condemned the press for supposedly treating badly the "many people" who, he claimed, weren't neo-Nazis and white nationalists but just came to Charlottesville to protest the taking down of a statue.

To anyone who had paid attention to Charlottesville's local media coverage and commentary in the run-up to the rally, these "both-sides" formulations and the emphasis on accusations of violence from antiracists would have been disconcertingly familiar.

The active support of the country's chief executive is enormously consequential for a social change movement. JFK and LBJ's support for the civil rights cause assured the movement's victories in the legislative arena and its significant, albeit debated, progress in race relations in American social, economic, and cultural realms. It matters if the president is on your side and is seen to be so. On August 15, 2017, at Trump Tower, the president of the United States made it very clear which side of the Charlottesville confrontations had his support.

The Descent: From JFK/LBJ to Trump

How did America descend from the soaring words of JFK and LBJ, and the powerful legislative remedies of the landmark legislation signaling a second Reconstruction that they supported, to a president a half century later giving support and succor to the white supremacist forces the civil rights revolution was supposed to have finally vanquished? Many Americans embrace a triumphalist popular narrative of the civil rights movement: Rosa Parks sat so Martin Luther King could walk, and now we are all free and equal.[11] PBS's hugely impactful 1987 *Eyes on the Prize* documentary, which culminates with the Selma campaign has perhaps assisted in cementing an affirmative victory narrative in the American imagination that obscures a more complicated trajectory.[12]

In the later 1970s and throughout the 1980s, with the rise of the New Right, the Reagan presidency, and an ascendant "color-blind" discourse of race relations, retrenchment was often harder to see. Lee Atwater, a Reagan aide in 1981, infamously explained the Republican Party's "Southern Strategy" in the post–civil rights era. After the passage of the Voting Rights Act, politicians wooing previous George Wallace voters and their ilk, Atwater explained, could no longer say "n—er, n—er, n—er." Those kinds of appeals would backfire. Politicians needed to get increasingly abstract, using code, focusing on economic cuts that would disproportionately impact Black people.[13] Republican politicians also refrained from speaking against the Voting Rights Act directly. To do so would signal, in a most visible and obvious way, a retreat from supporting racial equality. So congressional Republicans would ritualistically vote to reauthorize the Act whenever it came before Congress, but support the weakening and hollowing out of the Act in administrative and judicial venues that were not so visible—until the 2013 *Shelby County v. Holder* Supreme Court case in which the conservative majority blew a hole through the heart of the Act.[14] More generally, white America in the post–civil rights era practiced what sociologist Eduardo Bonilla-Silva has termed a "racism without racists." A new color-blind ideology arose, he argues, that "aids in the maintenance of white privilege without fanfare, without naming those who it subjects and those who it rewards."[15]

But then along came Donald Trump to rip the fig leaf off the "non-racist racism" practiced by a generation of right-wing politics in its efforts to undermine civil rights gains. Those Republican senators who took to Twitter to condemn Trump's words were hastily trying to reattach that fig leaf and assert their party's non-racism and cajole their leader to get back with the post-civil-rights-era program. White supremacists never went away, of course, but until Trump they had been appealed to mostly by abstracted dog whistles. Trump, however, enabled a new racial discourse less circumspect about displaying white racial animus and grievance. It began in 2011 with the "birther" conspiracy insinuating that the nation's first Black president wasn't born in the United States, was foreign, probably Muslim, alien, un-American. Trump's embrace of what we might now label "racist racism" culminated in Charlottesville with a Queens-born president deciding that it was worthwhile to put the force of his presidency behind the maintenance of Confederate statues. He'd eventually add Confederate-named military bases to his must-keep list.[16] This was no longer the abstracted color-blind racism of Lee Atwater and the Republicans' Southern Strategy. Trump was but a small step away from "n—er, n—er, n—er."

No legislative agenda followed Trump's response to the Unite the Right confrontations. Attempts to advance legislation to categorize white nationalist violence as domestic terrorism went nowhere during the Trump years.[17] However, two Republican senators in 2019 introduced resolutions to label antifa domestic terrorists, despite the fact that no antifascist activity has led to anyone's death. On the other hand, white nationalist extremists have killed hundreds in the past decade.[18]

But did Trump's non-condemnation of the alt-right really matter? Wasn't the Unite the Right rally a disaster for its organizers? As we've already seen, the alt-right was soundly out-organized by antiracist counterprotesters who wielded their media savvy in ways superior to those on the extreme and white-supremacist right. No-platforming campaigns effectively chased many alt-right big names and sites off the internet and have made it increasingly difficult for its adherents to raise funds. Many of the perpetrators of violence in Charlottesville sat languishing in jails for their crimes, and the *Sines v. Kessler* anti-conspiracy lawsuit against both Unite the Right organizers and participating groups succeeded in getting guilty judgments against all of them and saddled them with massive punitive and compensatory damages.

Scholar George Hawley in his influential 2017 primer on the alt-right phenomenon suggested that after an ascendancy period in 2015 and 2016, things were already declining for the alt-right even before Charlottesville. However, the Unite the Right rally fundamentally changed public perception of its members, he argues, from "a tech-savvy band of meme warriors, warping young minds and converting a new generation of white nationalists" to "a rowdy group of violent thugs, staging stunts designed to draw media attention."[19]

Ultimately the point of the Unite the Right rally was to create an actual bodies-in-the-street movement, one that would legitimate and normalize its adherents (no need to hide behind hoods anymore). It was about being visible, confrontational, media-genic, and attractive enough to encourage others to get off their mobile devices and laptops and come out into the open. That failed, at least in the short term. Unable to effectively organize, gather, or recruit in the real world, Hawley suggests, "the Alt-Right's hope of drawing great crowds of normal-looking people may never be realized."[20] Far-right extremists and racists slithered back into the ever-shadier dark web of platforms like 8chan (now 8kun) that are unreachable by Google searches. Unfortunately, the murderousness of these extremists didn't disappear, as attested by the terroristic mass-murder events at a mosque in Christchurch, New Zealand; synagogues in Pittsburgh and Poway, California; at an El Paso Walmart, deliberately targeting Latinos; and in 2022 against African Americans in a Buffalo supermarket. In all five cases, the white supremacist perpetrators posted online manifestos that circulated similar "Great Replacement" racist ideology foundational to alt-right thinking. Because the alt-right did not become a visible, embodied movement immediately following Unite the Right, these events could seem like isolated, "lone wolf" attacks rather than manifestations of a coherent worldwide phenomenon. Even the label "alt-right" seemed to have gone out of fashion after #Charlottesville.

But while the alt-right as an expanding, in-the-streets social change movement appeared to have collapsed in the streets of Charlottesville, largely because they were countered and outmaneuvered by progressives and antifascists, it is clearly premature to affirm as George Hawley did in 2019: "Whenever I talk about the alt-right at this point, I do so in the past tense." With the upsurge of massive antiracist protests in the summer of 2020 in the aftermath of the police killing of George Floyd, Black Lives Matter protesters were countered by Proud Boys and the new phenomenon of Boogaloo Bois, heavily armed, police-hating, Hawaiian shirt–wearing extremists wanting to foment a new civil war. The pronouncements of the alt-right's demise were premature, even as the antiracist movement exploded during the momentous summer of 2020 into the largest, most broad-ranging protest movement in US history.[21] Also premature were Hawley and other observers' suggestion that most white nationalists and those on the extreme right tended not to embrace Trump anymore.[22] In the aftermath of Trump's election loss, Proud Boys were at the forefront of violent pro-Trump rallies in Washington that included attacks on Black churches.[23] Trump had memorably refused to condemn the group earlier in the election campaign during a chaotic, calamitous presidential debate characterized by constant Trumpian interruptions and his declaration to the Proud Boys: "stand back and stand by." He immediately pivoted and condemned the left and antifa, just as he had done three years before in his third set of comments about the violence in Charlottesville. And just as alt-right figures saw his Charlottesville responses as support for their movement, so too did the Proud Boys, who gleefully took to social media to embrace Trump, with one Proud Boys group adopting his instructions as a new group logo.[24]

It ultimately culminated with a mass of Proud Boys and Oath Keepers (both groups who had marched in the 2017 Unite the Right rally), fervent Trump supporters, and followers of a bizarre QAnon conspiracy theory storming the US Capitol on January 6, 2021, at their defeated leader's behest in an insurrectionary act to stop legislators from declaring Joe Biden the duly elected new president. In both cases, as we'll explore more fully in the conclusion, this generation of violent, mostly white men had no qualms about engaging publicly in illegal activity with cameras everywhere recording their actions. Trump's embrace of white nationalism and disdain for democratic norms and values, already signaled with white hot rage in August 2017, came to maximum visibility in January 2021 in another violent and visually stunning media event.

How important is it if the president embraces some of the objectives and values of a social change movement? Hillary Clinton, running against Barack Obama in 2008, landed in political hot water for drawing a civil rights history lesson about presidential power in asserting, "Dr. King's dream began to be realized when President Johnson passed the Civil Rights Act. It took a president to get it done."[25] Her observation minimized the organizing and leadership of King and thoroughly ignored the grassroots work of activists in forcing legislators and the White House to take action. However, Clinton wasn't wrong in pointing out the political significance and power of the presidency in embracing a movement's goals. LBJ, and Kennedy before him, did so with the civil rights movement when the relentless media coverage of clashes between civil and voting rights activists and white segregationists made inaction no longer viable. In a distressing mirror-image fashion, Trump embraced significant aspects of the alt-right's goals, amplifying them on the national stage, even as the movement and its various leaders had their mass media platforms slipped out from under their feet.

White Supremacy in the Oval Office

Singing from the alt-right's songbook, Trump used the enormous media platform of the presidency to spread "Great Replacement" ideology. He characterized migration at the southern border as an "invasion," using language favored by white nationalists like Richard Spencer, who in the Charlottesville Statement labeled the refugee crisis in Europe with that term, calling it a war without bullets threatening the continent's very identity. Trump, like Spencer, extolled white Europeans, suggesting the United States should accept more immigrants from Scandinavia, while labelling African nations "shithole countries" and suggesting that a group of non-white American lawmakers "go back" to their "totally broken and crime infested" countries.[26] These and other comments echo alt-right pronouncements in the Charlottesville Statement: "Whites alone defined America as a European society and political order." In 2020 when Black Lives Matter protests against police brutality also called for the dismantling of Confederate monuments, Trump appeared to embrace white nationalism quite overtly, retweeting a video of Florida retiree supporters confronting opponents. In the video a counterprotester shouts to the Trump supporter, "Where's your white hood?" The retiree responds twice: "White power!"[27] Trump also trafficked in antisemitic rhetoric questioning American Jews' loyalties, mirroring alt-right assertions of Jews as a distinct ethno-religious group separate from, and at times hostile to, white Europeans and European states. And then there was the rampant misogyny.

The last time a president so overtly embraced white supremacy was in 1915. Woodrow Wilson not only provided a powerful platform for D. W. Griffith's paeon to the original Ku Klux Klan, *The Birth of a Nation*, by having it screened at the White House, but then went on to famously declare: "It is like writing history with lightning. And my only regret is that it is all so terribly true."[28] Wilson's defense of segregation and Lost Cause mythology (which he helped to popularize in his pre-presidential career as an academic), along with his support for the highly controversial Griffith epic, helped galvanize the rebirth of the Klan. Neither of his successors in the White House during the Klan's 1920s "second coming," Harding or Coolidge, were overt racists and Klan supporters like Wilson, but neither denounced the organization.[29] It didn't matter all that much, however. The Klan became mainstreamed, normalized, and politically potent until the eruption of internal Klan scandals, but also Klan-friendly legislative achievements shrank its membership by the later 1920s. By then, Jim Crow statutes were firmly in place throughout the South, and the Johnson-Reed Immigration Act ensured that the United States would close its doors to almost all immigrants, especially those from Asia and even much of Europe—at least southern and eastern Europe, where the people were darker-skinned, Jewish, or non-Protestant. Along with racist legislation, the built environment throughout the South—and even north of the Mason-Dixon Line—entrenched white supremacy as Confederate monuments began appearing in parks and in front of courthouses. In Charlottesville, a statue of Stonewall Jackson went up in 1921 in a new park expropriated from Black property owners.[30] That same year the Klan organized a local Charlottesville chapter.[31] Three years later, Robert E. Lee's statue was erected with great pageantry in another city park, and like the nearby Jackson Park, it was off-limits to the town's Black residents.

There are no records of any coordinated protest to the erection of the Jackson and Lee statues in Charlottesville in 1921 and 1924. And while there were significant demonstrations around the country against screenings of Griffith's *The Birth of a Nation*, with the nascent NAACP becoming a visible and national political organization through its robust attempts to ban the film, by the 1920s with the rise of the second Klan, coordinated protest against this manifestation of racism, nativism, antisemitism, and hatred of Catholics was surprisingly muted.[32] While some newspapers ran exposés to try to discredit the Klan, the coverage, as we have seen, tended to make the organization, with its bizarre rituals, garb, and terminology, fascinating and enticing. Rather than discredit the Klan, the coverage boosted its membership numbers. Black, Catholic, and Jewish publications tended to avoid providing coverage, refusing to get into debates with the Klan. As historian Felix Harcourt notes, the philosophy seemed to be: "The best way to defeat the Invisible Empire would be to deny it the oxygen of publicity."[33] He points out that "there was also no single, unified response to the Klan from members of these communities."[34]

That, of course, was not the case in 2017. There was the pushback from antiracist activists, clergy, and townspeople in Charlottesville, and even from Republican lawmakers, in response to Trump's lack of clear condemnation of the alt-right. Even with the cascade of outrageous remarks by Trump during his four years in office, which would blow up the media and everyone's attention only to dissipate until the next shocking or norm-defying statement erupted, Trump's Charlottesville comments have stuck. They serve as an enduring and defining episode, marking a presidency that tolerated, even celebrated, racism, aggrieved white masculinity, and violence against perceived "others." As an unprecedented figure to reach the Oval Office, Trump resists comparison to previous presidents. Nevertheless, it's necessary to compare how he comported himself in the office to his predecessors, in order to mark, document, and analyze democratic norm destruction.[35] His televised response to the violence in Charlottesville, so divergent from how JFK and LBJ responded to the white supremacist violence they confronted, marks yet another Trump-shattered norm of presidential behavior and leadership in the midst of a national crisis.

Biden/Charlottesville

It would take another politician seeking the presidency to model how presidents should assert moral leadership during moments of turmoil and reckoning about what the nation stands for. On April 25, 2019, former Vice President Joe Biden launched his ultimately successful bid for the Democratic nomination. As commentators noted, his opening appeal to voters differed markedly from that of other contenders in the crowded Democratic field.[36] He didn't talk about policies, he didn't recount his personal biography or his eight years serving with President Obama. Joe Biden used his first campaign-launch video to talk about Charlottesville, or rather #Charlottesville.

Biden's campaign ad evoking the Unite the Right rally would not be a one-off. His narration of what happened on August 11 and 12, 2017, and why it mattered, entered his stump speech and culminated in his address at the "virtual" Democratic Convention on August 20, 2020, accepting the party's presidential nomination. In rhetorical style and moral appeals to democracy and justice, Biden echoed JFK's and LBJ's televised addresses following the crises

Democratic presidential candidate Joe Biden's first campaign video: "Charlottesville" and the soul of the nation.

in Birmingham and Selma. Responses from local activists in Charlottesville to Biden's invocation of those two traumatic days also resonated with the way the more militant civil rights activists reacted to the words and actions of Kennedy and Johnson.

"Charlottesville" is the first word Biden speaks in the campaign video announcing his candidacy as we see him directly addressing the camera. Initially he links the town to Thomas Jefferson and the words of the Declaration of Independence. But he quickly pivots to Charlottesville's other distinction: "home to a defining moment for this nation." The video cuts away from Biden to footage of the August 11 tiki torch march through UVA's Central Grounds. That footage is interspersed with a few still photos from August 12 of white nationalists with shields and of neo-Nazis carrying Confederate and swastika flags. The video keeps returning to dramatic footage of alt-right marchers parading through the University's Lawn and down the steps of the Rotunda with their torches. We hear the "Jews will not replace us" chant. Biden narrates, making a linkage between these men with "crazed faces illuminated by torches, veins bulging, and baring the fangs of racism" to their forefathers spewing antisemitism in 1930s Europe. And then over footage of the confrontation between streaming groups of tiki torch marchers and the small group of students on the Rotunda plaza around the Jefferson statue, Biden elaborates further: "And they were met by a courageous group of Americans." There's a cut to a still image of the students hoisting up their banner, "VA Students Act Against White Supremacy." Biden continues: "A violent clash ensued," as we see more footage of tiki torch marchers and Chris "Crying Nazi" Cantwell beginning to throw punches. As the footage fades to black, we come back to Biden speaking to the camera as he concludes his narration: "And a brave young woman lost her life."

Wait—what? No one died in the tiki torch confrontation. The Biden video conflates the violence of August 11 and the more widespread, prolonged clashes of August 12 that culminated with the deadly car attack. What's going on here? Biden and his production team clearly made the decision to emphasize the visually more legible images of A11. As we've seen, the news film of the confrontations around Emancipation Park on A12 did not provide many images that clearly delineated "good guys" from "bad guys," neo-Nazis from antiracist counterdemonstrators. Trump was not entirely wrong in affirming that both sides behaved violently that day. Antifa groups, although in the minority among counterdemonstrators, did fight—and inevitably drew the cameras. The various videos of the car attack do provide more stark evidence of nonviolent, innocent marchers as victims of racist violence. But the car attack video, in its sheer horror, could be seen as too brutal for use in a campaign ad. The images from the tiki torch parade and confrontation provide visible moral clarity—like the Selma Bloody Sunday footage from the Edmund Pettus Bridge–whereas video from the next day's Unite the Right rally does not. That may be why Biden's video only briefly shows a few still photos from A12. Biden's collapsing

Biden's campaign ad emphasizing the tiki torch rally and the "courageous group of Americans" who stood in opposition: Conflating events of August 11 and August 12.

of the two days, while chronologically wrong, would likely only matter to those who were there that weekend and to those narrating the event as journalists or historians. Similarly, most Americans invoking the confrontations of the civil rights era are likely to conflate Birmingham and Selma, the Freedom Rides, and other high-profile events and moments from the 1960s.

The more important question is: what is Biden doing with this event? He is clearly and unequivocally aligning himself with the counterdemonstrators. In the immediate aftermath of the Unite the Right mayhem, Biden had published a short article in the *Atlantic*, which he references in the campaign ad and which provides much of its script. In that piece, published August 25, 2017, he was more specific about those who stood up to the neo-Nazis: "And we should never forget the courage of that small group of University of Virginia students who stared down the mob and its torches on that Friday night."[37] Biden, in both the article and the campaign video two years later, is doing the same thing that President Johnson did in 1965 when extolling civil rights activists' "actions and protests, his courage to risk safety and even to risk his life, have awakened the conscience of this Nation." In the Manichaean struggle between good and evil, right and wrong, Biden saw Charlottesville as Johnson saw Selma. Both were battlegrounds for the soul of America (for Biden) or the meaning of freedom in America (for Johnson). And in that battle, one needed to not only be on the right side but be able to articulate what that right side stood for. A president needed to convey moral leadership, something Trump was entirely incapable of doing as he engaged in mealy-mouthed assertions that there were "very fine people" on both sides and violence, hatred, and bigotry "on many sides," not to mention coming over and over again to the defense of those on the extreme right, who somehow were distinct from the neo-Nazis and white supremacists.

Biden's campaign ad excoriates Trump's response and his assertion of a moral equivalence "between those spreading hate and those with the courage to stand against it." Biden makes clear that his campaign was about the battle for the soul of the nation and the threat that Trump posed to its fundamental character. Cutting back to film footage, video, and photographic stills to illustrate "the core values of this nation," we see a series of archival images: the Statue of Liberty in New York harbor; suffragists parading for the right to vote; World War II soldiers at the beaches of Normandy and raising the US flag at Iwo Jima. And then as Biden extolls "everything that makes America, America," we cut to a photo from the civil rights movement showing Black and white marchers carrying a banner proclaiming "We Shall Overcome," followed by

Biden's campaign ad uses images of the civil rights movement to illustrate "what makes America America," linking those images to the students who confronted the tiki torch marchers.

footage of Martin Luther King at the March on Washington before we fade from King back to Biden. The video's montage of images connects those who stood up to the alt-right in Charlottesville to those who fought for women's rights, those who battled Nazis in World War II, and of course to civil rights movement activists. There's also a graphic similarity between the "We shall overcome banner" hoisted by the civil rights marchers and the "VA Students Act Against White Supremacy" sheet held by the 2017 students. Then, a fading of King's image to Biden's makes clear not only whose side Biden is on but whose mantle he metaphorically assumes.

Activists Respond

But just because the Democratic presidential candidate extolls the activists in Charlottesville who stood up against the alt-right doesn't necessarily mean that those activists would embrace Biden. Consider what happened in 1963 and 1965. The more militant activists in the civil rights movement maintained their criticism, distrust, and cynicism of the two presidents who appeared to be joining their cause.

Long before John Lewis became a sanctified civil rights movement hero and long-standing Georgia congressman loved and revered by both Democrats and Republicans, he was the uncompromising and militant president of SNCC, the youthful grassroots organization distrustful of top-down leadership, and often a thorn in the side of Martin Luther King. Lewis was one of the scheduled speakers at the March on Washington in August 1963, a mass gathering organized to push for the passage of Kennedy's Civil Rights Bill. The speech Lewis planned to deliver to the quarter of a million marchers who journeyed from around the country to press the government for "jobs and freedom" had been cowritten with other SNCC activists. Rather than thank the Kennedy administration for putting forth the bill, Lewis's speech castigated it as too little too late, complaining that it did nothing to protect against police brutality. The speech also accused JFK of "trying to take the revolution out of the street and put it into the courts."[38] Appalled and taken aback by SNCC's denunciations of Kennedy and his civil rights initiatives, other March on Washington leaders refused to participate if Lewis did not rewrite and tone down his incendiary remarks. He eventually did so, but the revised speech he delivered on that historic day remained sharp in its criticism of JFK's inadequate bill as well as both political parties and their woeful responses to the civil rights revolution.[39] SNCC activists had too much experience with Kennedy administration inaction during the Freedom Rides to trust it now.

In the wake of Johnson's Voting Rights Bill speech two years later, Selma activists and SNCC militants were no more impressed with this president. It was, after all, LBJ who at the 1964 Democratic Convention refused to allow the integrated Mississippi Freedom Democratic Party to be seated instead of the racist, segregated delegation. This was the president who had activist Fannie Lou Hamer cut off during her televised recounting of Mississippi racial terror, and who forever lost the already grudging support of Black and white young people who had agreed to go "part of the way with LBJ." Local activists feared that Johnson was co-opting the movement and outmaneuvering Martin Luther King. If the public viewed Johnson as responsible for civil rights victories, what would happen to the movement? Activists feared losing control of the agenda. SNCC members tended to be dismissive of LBJ's speech. James Foreman, a key SNCC leader, reacted to the president's use of "we shall overcome" in his speech to Congress by saying it "spoiled a good song."[40]

It should come as no surprise that local Charlottesville activists likewise responded to Biden's embrace of their activism with suspicion and distrust. Rev.

Seth Wispelwey, who maintained his mass media platform as a "go-to" spokesperson for local activists, castigated Biden as duplicitous: "For a presidential candidate like Joe Biden who has a disturbing legislative and policy history on race dating back to the 1970s to cite Charlottesville as a reason to launch his campaign is unwelcome." Jalane Schmidt, UVA professor and leader of Charlottesville's Black Lives Matter group, who also achieved high media visibility, tweeted, "We were meant to be his political prop." Don Gathers, another local leader in the Black community, asked why Biden hadn't come to Charlottesville right after A12 to show his solidarity.[41] Like the SNCC activists a half century before, the Charlottesville activists responded to decades-long skepticism of Democratic Party promises to Black voters that many had experienced as Lucy-and-the-football situations. With Biden in particular, there was his role in sponsoring the 1994 crime bill, which many BLM activists blame for the phenomenon of mass incarceration.

The Charlottesville figure who got most of the media attention in response to Biden's campaign video was, unsurprisingly, Susan Bro. Diplomatically, she refused to criticize the former vice president in her interviews with numerous media outlets including CNN. The cable news network's anchor Alisyn Camerota, in soliciting Bro's reaction, suggested that the focal point of Biden's campaign launch was "the story of Heather's death."[42] That's not quite accurate, but Camerota's framing serves as yet another example of the media's impulse to make Heather Heyer's martyrdom the main event of A12. Bro did her best to push back against this framing, asserting, as she had done many times, that it wasn't about Heather, it was about the hate. She also refuted a rumor that she was upset or traumatized by Biden's campaign video, while pointing out that others were distressed. After this comment, Camerota immediately jumped in asking Bro who she meant: "Heather's friends?" Again, it was as though everything about what happened that weekend must come back to Heather Heyer. Bro patiently pushed back, answering: "Survivors"—those who actually experienced the violence of August 11 and 12—"Actual living scenes, not just video." Bro's answer provides a way of understanding the response by activists like Wispelwey, Schmidt, and Gathers. These media images were ultimately representations of events that actually happened and that affected actual human beings in life-changing and traumatic ways. Biden's use of these images, and before him film director Spike Lee, who ended his Hollywood film *BlacKkKlansman* (2018) with a montage of images from A12—without first engaging with the community—can feel like a kind of theft.[43]

Remember "Charlottesville"

August 12, 2020: It was the third anniversary of the Unite the Right rally. On that day Biden introduced his running mate, Kamala Harris, a Black woman who also is part South Asian. As the Democratic candidate for the vice-presidency, hers was certainly an historic choice and served as the day's news hook. But in his remarks, Biden returned to what was now a standard element of his stump speech: "Charlottesville." He reminded voters of "the terrible day in Charlottesville. Remember? Remember what it felt like to see those neo-Nazis? Close your eyes. Those Klansmen, white supremacists. Coming out of fields carrying lighted torches." What was he asking Americans to remember? Emily Gorcenski and the other activists who were on the UVA Rotunda plaza that night would certainly remember what it felt like to see those neo-Nazis. But everyone else to whom Biden spoke was asked to remember the media event and the iconic images that three years later continued to define what happened in Charlottesville. He launched into a reiteration of remarks he'd first used in his inaugural campaign ad about Charlottesville, culminating with his campaign theme about being in a battle for the soul of the nation. He would repeat those words yet again at the culmination of the Democratic National Convention. Clearly "Charlottesville" was fundamentally tied to Biden's and the Democrats' appeal to voters.

When Biden joined the Democratic race in April 2019, he was one of a crowded field of candidates. The debut of his campaign was not a big-ticket event. Between that roll-out and his acceptance of his party's nomination over a year later, the world had fundamentally changed, with a crippling worldwide pandemic, economic collapse, and the most powerful racial justice movement since the civil rights era of the 1960s. The Biden campaign could have consigned the "Charlottesville" speech to the dustbin and pivoted elsewhere. But Biden made that searing event central to why he was running, and he returned over and over again to the words he first enunciated in his *Atlantic* magazine article in August 2017.[44]

Biden's acceptance speech and invocation of "Charlottesville" got the attention of Will.i.am of the Black Eyed Peas. In 2008, the rapper and music producer, inspired by the candidacy of Barack Obama, had put together a single and video in which he and an assortment of other celebrities sang along to Obama giving his "Yes We Can" speech. The video went viral on YouTube and amassed awards. In 2020, Will.i.am decided to go back to the same creative well and with singer Jennifer Hudson mashed together parts of Biden's speech with the Black Eyed Peas' 2003 hit protest song, "Where Is the Love?"

The video—and Biden's speech—starts with the civil rights movement. He quotes Ella Baker, the indispensable behind-the-scenes organizer of both the SCLC and SNCC. The video provides some rare footage of Miss Baker, a figure unlikely to be known to most Americans, as well as a more familiar image of the March on Washington. As Jennifer Hudson starts singing along to Biden's words about the third anniversary of the events in Charlottesville, we jump from the March on Washington to a horrific aerial shot of the car attack that culminated the violence of the Unite the Right rally. It's an image Biden's campaign ad had shied away from, but that Will.i.am, who did not coordinate with the Biden team, decided viewers needed to be reminded of in all its visceral violence. Biden and Hudson's duet then invites viewers to remember what they'd seen on television, as the video illustrates with images of the August 11 tiki torch parade and squads of neo-Nazis with shields from August 12, 2017, before the video pans out to include images of 2020, from the impact of the pandemic to numerous invocations of the George Floyd summer protests.

"Remember what you saw on television." Biden and Will.i.am appeal to camera images as "technologies of memory" that fix collective remembrance of national events. Marita Sturken, in her book *Tangled Memories,* argues that Americans as a national community use photographic and film images to "fix" collective memory and situate themselves as part of a national culture.[45] Our experience of traumatic events such as the Kennedy assassination or the 9/11 terrorist attacks were traumas most Americans experienced in front of television screens. Our personal memories become tangled up with the media imagery we engage with. Sturken grounded her discussion in Benedict Anderson's work and his concept of "imagined communities," which explains that modern nation-states are too complex and multifaceted to ever be experienced personally by their inhabitants. Mass media has functioned, in the twentieth century at least, to construct a cohesive and coherent idea of the nation. Individuals participate in an imagined idea of the nation through media engagement.

But the twenty-first century has so far fractured the very idea of an imagined community of Americans, through the intense polarization in US politics. Americans have increasingly been siloed into ever more narrow demographics and niches by new forms of media technologies, and in the Trump era they often failed even to agree on definitions of truth and reality. All of this has put into crisis the very concept of an American "imagined community" that shares collective memories through its technologies of remembrance. Nevertheless, Biden and Will.i.am appeal to precisely this idea of a collective American public that experienced the traumatic images from Charlottesville and then the despicable responses by Trump in the same way.

This imagined community of Americans sharing basic precepts of the nation's norms and values may have been as much of a fiction in 1963 and 1965, albeit masked by that era's consensus-oriented mass media ecosystem, as more clearly appeared to be the case in 2017. Nevertheless, in 2020 many millions more Americans got behind Biden's vision of the nation and ways of speaking about it than embraced Trump's white-grievance politics of division and discord. Just as the alt-right failed in the streets of Charlottesville, so too did Trump. Biden succeeded, like JFK and LBJ, by embracing antiracist activists. All three may have done so for politically calculated reasons, considering the response of at least some of those activists being embraced. However, all three harnessed the energy of a powerful movement for racial justice. Kennedy and Johnson used that energy to put forth and pass profoundly consequential legislation. Biden used that energy to win the White House and dislodge a Chief Executive who trumpeted the alt-right movement.

But, of course, political victories are only ever provisional. The alt-right had been vanquished in Charlottesville's streets in 2017. Trump and Trumpism went down to electoral defeat on November 3, 2020, in part because the winning candidate yoked Trump to "Charlottesville" and its fascistic and white supremacist signifiers. It didn't end there.

CONCLUSION

A12 to J6 and Beyond

As the year 2021 dawned, the struggle against white supremacy and right-wing extremism in the US appeared to be going well. The country had witnessed its largest and most geographically extensive popular uprising against racism and police brutality with the "Summer of George Floyd" protests. Unprecedented numbers of Americans seemed ready, finally, to grapple with systemic and institutionalized racism.

The perpetrator of the Charlottesville car attack sat moldering away in prison, having commenced his two life terms plus the extra 419 years tacked onto his sentence.[1] In an example of how right-wing extremists tend to eat their own, "Crying Nazi" Chris Cantwell got slapped with a three-year prison term in 2021 for extortion and threats against another white nationalist. Cantwell had already served time in jail for pepper-spraying counterprotesters at the August 11 tiki torch march.[2] Key groups that had organized the Unite the Right rally appeared defunct, including the Traditionalist Worker Party. Its high-profile head, Matthew Heimbach, following a number of run-ins with the law, announced in 2020 that he was leaving the neo-Nazi movement, but many were skeptical.[3] And although he abruptly relaunched his group in July 2021, which now imbibed anti-capitalist and Bolshevik politics along with hate, antisemitism, and calls to kill "elites," the move seemed more a desperate bid for attention than a sign of new relevance.[4] Identity Evropa, following a plunge in membership after Unite the Right, attempted to rebrand itself, but officially disbanded at the end of 2020.[5] Its erstwhile leader Eli Mosley (a.k.a. Elliot Kline), along with Richard Spencer and all the other leaders and organizations that organized the Unite the Right mayhem, came into 2021 facing significant legal peril. They were all named in the *Sines v. Kessler* lawsuit that would mobilize the little-used Reconstruction-era Ku Klux Klan Act of 1871 to argue that the UTR participants had conspired in advance to perpetuate racially motivated violence.[6] Mosley and Robert "Azzmador" Ray of the Daily Stormer destroyed and withheld evidence they were required to submit for the discovery portion of the case and found themselves slapped with "adverse inferences." That meant the jury for the October 2021 trial would be instructed to accept as fact the charges against the defendants.[7] The *Sines v. Kessler* case (whose outcome I discussed in chapter 3) appeared merely the next in a list of legal proceedings against those who had hoped to create an unstoppable movement for white masculinist power in the streets of Charlottesville.

Democratic institutions appeared to have held. Unprecedented numbers of voters turned out to cast ballots in the 2020 presidential election.[8] The repudiation of Trump and Trumpism seemed decisive, with the Democrats taking not only the presidency, but both Houses of Congress, even as Republicans added more congressional members, reducing the Democrats' previously commanding hold on that chamber. Candidate Biden's campaign platform of pointing to #Charlottesville as the symbol of the imperiled state of the soul of the nation clearly resonated with many voters.

But then came January 6, 2021. Thousands of enraged Trump supporters, far-right extremists, white supremacists, militia groups, QAnon conspiracy believers, and highly visible Proud Boys assembled in Washington, DC, at Trump's behest for a "Stop the Steal" rally at the Ellipse, followed by an unpermitted march to the Capitol. Confronted by a woefully underprepared US Capitol police force, hundreds violently attacked the Capitol, swarming into the building to stop Congress from dutifully certifying electoral votes to officially proclaim Joe Biden as the next president. Five people ended up dead, including a female insurrectionist shot while trying to clamber through a shattered glass door and a Capitol police officer who died after being sprayed with a chemical agent by rioters. Over a hundred overwhelmed police officers were injured trying unsuccessfully to hold back the mobs.

In the immediate aftermath of the insurrection, numerous media outlets began to draw linkages between #Charlottesville and #Capitol_Insurrection. There was the impunity given aggrieved white people to vent their anger violently, the lack of forceful police action to stop them, the support from Trump, and the fact that some of the same white nationalists who marched in Charlottesville marched on the Capitol.[9] January 6 echoed August 11 and 12 in many ways, but there was one stark difference. Antiracist and antifascist counterprotesters did not show up. The "Charlottesville model" of forcefully and massively countering neo-Nazis and white supremacists whenever and wherever they gather didn't happen in Washington, DC. And that mattered.

It's not that there weren't activist groups in DC similar to those in Charlottesville. ShutDownDC, All Out DC, and Black Lives Matter DC, along with other militant groups, had organized and clashed very publicly with Proud Boys who had descended on the District following the November presidential election. Most notably, in mid-December antiracists attempted to prevent Proud Boys from entering Black Lives Matter Plaza and from defacing the fencing at Lafayette Square, which was adorned with protest posters and artwork. The white nationalists ended up stealing and burning BLM flags from historic African American churches and engaging in violent confrontations with counterprotesters, leading to serious injuries and arrests. Proud Boy contingents outnumbered counterprotesters at least six to one.[10] This disparity proved daunting to antiracist organizers as the prospects of another big pro-Trump rally slated for January 5 and 6 rapidly came together.

During Charlottesville's Summer of Hate, the counterprotesters almost always outnumbered the white nationalists: when Richard Spencer's alt-right group staged its first tiki torch photo op in Lee Park on May 13, 2017, the community's candlelit counter-rally the following night brought out double to triple as many participants. Two months later, the fifty or so Klansmen rallying in Jackson (then Justice) Park were met with a thousand counterprotesters. And on August 12, the Unite the Right rally participants were confronted with more than equal numbers of opponents.

But in the days before January 6, All Out DC and BLM DC pointed to difficulties in mobilizing counterdemonstrators. One organizer from All Out DC explained, "I think at the moment we're mobilizing as liberal apathy is setting in." BLM DC urged people not to counterprotest, considering the ratio of Proud Boys to antiracists in confrontations over the past two months. "We will be outnumbered," noted a BLM spokesperson; the focus needed to be on keeping their own people safe from racist violence.[11] The group tried to get DC hotels to deny bookings to extremist groups, and one that had been the Proud Boys' favored hotel and gathering spot agreed to close its doors on January 5 and 6.

NBC Nightly News footage of insurrectionists at the Capitol Building: Echoes of the alt-right at UVA's Rotunda.

When the actions of that day became the media event we now know as "January 6," the work of local antiracist and antifascist activists was largely invisible. The media images that circulated around the world brought to maximum visibility large groups of apparently unstoppable, mostly white men conquering the seat of American governmental power. Police were depicted looking weak, defeated, and even victimized by the insurrectionists. Ubiquitous news images showed rioters swarming all over the iconic Capitol building. Those pictures echoed the iconic images of enraged white men in front of another well-known American Greco-Roman edifice: Unite the Right marchers at UVA's Rotunda.

As we saw, Unite the Right organizers planned the tiki torch rally as an organizing event—the images were supposed to serve as attractive propaganda, the architectural backdrop carefully chosen. It's unclear whether January 6 rally organizers were thinking much about media coverage, the semiotic meanings of the architecture, or about using the event to build a movement.[12] Nevertheless, the media effect was similar to what alt-right organizers in 2017 had hoped for: triumphant images of unleashed white male power mass-disseminated. On the night of August 11, it initially appeared that white nationalists had achieved "total victory," as one tiki torch marcher proclaimed in his livestream, the group of counterprotesters was so small and easily overpowered. But, of course, that's not how the narrative played out.

CONCLUSION 179

Media coverage of the Capitol insurrection initially featured no images or narratives of opposition. Eventually, however, footage of a lone African American Capitol police officer who appeared to be chased and imperiled by rampaging insurrectionists did provide a narrative similar to that offered by the students at the Thomas Jefferson statue on UVA's Rotunda plaza. When initially broadcast, the footage of Officer Eugene Goodman appeared to fit into the long tradition of American media imagery and racialized melodramatic narratives of evil white men with power and beleaguered, victimized Black people.[13] But Officer Goodman wasn't running from the forces of white power unleashed. Very cannily he was leading the marauders away from US senators and their unprotected Senate chambers. The cell phone footage provided by a *Huff Post* reporter documenting Goodman's actions took a while to get analyzed and fully narrated. When that happened, the story exploded. Goodman pushes lightly at a QAnon sweatshirt-wearing man, in a calculated ploy to get him and the throng behind to follow Goodman up a set of marble stairs away from the Senate chambers. Like the students who stood up to the tiki torch wielding neo-Nazis in Charlottesville, Officer Goodman quickly got hailed as a hero in media accounts.[14] He was subsequently awarded the Congressional Gold Medal for his bravery.

However, except for this much-touted moment of successful pushback to

Capitol Police Officer Eugene Goodman appears to be a Black imperiled victim of empowered whites; actually, he cannily leads the Capitol rioters away from the unprotected Senate chambers.

"You Have Been Replaced." Capitol insurrectionist gets comfortable in Speaker of the House Nancy Pelosi's office.

the forces of insurrection and white riot, most of the soon-to-be iconic images of January 6 gave the public representations of white nationalist and antidemocratic masculine triumphalism. There was the photo of a middle-aged, white-bearded man comfortably lounging back in the office chair of Speaker of the House Nancy Pelosi, with his heavy work boot propped up on her desk. His casual stance communicated his right to be there; his boot on her papers signifying contempt for her. We're already past "You Will Not Replace Us." The photo implies, "You Have Already Been Replaced."

Among the most widely circulated images of the insurrection were pictures and film of the "QAnon Shaman," later identified as Jacob Chansley (a.k.a. Jake Angeli). The most colorful and visually striking of all the insurrectionists, Chansley sported a Viking-like fur headdress with horns, a cape, a US flag on a spear, and a bared, well-muscled torso adorned with large tattoos. He eventually made his way into the well of the Senate, as did other rioters, who took selfies of themselves there, while others ransacked senators' desks. Once he and other insurrectionists left the building, he gleefully proclaimed to a journalist, "We won the fucking day! We won!"[15] Tiki torch marchers had said the same thing.

This triumphalism was certainly understandable. The media imagery suggested as much. And without Black Lives Matter or antifa opponents to con-

CONCLUSION 181

The photogenic "QAnon Shaman": Representing triumphalist white hypermasculinity, but also looking a tad ridiculous.

tend with, some participants on right-wing extremist social media sites began to see DC law enforcement as their enemy: they were "coptifa" and yet another impediment to be overcome in the insurrectionists' goal of achieving total victory.[16] But as a visual representation of the Capitol invaders, Chansley presents an odd image. On the one hand, he's the incarnation of the kind of unrestrained hypermasculine ideal called for by the Proud Boys and other alt-right "manosphere" groupings.[17] On the other hand, his primitivist costume, along with his penchant for bellowing in guttural tones, is rather ridiculous. But so were the faux-Polynesian backyard barbecue props wielded by alt-right marchers at UVA's Rotunda. The point was, they could get away with it.

Until they couldn't. Like the perpetrators of white riot and violence in Charlottesville, the Capitol insurrectionists acted fully out in the open. Like in Charlottesville, as Emily Gorcenski had warned, there were cameras everywhere. And Capitol insurrectionists were quite happy to film themselves and snap selfies, creating even more visual evidence.[18] And like the violent Unite the Right participants, the Capitol rioters found themselves facing serious legal sanction. As this book goes to press, there have been nine hundred arrests, out of an estimated two thousand who illegally breached the Capitol. Over three hundred have pled guilty, mostly to misdemeanor crimes. A smaller group have so far been convicted of more serious charges, especially for assaulting police officers, garnering months- and years-long jail sentences. The most serious charges filed against Oath Keepers and Proud Boys, seditious conspiracy, await prosecution.[19]

As in the aftermath of #Charlottesville, Republican lawmakers condemned the rioters as un-American and called on Trump to do more to stop the violence and the assault on the law and the Constitution.[20] In 2017 the GOP politicians moved on, never really holding Trump accountable for his refusal to fully condemn the neo-Nazis and white supremacists who descended on Charlottesville. The aftermath of January 6 was even more disturbing, as Republican elected officials began backtracking on their condemnation of the insurrectionists, with some claiming the rioters' behavior was like a "normal tourist visit," or that the rioters may actually have been left-wing agitators, or, finally, that what happened at the Capitol was certainly not an insurrection, or even necessarily unpatriotic.[21] The handful of Republican senators and members of Congress who continued to condemn Trump's instigating of the mob and perpetrating the Big Lie about a stolen election found themselves punished by their colleagues. At the state level, Republicans launched hundreds of initiatives to make voting more difficult, especially for voters of color, while their counterparts in Washington refused to move on legislation, including the John Lewis Voting Rights Advancement Act. And then the Supreme Court took the ragged remains of the Voting Rights Act and tore it up some more. Now it would be even more difficult for voters of color to claim racial discrimination, because the Court's conservative majority decided that the cause of hypothetical voter fraud was more important.[22]

And so we are back to that pivotal year 1965, when who could vote and how voting could be regulated at the federal level changed the nation (along with the other momentous rights expansions and immigration changes written into law in that brief period). We've already explored how the Unite the Right rally as a media event brought to maximum visibility a political movement whose foundational purpose was the eradication of all those expansions. It wasn't entirely clear in 2017 just how fully Trump embraced the white supremacist, antidemocratic alt-right cause. He was canny enough to provide himself ideological wiggle room with his "both sides" rhetoric. The January 6 media event brought to maximum visibility that Trumpism and the alt-right of 2017 were ultimately the same movement. What did "Stop the Steal" mean? The same thing as "You/Jews Will Not Replace Us." It meant the country had been "stolen" from white people since the aftermath of Birmingham and Selma. And while "only" 17 percent of those arrested to date were clearly connected to far-right extremist groups, according to an NPR investigation, researchers examining the identities of the insurrectionists have "raise[d] concerns about how extremist ideologies have moved increasingly into the mainstream."[23] Political scientist Robert Pape, in an analysis of where the arrested rioters came from, discovered that most lived in counties across the nation experiencing the most significant declines in white population in recent years. They were from places "awash in fears that the rights of minorities and immigrants were crowding out the rights of white people in American politics and culture."[24]

Then, a few days after Pape's research hit the pages of the *New York Times* and the *Washington Post*, Fox News's most popular prime-time star, Tucker Carlson, helpfully laid out the white supremacist thinking that undergirded "Stop the Steal." Claiming to argue a voting rights question, Carlson forthrightly wielded "Great Replacement" theory in charging the Democratic Party with "trying to replace the current electorate, the voters now casting ballots, with new people, more obedient voters from the third world." This "replacement" thereby lessened Carlson's political power "because they're importing a brand new electorate. Why should I sit back and take that? The power that I have as an American, guaranteed at birth, is one man, one vote. And they are diluting it."[25] The Fox News pundit didn't have to clarify that by "one man" he really meant one white man.

In 2017 the alt-right attempted to create a social change movement using Charlottesville as its stage set; it appeared to have collapsed rather decisively. Three and a half years later, #Charlottesville 2.0 erupted in Washington, DC. The participants this time were far more desperate, not well organized (they had a tough time figuring out where they were going once they crashed and smashed their way into the Capitol building), and did not appear focused on building a movement. They already were a movement, albeit one with a leader about to lose all his platforms.[26] Did it ultimately matter that counterprotesters didn't show up? The resulting confrontations would likely have been even more deadly than what resulted. The lack of an oppositional movement can only raise questions about the antiracist and antifascist movement "muscle" that Zeynep Tufekci discusses. On the other hand, that movement muscle was powerfully on display all through the Summer of George Floyd.

There will be future media events centered on racism, white supremacy, and the struggles for democracy and diversity, as those issues are this nation's unfinished business and ongoing conflict, often buried only to erupt again and again demanding attention and action. John Fiske argued that the significance of the media event was "the inevitability of its recurrence."[27] In the civil rights era, when the postmodern concept of the media event was still new, Birmingham and Selma signaled a nation grappling with race and rights and the expansion of those rights, because large enough numbers of Americans found themselves compelled to confront media imagery of the sheer ugliness and brutality of white supremacy. Fifty years later, Charlottesville and most recently the Capitol insurrection became media events suggesting how imperiled the expansion of those rights was as a white empowerment movement attempted to do what the civil rights movement did decades previously. The images this time were also ugly, brutal, and inevitably violent, since that's the essence of white supremacy, both when it was dominant, as it was a half century ago, and weakened and lashing out, as is the situation now. In both cases, large numbers of Americans, along with their elected representatives, had to confront what their nation was and what they wanted to do about it. "Charlottesville" provided a useful model for how to respond: those opposed to white supremacy and its existential threat to democracy need to show up and confront it. The threat is always greater than we think it is.

Winning?

It was a Friday afternoon, July 9, 2021, when the press release from the City of Charlottesville landed in residents' email in-boxes and social media feeds. The Robert E. Lee and Stonewall Jackson statues would be coming down the next day. I was finishing up final revisions for this book when I got the news. Why such a late notice? Oh, right: can't give too much lead time for any neo-Confederates or white supremacists who might want to make one last stand in defense of their racist Lost Cause. The press release didn't give the community much time to organize itself either. And the notice didn't say anything about what time on Saturday the statues would finally come down. I texted with friends and activists trying to figure out when we should gather on Saturday.

The African American–owned removal company, Team Henry Enterprises, made quick work of the Robert E. Lee statue early the next morning. They'd had experience removing Richmond's Confederate statues in 2020.[28] Those gathered to watch and cheer the removal were all community members, many of them activists who had been engaged in the struggle against systemic racism in Charlottesville for some time. Many of the people celebrating this day had been featured in the Inside Out Charlottesville project. For those watching the

CONCLUSION 185

speedy removal of the Lee statue and the slower process to take down the Jackson monument, the experience was clearly cathartic. Community members and activists cheered, hugged each other, and cheered some more.

We'd won. Almost four years ago, our town had become a worldwide media event and hashtag when waves of far-right extremists, Klansmen, and neo-Nazis came to town on the pretext of protesting the city's plan to take down these statues. The statues served as the vehicle for their movement-building. Now those alt-right white nationalists were nowhere to be seen—and wouldn't be seen until some returned to face trial in October–while the statues they so revered were coming down at last, following so many other Confederate monuments toppled in the aftermath of the Unite the Right disaster.

After watching the Jackson statue get placed facing backwards on Team Henry's flatbed truck and hauled ignominiously out of town, I wandered back, past the synagogue, toward Market Street (formerly Emancipation) Park. Gazing at the empty pedestal, I took a photo. At home, I posted that photo juxtaposed with an image from the alt-right's first tiki torch rally in front of the Lee statue from May 2017.

Author's Facebook post.

Yes, we won. But what did that ultimately mean? Former mayor Mike Signer, in his 2020 memoir about the Summer of Hate, raised concerns that some community members during that period were getting caught up in the "politics of symbolism" rather than substance, focusing on symbolic victories rather than changes in policy.[29] Signer might be right, if the only thing that results from the removal of monuments to the Confederacy is the sudden availability of more open space in parks and public places and momentary feel-good vibes. But the statues were always about much more. The alt-right used them to launch an "in real life" movement. Their antiracist opponents used them to mobilize a countermovement. It remains to be seen how successful that countermovement will be, either in Charlottesville or elsewhere, but the person who sparked it all certainly understood the larger issues.

Zyahna Bryant, the fifteen-year-old African American high school student who started the countermovement in Charlottesville has much in common with the Black girls and women whose actions were crucial—but often unseen or forgotten—during the civil rights era. Sixteen-year-old Barbara Johns led a walk-out in protest of conditions in her Farmville, Virginia, segregated school in 1951. Her activism, leading to a school desegregation case that got folded into the landmark 1954 *Brown v. Board of Education* Supreme Court decision, served as one impetus for the modern Black freedom movement.[30] Another teenager, fifteen-year-old Claudette Colvin, refused to give up her seat to a white person on a Montgomery bus in 1955 nine months before Rosa Parks took the same action. Local Black leadership decided to launch a movement around Parks because she presented a more media-ready image. We've already seen other Black female activists—the Selma campaign's Amelia Boynton, Annie Lee Cooper, Diane Nash—who were crucial to the movement but remained largely invisible in media accounts. Bryant was also mostly unseen in major media coverage of the Summer of Hate and its aftermath.

But things changed notably when the statues came down. Major outlets like CNN, NBC, and CBS clambered to give the now twenty-year-old rising third-year University of Virginia student a platform to explain what the removal of the statues meant, and the *Washington Post* spotlighted Bryant in a major profile.[31] The press were not going to Susan Bro or to former Mayor Mike Signer, both of whom have maintained significant media platforms since 2017.[32] The media did not spotlight Rev. Seth Wispelwey or even former Vice-mayor Wes Bellamy, the most high-profile African American figure interviewed during and, especially with some frequently, right after the Summer of Hate.

CONCLUSION 187

In #Charlottesville's follow-up chapter in 2021, media treatment diverged quite significantly from one key characteristic of how press covered Birmingham and Selma. Then, Martin Luther King was typically the sole Black activist the press relied on to frame the stakes and the meanings of the Black freedom movement. During the Selma campaign if it wasn't King, in network TV coverage at least, viewers would often see a white figure given the microphone.[33] King fit the role in seeming to look and sound relatively unthreatening to white liberals. A product of the Atlanta Black elite, holder of a Boston University Ph.D., with a public persona of formality, gravitas, and modesty, King appeared older than his years and his status as a clergyman made him almost unassailable. Throughout the Southern civil rights years, Black women were almost never handed the mass media microphone. When Fannie Lou Hamer seized it in 1964 on behalf of the Mississippi Freedom Democratic Party's attempt to seat an integrated delegation at the Democratic National Convention, the anomaly of a working-class woman with none of King's pedigree or refinement representing the movement was the exception that proved the rule.

In 2021, Zyahna Bryant self-consciously positioned herself in a lineage from these mostly unheralded Black women activists.[34] Like many of them, she would not have been considered "media-ready" in an earlier time. Yet with the powerful nation-wide platforms she suddenly commanded, she drew out

NBC News, among the numerous mass media platforms for Zyahna Bryant.
In 2021, a young Black woman gets the microphone to frame the stakes and the meaning of Confederate statues' removal in Charlottesville.

the connections from the statues to the political-economic situation for Black and Brown communities. Speaking to national and international media in front of the about-to-be-felled Lee statue, she said, "We are standing in a park where the city is still refusing to address systemic issues. And the work of removing the statues is only the tip of the iceberg. There's so much work left to do to address affordable housing, to address policing, to address the wealth gap."[35] Interviewed by CBS News, she argued that "by addressing those deeper systems [communities are] able to match the politics with the physical changes we're making in the landscape and the infrastructure of these places."[36]

Time, and the perspective of history, will tell whether the movements for racial justice and expanded democracy that the nation first grappled with seriously during civil rights–era media events like Birmingham and Selma, and then confronted again beginning with #Ferguson and then with searing horror during #Charlottesville, have the abiding "movement muscle" to do what Zyahna Bryant calls for. Martin Luther King famously proclaimed, "the arc of the moral universe is long, but it bends towards justice." The nation may want to keep its eyes on Charlottesville to see the progress of that bending.

AFTERWORD

My Summer of Hate—A Personal Narrative

"I hope those guys think this is a church."

The thought went through my mind on the morning of August 12, 2017, as I looked out the big windows of my synagogue down onto Jefferson Street in downtown Charlottesville. Neo-Nazis with Confederate flags, swastikas, shields, and poles paraded by our front entrance. One happened to glance up. Our building, constructed in the 1880s and located between the two city parks dominated by Confederate monuments, looks a lot like the Catholic church across the street. Both were built by the same architect. Ours has fleur-de-lis decorations atop Gothic Revival spires. From the ground, they sort of look like crosses.

Services for that Saturday had been scheduled an hour earlier than usual so that congregants would be able to finish worship and leave the building before the noontime Unite the Right rally got started at the former Lee Park, recently renamed Emancipation Park, a little over a block away. Post-service conversation focused on how to protect ourselves, the synagogue, and our Torah scrolls from the people marching down our street. The scrolls needed to be removed for safekeeping. What about the Holocaust scroll—rescued from a Nazi-destroyed synagogue near Prague in 1939 and on permanent loan to our congregation—which might be too fragile to move?[1] Our rabbi instructed all of us to exit out the back entrance, not out front. Go in groups.[2]

I'd gotten up early that morning to participate in a march of community people and religious groups. The march started at the Jefferson School Community Center, west of the downtown center. Originally it was Charlottesville's segregated school for Black children. We marched through what had once been Vinegar Hill, an African American segregated neighborhood right by downtown. It had been literally blasted away and demolished in 1965, its residents, businesses, and homeowners forced to leave in the (white) interests of urban renewal.[3] We ended up rallying a block east of Emancipation Park in McGuffey Park, which was right next to a 1916 Colonial Revival building with red bricks and white columns now serving as an arts center. In its previous incarnation, the building had been a segregated elementary school: white kids only. It was much grander looking than the Jefferson School. Our half-hour march to protest white supremacy in 2017 had taken us through Charlottesville's built environment of segregation and Black community destruction.[4]

McGuffey Park had been designated by activists a safe space for the local community. It didn't have a Confederate monument, just a lot of children's play equipment, and no markers to its segregationist past. Vice-mayor Wes Bellamy, a lightning rod for alt-right forces because of his leadership role in advocating for the removal of Confederate statues, led the assembled crowd in chants of "No hate! No fear! White supremacy's not welcome here!"

When the rally broke up, I ventured forth alone to the synagogue for that unusually early service. Furtively looking out for alt-right types as I walked, I felt a bit vulnerable, especially since I'd decided to wear a Star of David pendant. There'd been groups of young men around downtown in the previous days decked out in neat suits, white polo shirts, and short Hitler-Youth haircuts. They were easy to spot.

So were the media trucks. When was the last time there'd been so much media presence in my town? Was it in 2014, when UVA nursing student Hannah Graham was murdered? Was it during the 2012 trial of George Hugueley for killing fellow UVA student Yeardley Love? The violent death of young white women in this visually bucolic Southern town did seem to bring national media attention.

As our post-worship service gathering time wrapped up, some congregants planned to get home as quickly as possible. I, however, was staying downtown. In this latest manifestation of what local Black Lives Matter activist and UVA professor Jalane Schmidt coined Charlottesville's "Summer of Hate," I'd decided to join those in the community standing up, counterprotesting, putting bodies on the line. Schmidt had published an article on Medium at the end of June 2017 that became required reading for everyone in the town concerned about the rise of extremist "alt-right" activity in our midst. Memorably titled, "Excuse Me, America, Your House Is on Fire," she laid out the challenge to people who liked to imagine the stands they would have taken against slavery or the Third Reich or what they would have done during the civil rights movement: "Now is a historical moment to cast one's lot. Whatever you are doing (or not doing) today is what you would have been doing then."[5] As a scholar of the civil rights movement and the daughter-in-law of a Holocaust survivor, I decided I couldn't go home.[6] But now as the Unite the Right rally participants were converging on Emancipation Park, what would those who had decided to counterprotest encounter? What would happen when hundreds of antiracist and antifascist activists stood up to hundreds of emboldened neo-Nazis and white supremacists?

The Summer of Hate began for me on July 8 with the permitted rally of a North Carolina KKK chapter in the park a block east of the synagogue, which featured a statue of Confederate General Stonewall Jackson. Antiracist and antifascist activists had been mobilizing in town for more than a year, since our Confederate statues had become a lightning rod with the 2016 petition by fifteen-year-old Black high schooler Zyahna Bryant calling for the removal of the Robert E. Lee statue and the renaming of Lee Park. I followed the news about the city's fraught decision-making about the monuments but didn't feel personally compelled to get involved. The local media infrastructure certainly didn't help encourage activist participation.

It was hard to get quickly plugged into the activism and organizing in the community. Where were the local activist media sources of information? A friend told me about the online newsletter *Solidarity Cville*. This anonymous community defense and activist media collective would prove to be indispensable throughout the summer. Meeting up with two friends, I joined a thousand anti-Klan protesters to yell at the small contingent of Klansmen decked out in their garish robes and pointy hats who paraded into the newly named Justice Park. Facing us were body armor–clad Virginia state police there to protect the Klan and their First Amendment rights.

That was the first jolt: law enforcement wasn't there to serve and safeguard us, the counterprotesters, nor the Charlottesville community. The more seasoned activists knew that, as did most local African Americans. For instance, while Black people were less than 20 percent of Charlottesville's population, they constituted 70 percent of the warrantless stop-and-frisk encounters with police.[7] Eventually, after I had left, the police let loose tear gas on the remaining demonstrators who didn't disperse quickly enough. Local activists were manhandled and arrested. The Klan received escort service by police back to their vehicles.

The second jolt: most of the KKK's signs targeted Jews. "Communism = Judaism." Other signs said something about Jews and Satan, and the Talmud and child molestation. Rather than center their white hate on Black people and other racial minorities, on this day Klan hatred targeted Jews. One month later, on the night of August 11, tiki torch–carrying neo-Nazis would chant "Jews will not replace us" as they paraded across the Grounds of my university. Why the venomous focus on Jews? While many factions of American white supremacists historically didn't consider Jews to be white, the more recent strands of antisemitism animating the alt-right argued that Jews were actively promoting "white genocide" by championing non-European immigration, multiculturalism, feminism, and "globalist" values. Jews, in this way of thinking, deviously partnered with other non-white people to destroy white civilization.[8]

Following the KKK rally, like many others in Charlottesville I spent the next month figuring out what I would do come August 12th. Heeding the admonition by organizers and activists that anyone planning to be anywhere near Emancipation Park that day undergo nonviolent direct-action training, I joined hundreds of people on the afternoon of August 11 at St. Paul's Memorial Church to learn some basic skills just in case we got swept up with frontline activists from here and elsewhere planning to confront and physically disrupt the Unite the Right rally. I knew a lot about nonviolent protest from my scholarly work on the civil rights and protest movements of the 1960s and had engaged in protest activity during my 1980s student days. This wasn't entirely unfamiliar to me. But standing there in that big room learning how to link arms with other protesters to hold space and protect each other, I realized what local activists had been warning for months: this is for real. Things could get bad. I still didn't know quite what I was prepared to do the next day beyond an early morning march. What if I got arrested? I carried far more privilege than many who would face the fascists the next day, but as an expatriate Canadian, I wasn't convinced my green card would necessarily protect me against deportation from Trump's America.

I discovered my role supporting frontline activists pretty much at the last minute. Partnering with my fellow congregant and UVA colleague, Cora, I joined her, her son, and his girlfriend, who had set up an activist snack station in McGuffey Park. Above their "Snack Squad" tent flapped a red flag with a black raised fist clenching a fork. We were all "care bears." Activists putting themselves in harm's way need all manner of support from other activists assuming non-frontline roles: medics, legal observers, communications personnel, and community care volunteers who ensure that marchers and demonstrators are hydrated and fed. In the heat and intensity of a demonstration, protesters often don't pay attention to their physical needs. Care bears, like attentive moms, tend to that. It was all characteristic of the mutual aid, "we take care of us" ethos of antiracist and antifascist movements. The alt-right subscribed to different principles.

Cora and I filled up our backpacks with provisions and headed down from McGuffey Park toward Market Street.[9] We passed a contingent of black-clad antifa fighters suiting up. Their battle gear of goggles, gloves, batons, and face respirators made them look fierce. Their demeanor towards us, two middle-aged white lades bearing water and energy bars, was incongruously polite and almost tender. My politics of nonviolence weren't in accord with theirs, but over the course of that day, I took some comfort from the presence of these antifa groups. They provided protection.

Market Street was a chaotic battleground as alt-right forces with poles and shields clashed with counterprotesters. In front of us were scenes that would play out over and over again in subsequent media coverage of "#Charlottesville." In the crush of bodies we surveyed from our vantage point up an incline from the street, it was hard for me to immediately distinguish who was who. There was little, if any, police presence that I could see. Counterprotesters were trying to stop the white nationalists and neo-Nazis from getting to Emancipation Park, a block east of us. Then we saw gas wafting up. Cora dragged me further up the incline, yelling and coughing that we had to get away from it.[10]

Back at the sanctuary of our "Snack Squad" tent, two neo-Nazi figures suddenly lumbered into our park. McGuffey was supposed to be a safe haven only for "our" people. One neo-Nazi was bellowing and yelling and crying. He'd clearly been overcome by gas, as had his less vocal companion. A medic tent was just a stone's throw from ours. And there were "our" medics tending to these fascists. I watched as one of them yanked off his shirt, blubbering away while the medics poured milk into his eyes. Were more of his comrades going to invade our sanctuary? The two quickly left, and no others appeared. Why were our medics providing aid to our enemies? I certainly wouldn't have provided water or food to Nazis in need. As health care professionals, were the medics required to give medical assistance? What were the ethics of the situation? I was still sitting with this a day later at a small gathering at a local church for activists who wanted to talk about what they'd seen and experienced. After recounting the story and my ethical quandary, an elderly man took me aside, smiling knowingly: "We got his phone. We followed their communication the rest of the day."[11]

Our care bear duties kept us behind the front lines the rest of that day. Overhead we heard the nonstop whirring of a police helicopter. Its incessant, oppressive humming formed a sonic backdrop to our activities. We knew we were under constant surveillance. Hours later that Virginia State Police chopper went down in a horrible accident, killing both officers who had spent their day monitoring us.

Our snack squad crew ventured over to Justice Park with more provisions, handing them out, feeding ourselves, listening as local musician John D'earth played a mournful trumpet off in a shady corner, and then hastening ourselves out of the park because there was a guy with an automatic weapon walking around the area. Who was he? We didn't want to find out. He might have been a member of Redneck Revolt, an anti-capitalist, antiracist, antifascist militia that came to Charlottesville to protect the counterprotesters. But how would we have been able to tell? All we saw was a frightening military weapon toted by a white man in a dark shirt.

First United Methodist Church, a stately edifice with tall white columns, elaborate spire, and a broad sweep of marble steps facing Emancipation Park, functioned as another safe space for counterprotesters. We ventured there for a bathroom break, making our way through the elaborate security protocol more easily than the young white men who encountered enhanced screenings and pat-downs in the church's driveway. On the sidewalk, a group of Quaker women sang freedom songs. Across the street, a contingent of antifa kept watch.

No sooner had we entered, when the church went on lockdown. The Unite the Right rally had finally been declared an unlawful assembly after about forty-five minutes of melee, and Virginia State Police had begun their dispersal tactic of pushing alt-right forces throughout the downtown area. Neo-Nazis were scattering everywhere, including by the church. As we sheltered inside sharing stories, we had no idea what was happening outside. Finally given the all-clear, Cora wanted only to meet up with her son. Getting back to McGuffey Park, we discovered that he and his girlfriend had joined a contingent of people marching down toward Friendship Court, a predominantly African American low-income housing complex just south of Market Street. There was fear that neo-Nazis might be heading there to terrorize the community. What should we do? Go in support? We never got to make a decision.

An incident had just happened near Market Street, we were told. Something with a car. People were injured. Cora frantically tried to text and phone her son. No answer. McGuffey Park was oddly serene and peaceful. A few minutes later he and his girlfriend came reeling into the park, trauma plainly visible on their faces. Someone had deliberately driven a car into a crowd of counterprotesters. They had seen it. Nobody knew how many were hurt or how badly.

Eventually I made my way out of downtown with another friend, who'd parked just outside the barricaded perimeter. Taking a circuitous route to my car at the Jefferson School, we saw the familiar streets that looked so—normal. Back at my own car, I drove away from the downtown core to my home outside the town center, anxiously scanning for neo-Nazi contingents. It all looked so—normal. A beautiful, sunny, warm day in Charlottesville.

Driving to the UVA side of town, I passed a traditionally African American neighborhood in the throes of gentrification as the ever-growing University community of professors, administrators, and affluent students gobbled up housing that local people, many who worked low-paid service sector jobs at the University, could no longer afford. I drove into my neighborhood with its wide streets, mature trees, flowers, cultivated lawns. Built in the postwar era of University expansion, it was meant for white homeowners. Charlottesville, in the Jim Crow era and beyond, had built itself on racial covenants.[12] Sixty years on, my neighbors were still largely white. It was as placid as ever.

Opening my front door, my husband, nursing a summer cold, greeted me from the living room couch. The TV was on. CNN. MSNBC. Back to CNN. It was all Charlottesville, he told me. I sat down and watched looped footage of the mayhem on Market Street, with one activist hoisting a *C-ville Weekly* news box through the air. Trump was scheduled to say something about it all at any time. The wall-to-wall coverage would continue for weeks. The anguish of my town had become a worldwide media event. Its name became a symbol. My Summer of Hate was now #Charlottesville.

I would spend the next four years trying to understand what "#Charlottesville" meant. This book is the culmination of that frequently painful effort.

NOTES

INTRODUCTION

1. The story is told most compellingly and comprehensively in Raymond Arsenault, *Freedom Riders* (New York: Oxford University Press, 2006), 229–42.
2. One of the most quoted lines from the 2013 inaugural address, partly because it acknowledges the struggle for gay rights, is the invocation of the place names that appears here: "We, the people, declare today that the most evident of truths—that all of us are created equal—is the star that guides us still; just as it guided our forebears through Seneca Falls, and Selma, and Stonewall; just as it guided all those men and women, sung and unsung, who left footprints along this great Mall, to hear a preacher say that we cannot walk alone; to hear a King proclaim that our individual freedom is inextricably bound to the freedom of every soul on Earth." https://obamawhitehouse.archives.gov/the-press-office/2013/01/21/inaugural-address-president-barack-obama.
3. Nikole Hannah-Jones, "Our Democracy's Founding Ideals Were False When They Were Written. Black Americans Have Fought to Make Them True," *New York Times Magazine*, August 14, 2019, https://www.nytimes.com/interactive/2019/08/14/magazine/black-history-american-democracy.html.
4. The Thirteenth Amendment abolished slavery throughout the nation, the Fourteenth Amendment granted citizenship to all those born or naturalized in the United States and provided them with "equal protection under the law," and the Fifteenth Amendment prohibited disenfranchisement of voters based on race, colour, "or previous condition of servitude."
5. See for instance Gabriel J. Chin and Rose Cuison Villazor, eds., *The Immigration and Nationality Act of 1965: Legislating a New America* (Cambridge University Press, 2015).
6. A good overview of this short, remarkable period of congressional lawmaking is Julian E. Zelizer, *The Fierce Urgency of Now: Lyndon Johnson, Congress, and the Battle for the Great Society* (New York: Penguin, 2015).

7. Alexandra Minna Stern, *Proud Boys and the White Ethnostate: How the Alt-Right Is Warping the American Imagination* (Boston: Beacon Press, 2019), 47.
8. Ibid.
9. Shelby County v. Holder, 570 U.S. 529 (2013).
10. Steven Levitsky and Daniel Ziblatt, *How Democracies Die* (New York: Broadway Books, 2018).
11. Daniel J. Boorstin, *The Image or What Happened to the American Dream* (New York: Atheneum, 1961), 11.
12. Aniko Bodroghkozy, *Equal Time: Television and the Civil Rights Movement* (Urbana: University of Illinois Press, 2012). See also Sasha Torres, *Black, White, and in Color: Television and Black Civil Rights* (Princeton, NJ: Princeton University Press, 2003); and Gene Roberts and Hank Klibanoff, *The Race Beat: The Press, the Civil Rights Struggle, and the Awakening of a Nation* (New York: Knopf, 2006).
13. See for instance Jean Baudrillard, *Simulacra and Simulation* (Ann Arbor: University of Michigan Press, 1994); Fredric Jameson, *Postmodernism, or the Cultural Logic of Late Capitalism* (Durham: Duke University Press, 1991).
14. John Fiske, *Media Matters: Race and Gender in U.S. Politics* (Minneapolis: University of Minnesota Press, 1996), 2. Fiske isn't the only media studies scholar in the 1990s to put forth a definition of the media event. Elihu Katz and Daniel Dayan did so as well. In their formulation, a media event is a live broadcasting of historical momentousness that audiences watch in a ceremonial manner. They aren't so much news events, but rather ritualized televisual experiences that audiences undergo as akin to holidays or other experiences outside the routines of everyday life. Their examples include JFK's funeral (but not coverage of his assassination, which they consider a news event rather than a media event), Prince Charles and Princess Diana's wedding, the Olympic Games, etc. While a useful way of understanding certain modes of television, their definition is not relevant to media coverage of the events I am discussing here. See Elihu Katz and Daniel Dayan, *Media Events: The Live Broadcasting of History* (Cambridge, MA: Harvard University Press, 1992).
15. Fiske, *Media Matters*, 7.
16. Ibid., 8.
17. Adam Fairclough, *To Redeem the Soul of America: The Southern Christian Leadership Conference and Martin Luther King, Jr.* (Athens: University of Georgia Press, 1987), 229.
18. Ibid., 126.
19. See chapter 2 for more on the inherent violence of the alt-right.
20. In his landmark sociological study of CBS's and NBC's news divisions and the weekly newsmagazines *Time* and *Newsweek*, Herbert Gans argued, "insofar

as the news has an ideology of its own, it is moderate." Herbert Gans, *Deciding What's News* (New York: Random House, 1979), 52. CBS News President Richard Salant's quote serves as an epigraph to another landmark book about network TV news in the classical network television era: Edward Jay Epstein, *News from Nowhere: Television and the News* (New York: Random House, 1973).

21. Some scholars have questioned the "most trusted" title, based on polling methods that initially grouped Cronkite with politicians. See W. Joseph Campbell, *Getting It Wrong* (Berkeley: University of California Press, 2010). According to Gallup polling that began to sample the American public's trust of the news media in the early 1970s, approximately 70 percent reported a great or fair amount of trust in the media. Since 2008, that trust has wallowed, with a low of 32 percent the year Trump was elected in 2016 and remaining in the low fortieth percentiles thereafter: https://news.gallup.com/poll/321116/americans-remain-distrustful-mass-media.aspx.
22. Philip Napoli, *Social Media and the Public Interest: Media Regulation in the Disinformation Age* (New York: Columbia University Press, 2019).
23. Lynn Spigel, "Entertainment Wars: Television Culture after 9/11," *American Quarterly* 56, no. 2 (June 2004): 257. See also Brian A. Monahan, *The Shock of the News: Media Coverage and the Making of 9/11* (New York: New York University Press, 2010).
24. See chapter 7 for a discussion of Republican senators' responses to the events in Charlottesville.
25. Fiske, *Media Matters*, 263.
26. Felix Harcourt, *Ku Klux Kulture: America and the Klan in the 1920s* (Chicago: University of Chicago Press, 2017).
27. Zeynep Tufekci, *Twitter and Tear Gas: The Power and Fragility of Networked Protest* (New Haven, CT: Yale University Press, 2017).
28. Linda Williams, *Playing the Race Card: Melodramas of Black and White from Uncle Tom to O. J. Simpson* (Princeton, NJ: Princeton University Press, 2001).
29. For instance, on Birmingham, see the Pulitzer Prize–winning book by Diane McWhorter, *Carry Me Home: Birmingham, Alabama: The Climactic Battle of the Civil Rights Revolution* (New York: Simon and Shuster, 2001). Important historical monographs include Glenn T. Eskew, *But for Birmingham: The Local and National Movements in the Civil Rights Struggle* (Chapel Hill: University of North Carolina Press, 1997). Well-known among young readers, see the Newberry Honor children's book by Christopher Paul Curtis, *The Watsons Go to Birmingham—1963* (New York: Random House, 1995). On Selma, see Gary May's two books, *Bending toward Justice: The Voting Rights Act and the Transformation of American Democracy* (Durham, NC: Duke University Press,

2005); and *The Informant: The FBI, the Ku Klux Klan, and the Murder of Viola Liuzzo* (New Haven, CT: Yale University Press, 2011). See also the memoir by child activists Sheyann Webb and Rachel West Nelson, *Selma, Lord, Selma* (Tuscaloosa: University of Alabama Press, 1997). It was turned into a Disney movie. There's also Ava DuVernay's acclaimed major motion picture, *Selma* (2105). The landmark 1987 six-part PBS documentary series, *Eyes on the Prize*, which helped solidify the mainstream narrative of the civil rights movement, devotes two episodes specifically to these two campaigns.

30. See for instance Spike Lee's *BlacKkKlansman* (2018), which ends with footage of the car attack (discussed in chapter 4); the Black Eyed Peas' Will.i.am, who also used #Charlottesville footage in his 2020 pro-Biden music video with Jennifer Hudson, "Where Is the Love" (discussed in chapter 7); Vice Media's *Charlottesville: Race and Terror* (2017); PBS *Frontline* / ProPublica's *Documenting Hate* (2018); Netflix's *Alt-Right: Age of Rage* (2018); and Discovery's *Impact of Hate: Charlottesville* (2020).

1. CHOOSING THE SET

1. This was also the great lesson the SCLC learned during the 1962 Albany, Georgia, campaign when the local sheriff strategically avoided using force on civil rights demonstrators. Sheriff Laurie Pritchett was as much a racist as Bull Connor or Jim Clark, but he refused to allow himself or his police officers to behave brutally while news cameras were in town. And because there was no violence, news crews left, and the movement suffered one of its most significant defeats, with Albany remaining a citadel of segregation. See Bodroghkozy, *Equal Time*, 57–58.

2. Aniko Bodroghkozy, *Equal Time: Television and the Civil Rights Movement*. (Urbana: University of Illinois Press, 2012). See also Sasha Torres, *Black, White, and in Color: Television and Black Civil Rights* (Princeton, NJ: Princeton University Press, 2003).

3. See Glenn T. Eskew, *But for Birmingham: The Local and National Movements in the Civil Rights Struggle* (Chapel Hill: University of North Carolina Press, 1997). See also Diane McWhorter, *Carry Me Home: Birmingham, Alabama: the Climactic Battle of the Civil Rights Revolution* (New York: Simon & Schuster, 2001). Her work is particularly comprehensive. With a focus on King, there's the classic first volume of Taylor Branch's trilogy, *America in the King Years: Parting the Waters* (New York: Simon & Schuster, 1988). Pushing back a bit against the emphasis on activists and suggesting that Black moderate leadership was ultimately more significant in both Birmingham and later Selma, see J. Mills Thornton, *Dividing Lines: Municipal Politics and the Struggle for Civil*

Rights in Montgomery, Birmingham, and Selma (Tuscaloosa: University of Alabama Press, 2002).
4. Harrison Salisbury, "Fear and Hatred Grip Birmingham," *New York Times*, April 12, 1960, 1.
5. The definitive history of the Freedom Rides is Raymond Arsenault's *Freedom Riders* (New York: Oxford University Press, 2006).
6. See "Who Speaks for Birmingham," *CBS Reports*, May 18, 1961; Bodroghkozy, *Equal Time*, 85–87.
7. Eskew, *But for Birmingham*, 15.
8. S. Jonathan Bass, *Blessed Are the Peacemakers: Martin Luther King Jr., Eight White Religious Leaders, and the Letter from Birmingham Jail* (Baton Rouge: Louisiana State University Press, 2001).
9. Martin A. Berger, *Seeing through Race: A Reinterpretation of Civil Rights Photography* (Berkeley: University of California Press, 2011). This topic is discussed further in chapter 4.
10. See for instance Steven Levingston, *Kennedy and King: The President, the Pastor, and the Battle over Civil Rights* (New York: Hachette, 2017).
11. John Lewis, *Walking with the Wind: A Memoir of the Movement* (New York: Simon & Schuster, 1998), 310.
12. Andrew Young, *An Easy Burden: The Civil Rights Movement and the Transformation of America* (New York: HarperCollins, 1996), 338. Young, Executive Director of the SCLC, was particularly astute about crafting media campaigns for the movement. Having worked in television in the 1950s, Young appeared on CBS's Sunday morning religious show *Look Up and Live*.
13. On press treatment of the civil rights movement, see Gene Roberts and Hank Klibanoff, *The Race Beat: The Press, the Civil Rights Struggle, and the Awakening of a Nation* (New York: Knopf, 2006). This comprehensive history focuses mostly on print media.
14. Bernard Lafayette Jr. and Kathryn Lee Johnson, *In Peace and Freedom: My Journey in Selma* (Lexington, KY: University Press of Kentucky, 2013).
15. Young, *Easy Burden*, 338.
16. Gary May, *Bending toward Justice: The Voting Rights Act and the Transformation of American Democracy* (Durham, NC: Duke University Press, 2013). Single-volume studies of the Selma campaign include Charles Fager, *Selma, 1965* (New York: Scribner, 1974); David J. Garrow, *Protest at Selma: Martin Luther King, Jr, and the Voting Rights Act of 1965* (New Haven, CT: Yale University Press, 1979), Robert A. Pratt, *Selma's Bloody Sunday: Protest, Voting Rights, and the Struggle for Racial Equality* (Baltimore, MD: Johns Hopkins University Press, 2017). See also Joe Street and Henry Knight Lozano, eds., *The Shadow of Selma* (Gainesville: University Press of Florida, 2018).

17. Bodroghkozy, *Equal Time*, 115.
18. See for instance Todd Gitlin, *The Whole World Is Watching: Media in the Making and Unmaking of the New Left* (Berkeley: University of California Press, 1980).
19. See for instance Bonnie J. Dow, *Watching Women's Liberation 1970: Feminism's Pivotal Year on the Network News* (Urbana: University of Illinois Press, 2014); and Larry P. Gross, *Up from Invisibility* (New York: Columbia University Press, 2001).
20. Ginna Husting, "Neutralizing Protest: The Construction of War, Chaos, and National Identity through US Television News on Abortion-Related Protest, 1991" *Communication & Critical/Cultural Studies* 3, no. 2 (June 2006): 162–80. See also the documentary *How to Survive a Plague* (2012).
21. Both the Southern Poverty Law Center and the Anti-Defamation League provide useful descriptions of the alt-right on their websites. See chapter 2 for more discussion about the alt-right and relevant literature.
22. "Baltimore Could Follow New Orleans by Removing Confederate Statues," *Guardian*, May 28, 2017, https://www.theguardian.com/us-news/2017/may/28/baltimore-remove-confederate-monuments-mayor-new-orleans.
23. Lisa Provence, "'Capital of the Resistance' Rally Draws Hundreds," *C-ville Weekly*, January 31, 2017, https://www.c-ville.com/capital-resistance-rally-draws-hundreds. See also Derek Quizon, "Signer Declares City a 'Capital of Resistance' to Trump," *Daily Progress*, January 31, 2017, https://www.dailyprogress.com/news/politics/signer-declares-city-a-capital-of-resistance-against-trump/article_12108161-fccd-53bb-89e4-b7d5dc8494e0.html; Michael Signer, *Cry Havoc: Charlottesville and American Democracy under Siege* (New York: PublicAffairs, 2020), 99–102.
24. "Anti-White Profile: Mayor Mike Signer of Charlottesville, VA," Occidental Dissent, May 14, 2017, http://www.occidentaldissent.com/2017/05/14/anti-white-profile-mayor-mike-signer-of-charlottesville-va/.
25. Wes Bellamy, *Monumental: It Was Never about a Statue* (Middletown, DE: Black Gold Publishing, 2019).
26. Zy B, "Change the Name of Lee Park and Remove the Statue," Change.com, https://www.change.org/p/charlottesville-city-council-change-the-name-of-lee-park-and-remove-the-statue-in-charlottesville-va.
27. John Edwin Mason, "History, Mine and Ours: Charlottesville's Blue Ribbon Commission and the Terror Attacks of August 2017," in *Charlottesville 2017*, edited by Louis P. Nelson and Claudrena N. Harold (Charlottesville: University of Virginia Press, 2018), 19–22. See also Hawes Spencer, *Summer of Hate: Charlottesville, USA* (Charlottesville: University of Virginia Press, 2018), 58–61.
28. Andrew Anglin and Robert "Azzmador" Ray, Daily Stormer, August 8, 2017.

29. Lisa Provence, "Who's a Racist? Wes Bellamy and Jason Kessler Speak Out at City Council," *C-ville Weekly*, December 6, 2016. See also the Southern Poverty Law Center's page about Kessler: https://www.splcenter.org/fighting-hate/extremist-files/individual/jason-kessler.
30. Timothy J. Heaphy, *Independent Review of the 2017 Protest Events in Charlottesville, Virginia* (Richmond, VA: Hunton & Williams, 2017), 25–28. It is known popularly and will be referred to in the main text as "the Heaphy Report," after US Attorney Timothy J. Heaphy, who conducted the review.
31. Spencer, *Summer of Hate*, 110.
32. The Sharon Statement (1960) mapped out the conservative principles of a new generation of right-wing activists, Young Americans for Freedom, and was composed in Sharon, Connecticut, at the estate of William F. Buckley. The Port Huron Statement (1962), drafted at the eponymously named union retreat in Port Huron, Michigan, was the founding document for the New Left's Students for a Democratic Society (SDS).
33. Branch, *Parting the Waters*, 804. See also Martin Luther King Jr., *Why We Can't Wait* (New York: Penguin, 1964).
34. In a follow-up post, he did mention both the Sharon and Port Huron Statements. The post is available on his Altright.com website. If a 2020 Google search is any reliable guide, the Statement's impact has been negligible at best.
35. George Hawley, *The Alt-Right: What Everyone Needs to Know* (New York: Oxford University Press, 2019), 10.
36. Heaphy, *Independent Review*, 30.
37. See chapter 3.
38. As recounted in the afterword, I was one of the counter-protesters on the street that day.
39. *Operation Unite the Right Charlottesville 2.0*, https://www.unicornriot.ninja/wp-content/uploads/2017/08/OpOrd3_General.pdf. This document, written by racist Eli Mosley (a.k.a. Elliot Kline) of Identity Evropa was uncovered by the media collective Unicorn Riot, which gained access to Unite the Right planning and discussion chats on the social media platform, Discord, as discussed further in chapter 2: See Chris Schiano, "LEAKED: The Planning Meeting that Led Up to Neo-Nazi Terrorism in Charlottesville," Unicorn Riot, August 16, 2017, https://unicornriot.ninja/2017/leaked-planning-meetings-led-neo-nazi-terrorism-charlottesville/.

2. BEING MEDIA-SAVVY

1. See for instance Angela Nagle, *Kill All Normies: Online Culture Wars from 4chan and Tumblr to Trump and the Alt-Right* (Winchester, UK: Zero Books,

2017); Mike Wendling, *Alt-Right: 4chan to the White House* (London: Pluto Press, 2018).
2. Jessie Daniels, "The Algorithmic Rise of the 'Alt-Right,'" *Contexts* 17, no. 1 (2018): 62. Unfortunately, Daniels misdates the Unite the Right rally as August 13, as does the striking illustration that accompanies her article.
3. Felix Harcourt, *Ku Klux Kulture: America and the Klan in the 1920s* (Chicago, IL: University of Chicago Press, 2017), 11.
4. Ibid., 27.
5. Harcourt's book includes informative chapters about the Klan's forays into national newspaper publishing and radio broadcasting, along with other forms of new mass culture. Also, Reveal Digital's "Understanding Hate in America" provides an online repository of digitized copies of many Klan newspapers of the 1920s: https://uhia.revealdigital.org/?a=p&p=home&-------en-20--1--txt-txIN---------------1
6. The passage of the 1924 Johnson-Reed Immigration Act, which slammed the doors on all Asians and on most immigrants from southern and eastern Europe, fulfilled a key goal of the Klan and paradoxically took some of the wind out of the organization's white sails as they now had one less hot-button issue to organize around.
7. In his classic study of the news media in this era, Herbert Gans argued that moderatism was as close to an ideology as the industry had. See Gans, *Deciding What's News* (New York: Random House, 1979), 51–52.
8. David J. Garrow, *Protest at Selma* (New Haven, CN: Yale University Press, 1978), 111. See also Bodroghkozy, *Equal Time: Television and the Civil Rights Movement* (Urbana: University of Illinois Press, 2012), 2.
9. Stephanie R. Rolph, *Resisting Equality: The Citizens' Council, 1954–1989* (Baton Rouge: Louisiana State University Press, 2018), 10.
10. Mary Ann Watson, *The Expanding Vista: American Television in the Kennedy Years* (Durham, NC: Duke University Press, 1994), 144–52.
11. Peter Baker, "A Half-Century after Wallace, Trump Echoes the Politics of Division," *New York Times,* July 30, 2020, https://www.nytimes.com/2020/07/30/us/politics/trump-wallace.html.
12. David Greenberg, "The Idea of 'The Liberal Media' and Its Roots in the Civil Rights Movement," *The Sixties: A Journal of History, Politics, and Culture* 1, no. 2 (2008): 179.
13. Ibid., 169.
14. Susan J. Douglas, *Listening In: Radio and the American Imagination* (Minneapolis: University of Minnesota Press, 2004), 290.
15. Madeline Peltz, "Tucker Carlson's Descent into White Supremacy: A Timeline," mediamatters.org, August 20, 2020, https://www.mediamatters.org/tucker

-carlson/tucker-carlsons-descent-white-supremacy-timeline. See also Tim Elfrink, "'It's Not Actually a Real Problem in America': Tucker Carlson Calls White Supremacy a 'Hoax,'" *Washington Post*, August 7, 2019, https://www.washingtonpost.com/nation/2019/08/07/tucker-carlson-white-supremacy-hoax-lie-not-real-problem/.
16. Daniels, "Algorithmic Rise," 64.
17. Adam Klein, *Fanaticism, Racism, and Rage Online* (Cham, Switzerland: Palgrave Macmillan, 2017), 57.
18. Ibid., 3.
19. For more information about Identity Evropa, see Anti-Defamation League, "Identity Evropa/American Identity Movement," https://www.adl.org/resources/profiles/identity-evropa. See also Ben Davis, "The New White Nationalism's Sloppy Use of Art History Decoded," Artnet News, March 7, 2017, https://news.artnet.com/art-world/identity-evropa-posters-art-symbolism-881747.
20. Klein, *Fanaticism, Racism, and Rage Online*, 101.
21. Bailey Poland, *Haters: Harassment, Abuse, and Violence Online* (Lincoln, NE: Potomac Books, 2016).
22. Aja Romano, "What We Still Haven't Learned from Gamergate," Vox, January 20, 2020, https://www.vox.com/culture/2020/1/20/20808875/gamergate-lessons-cultural-impact-changes-harassment-laws.
23. Heather Suzanne Woods and Leslie A. Hahner, *Make America Meme Again: The Rhetoric of the Alt-Right* (New York: Peter Lang, 2019), 2.
24. Ibid., 27.
25. The 2020 major-release documentary, *Feels Good Man*, chronicles Furie's attempts to wrest control of his cartoon creation from the alt-right forces who hijacked his character.
26. Woods and Hahner, *Make America Meme Again*, 79.
27. Mostly associated with internet trolls, "lulz" means gaining amusement or a sense of fun from the emotional distress of a targeted victim.
28. See for instance Donna Zuckerberg, *Not All Dead White Men: Classics and Misogyny in the Digital Age* (Cambridge, MA: Harvard University Press, 2018). The alt-right penchant for Greco-Roman classicism extends to architecture as well, as we'll discuss later. See Jalane Schmidt, "Material Markers of Whiteness at Mr. Jefferson's University," Medium, https://medium.com/@JalaneSchmidt/uva-rotunda-whiteness-c8ecd289244d.
29. Andrew Anglin, "A Normie's Guide to the Alt-Right," Daily Stormer, August 31, 2016. See also Viveca S. Greene, "'Deplorable' Satire: Alt-Right Memes, White Genocide Tweets, and Redpilling Normies," *Studies in American Humor* 5, no. 1 (2019): 31–69.

30. See Civil Rights Movement Archive, "WATS & Incident Reports," https://www.crmvet.org/docs/wats/watshome.htm.
31. Bijan Stephen, "Get Up, Stand Up," *Wired*, November 2015, 122.
32. See for instance court documents in the successful civil case against Jason Kessler, Richard Spencer, and other Unite the Right organizers on behalf of counterprotesters who suffered injury, *Sines v. Kessler*, Civil Action No. 3:17 (2019), 26. The case, filed in federal court in Charlottesville, led to a jury trial in 2021. The jury found the defendants conspired to deny plaintiffs their civil rights and awarded significant compensatory and punitive damages. The civil action court document provides extensive documentation of the Unite the Right organizers' use of Discord. See Integrity First for America, "IFA's Charlottesville Case: Sines v. Kessler," https://www.integrityfirstforamerica.org/our-work/case/charlottesville-case. Note that in alt-right nomenclature, "Charlottesville 1.0" referred to the May 13–14, 2017, impromptu gatherings in Jackson and Lee parks.
33. Chris Schiano, "DATA RELEASE: 'Unite The Right' Planning Chats Demonstrate Violent Intent," Unicorn Riot, August 22, 2017, https://unicornriot.ninja/2017/data-release-unite-right-planning-chats-demonstrate-violent-intent/.
34. Chris Schiano, "DATA RELEASE: Discord Chats Planned Armed Neo-Nazi Militia Operations in Charlottesville," Unicorn Riot, August 18, 2017, https://unicornriot.ninja/2017/data-release-discord-chats-planned-armed-neo-nazi-militia-operations-charlottesville/. The *Sines v. Kessler* civil case against the organizers and organizations that planned the Unite the Right rally successfully argued in court that violence was expected and promised.
35. Schiano, "'Unite The Right' Planning Chats."
36. Lauren Berg, "Fogel Charged after Confrontation Involving Kessler, SURJ," *Daily Progress*, June 2, 2017; Staff, "Kessler Discusses KKK, Unite the Right Rallies and His Political Beliefs," *Daily Progress*, July 11, 2017.
37. Staff, "Kessler Discusses KKK."
38. See for instance: Solidarity C-ville, "Before August 12th," https://solidaritycville.wordpress.com/before-august-12th-2/.
39. Chris Suarez, "Unite the Right Rally Attracting Increasingly Radical Attention," *Daily Progress*, July 22, 2017.
40. Anti-Defamation League, "From Alt Right to Alt Lite: Naming the Hate," https://www.adl.org/resources/backgrounders/from-alt-right-to-alt-lite-naming-the-hate.
41. Daniel C. Hallin, *The "Uncensored War": The Media and Vietnam* (Berkeley: University of California Press, 1989), 116–18. See also Todd Gitlin, *The Whole World Is Watching: Media in the Making and Unmaking of the New Left* (Berke-

ley: University of California Press, 1980). The media ecosystem has changed dramatically since the 1960s, but I would argue that mainstream journalism that presents itself as nonpartisan and "serious" continues to espouse the ideals and codes of balance and notions of objectivity that have guided the business since its institutionalization as a profession. They remain operative as ideals even if frequently found wanting in practice.

42. For a good study of how the press grappled with covering the alt-right and white supremacy, see "Reporting White Supremacy: The State of the Beat," Center for Media at Risk, Annenberg School of Communication, University of Pennsylvania, December 11, 2018, https://www.ascmediarisk.org/2018/12/reporting-white-supremacy-the-state-of-the-beat/.
43. Lisa Provence and Samantha Baars, "The Kids Are Alt-Right," *C-ville Weekly*, August 9, 2017, 18–21.
44. "Opinion/Editorial: Councilor Should Speak Up Now to Calm Raging Fire," *Daily Progress*, August 10, 2017. The editorial received national, withering criticism in the aftermath of the Unite the Right mayhem. See Brendan Fitzgerald, "The Outrageous Editorial by a Charlottesville Daily that Preceded Violence," *Columbia Journalism Review*, August 15, 2017, https://www.cjr.org/united_states_project/charlottesville-daily-progress-editorial.php.
45. British Pathé, "40,000 Ku Klux (1925)," https://www.youtube.com/watch?v=BnI8SUQPB4k&t=108s. All Pathé News items created between 1910 and 1970 have been released publicly.
46. The 1937 Hindenburg disaster is a particularly notable example.
47. Bodroghkozy, *Equal Time*, 94–95.
48. *Operation Unite the Right Charlottesville 2.0*, https://www.unicornriot.ninja/wp-content/uploads/2017/08/OpOrd3_General.pdf.
49. Ibid.
50. Bodroghkozy, *Equal Time*, 94.
51. The concept of "the politics of respectability" was first explored by historian Evelyn Brooks Higginbotham in *Righteous Discontent: The Women's Movement in the Black Baptist Church, 1880–1920* (Cambridge, MA: Harvard University Press, 1993).
52. Schmidt, "Material Markers of Whiteness."
53. Walter Benjamin's argument that fascism aestheticizes politics is relevant here. See Benjamin's classic article, "The Work of Art in the Age of Mechanical Reproduction," in *Illuminations*, ed. Hannah Arendt (New York: Schocken, 1969), 19–20.
54. Heaphy, *Independent Review*, 118.
55. The alt-right tend to term any counterprotesters as "antifa." The name actually refers to anyone who protests or stand up against fascism.

56. "Unite the Right Torchlit March toward Lee Park through Charlottesville, VA," posted August 13, 2017, YouTube video, 23:32, https://www.youtube.com/watch?v=4PVnLA3QglU.
57. Julia Reinstein, "People Are Mocking White Nationalists for Marching with Literal Tiki Torches," BuzzFeed News, August 12, 2017, https://www.buzzfeednews.com/article/juliareinstein/citronazi-candles. The article was posted at 10:32 a.m., before the mayhem of that day.
58. Solidarity CVille, "Solidarity Cville Documents Threats of Violence Planned for August 12," July 17, 2017, https://solidaritycville.wordpress.com/2017/07/17/solidarity-cville-documents-threats-of-violence-planned-for-august-12/. This set of documents is different from what Unicorn Riot obtained, but of course provides the same evidence of violent intent.

3. BEING MORE MEDIA-SAVVY

1. In February 2020, ABC News in its *Live Prime* series provided an in-depth story about the Smith case—and the lack of media attention given the disappearance: https://www.youtube.com/watch?v=OMRI1aSOcOM.
2. The action received coverage by Charlottesville's local television news, but not in print media such as the *Daily Progress* or *C-ville Weekly*.
3. While I know many of the antiracist activists in Charlottesville, few were willing to be interviewed for this book. This chapter is grounded in publicly available documents such as primary-source media artifacts, social media texts, activist-produced material, and journalistic coverage.
4. The White House chief strategist in 2017, Steve Bannon, was the former chairman of Breitbart News and declared the website "the platform for the alt-right." The deputy assistant to the president, Sebastian Gorka, ousted like Bannon shortly after the Unite the Right debacle, had similar far-right views. Stephen Miller, the White House senior policy advisor throughout Trump's four-year term, displayed clear affinities with far-right extremism. Michael Edison Hayden, "Stephen Miller's Affinity for White Nationalism Revealed in Emails," Southern Poverty Law Center, November 12, 2019, https://www.splcenter.org/hatewatch/2019/11/12/stephen-millers-affinity-white-nationalism-revealed-leaked-emails.
5. Jacey Fortin, "Jeff Sessions Limited Consent Decrees. What about the Police Departments already under Reform?" *New York Times*, November 15, 2018, https://www.nytimes.com/2018/11/15/us/sessions-consent-decrees-police.html.
6. See for instance: Sarah Ganim and Chris Welch, "Unmasking the Leftist Antifa Movement," CNN, updated May 3, 2019, https://www.cnn.com/2017/08/18/us/unmasking-antifa-anti-fascists-hard-left/index.html.

7. Zeynep Tufekci, *Twitter and Tear Gas: The Power and Fragility of Networked Protest* (New Haven, CT: Yale University Press, 2017).
8. "#OccupyCville," Internet Archive Wayback Machine, October 24, 2011, https://web.archive.org/web/20111024230342/http://occupycville.org/?page_id=2. As mentioned in the previous chapter, Jason Kessler participated in Charlottesville's Occupy movement before shifting his allegiances.
9. Tufekci, *Twitter and Tear Gas*, 193–99.
10. See the conclusion for a consideration of how the January 6, 2021, insurrection at the US Capitol connects to the Unite the Right rally and the possibility of renewed movement "muscle" for the extremist, white nationalist cause.
11. Showing Up for Racial Justice, "Chapters," https://surj.org/our-work/chapters/.
12. Maya Dukmasova, "What Does It Mean to Be a White Ally?" *Chicago Reader*, July 21, 2016, https://www.chicagoreader.com/Bleader/archives/2016/07/21/what-does-it-mean-to-be-a-white-ally.
13. For a history of the original Highlander, see John M. Glen, *Highlander: No Ordinary School, 1932–1962* (Lexington: University Press of Kentucky, 1988).
14. In 2021, the organization changed and updated its website and no longer carries Braden's quote.
15. Catherine Fosl, *Subversive Southerner: Anne Braden and the Struggle for Racial Justice in the Cold War South* (New York: Palgrave Macmillan, 2002).
16. Chris Suarez, "Rally Brought Statue Debate to Boiling Point," *Daily Progress*, May 21, 2017, https://dailyprogress.com/rally-brought-statue-debate-to-boiling-point/article_fc90b552-fa66-5033-9723-29de8fca016b.html.
17. See for instance Mark Bray, *Antifa: The Anti-Fascist Handbook* (Brooklyn, NY: Melville House, 2017).
18. Thomas Fuller, "Berkeley Cancels Ann Coulter Speech over Safety Fears," *New York Times*, April 19, 2017, https://www.nytimes.com/2017/04/19/us/berkeley-ann-coulter-speech-canceled.html.
19. Joshua Eaton, "Before the Torches and After: The Activists Fighting White Supremacy in Charlottesville," *ThinkProgress*, October 31, 2017, https://archive.thinkprogress.org/cville-fighting-right-9e82a5d4b768/.
20. Press Statement of Showing Up for Racial Justice (SURJ) Charlottesville on Media Coverage of White Supremacy in Charlottesville, February 16, 2017. https://solidaritycville.wordpress.com/before-august-12th-2/.
21. Aniko Bodroghkozy, *Equal Time: Television and the Civil Rights Movement* (Urbana: University of Illinois Press, 2012), 144.
22. Ibid., 141–42.
23. Lisa Provence, "Tactical Change: Not Your Grandpa's Protest," *C-ville Weekly*, May 31, 2017, https://www.c-ville.com/tactical-change-not-grandpas-protest/.
24. Ibid.

25. Chris Suarez, "Tensions Simmer at Lee Park Rally against Racism," *Daily Progress*, May 31, 2017. For further discussion of media treatment of Fitzhugh, see chapter 5.
26. Provence, "Tactical Change."
27. Gene Roberts and Hank Klibanoff, *The Race Beat* (New York: Knopf, 2006), 310.
28. Richard Lentz, *Symbols, the News Magazines, and Martin Luther King* (Baton Rouge: Louisiana State University Press, 1990), 80.
29. Ibid., 85.
30. Ibid., 87–88.
31. Ibid., 78.
32. See chapter 7 for discussion of how Joe Biden used his presidential campaign to extol Charlottesville's antiracist activists.
33. Eaton, "Before the Torches."
34. UVa Students United, "Richard Spencer rally at Jackson Park," Facebook, May 13, 2017.
35. Kessler's penchant for living on camera did not serve him very well in the aftermath of the Unite the Right debacle. During a livestream interview with a fellow alt-righter, Kessler got yelled at by his father and ordered to get out of his parents' room. The humiliating but comical incident garnered copious and gleeful media attention. See for instance Zach Beauchamp, "The Organizer of the Charlottesville Rally Just Got Humiliated by His Own Father," Vox, August 15, 2018, https://www.vox.com/policy-and-politics/2018/8/15/17692552/charlottesville-unite-the-right-jason-kessler-father.
36. Laura Vozzella, "White Nationalist Richard Spencer Leads Torch-Bearing Protesters Defending Lee Statue," *Washington Post*, May 14, 2017, https://www.washingtonpost.com/local/virginia-politics/alt-rights-richard-spencer-leads-torch-bearing-protesters-defending-lee-statue/2017/05/14/766aaa56-38ac-11e7-9e48-c4f199710b69_story.html.
37. Spencer, *Summer of Hate*, 115.
38. See for instance Brandon Griggs, "Protest over Confederate Statue Shakes Charlottesville," CNN, May 15, 2017, https://www.cnn.com/2017/05/15/us/charlottesville-lee-monument-spencer-protests-trnd/index.html. Other national media outlets who covered the story in similar ways include the *Washington Post* and NBC News.
39. George Lewis, "Sidelining Selma's Segregationists: Memory, Strategy, Ideology, and Agency," in *The Shadow of Selma*, ed. Joe Street and Henry Knight Lozano (Gainesville: University Press of Florida, 2018), 179, 181.
40. See for instance David Levering Lewis, *King: A Biography Third Edition* (Urbana: University of Illinois Press, 2013 [1970]). This very early King biogra-

phy, unlike some others to come, notes the important contributions of Robinson and other women activists.
41. Brian Ward, *Radio and the Struggle for Civil Rights in the South* (Gainesville: University Press of Florida, 2004), 7.
42. Ibid., 24.
43. Ibid., 183.
44. Julian Williams, "Black Radio and Civil Rights: Birmingham 1956–1963," *Journal of Radio Studies* 12, no. 1 (May 2005): 59.
45. Eaton, "Before the Torches."
46. Thanks to Jalane Schmidt for this information.
47. Aleurophile, "Charlottesville #RESISTS White Supremacists! DAVE BRAT: Where Do YOU Stand?" Daily Kos, May 16, 2017. https://www.dailykos.com/stories/1662363.
48. Solidarity Cville, "First Time? Preparations Tips for August 12," August 5, 2017, https://solidaritycville.wordpress.com/2017/08/05/first-time-preparation-tips-for-august-12/.
49. Solidarity Cville, "History of Solidarity Cville Media Collective," https://solidaritycville.wordpress.com/history-of-solidarity-cville-media-collective/.
50. Bodroghkozy, *Equal Time*. See also Sasha Torres, *Black, White, and in Color: Television and Black Civil Rights* (Princeton, NJ: Princeton University Press, 2003).
51. Heather Suzanne Woods and Leslie A. Hahner, *Make America Meme Again: The Rhetoric of the Alt-Right* (New York: Peter Lang, 2019). See also Whitney Phillips, "The Oxygen of Amplification," *Data & Society*, May, 22, 2018, https://datasociety.net/library/oxygen-of-amplification/.
52. Woods and Hahner, *Make America Meme Again*. See also the website Know Your Meme and its item "The Left Can't Meme," https://knowyourmeme.com/memes/the-left-cant-meme.
53. Heaphy, *Independent Review*, 56.
54. Chris Suarez, "City Leaders Hoping to Overshadow KKK Rally on Saturday," *Daily Progress*, July 5, 2017.
55. Community #BlocKKKParty, Facebook post, July 7, 2017.
56. Jalane Schmidt, "Excuse Me, America, Your House Is on Fire: Lessons from Charlottesville on the KKK and 'Alt-right.'" Medium, June 27, 2017, https://medium.com/resist-here/excuse-me-america-your-house-is-on-fire-lessons-from-charlottesville-on-the-kkk-and-alt-right-84aafddca685.
57. Solidarity Cville circulated the poster in its media campaign. See for instance on its Twitter feed: @SolidCville, tweet, June 28, 2017.
58. By 2021, her Twitter following had grown to over 100,000.
59. Spencer, *Summer of Hate*, 127–28.

60. See Emily G, @EmilyGorcenski, tweet, July 9, 2017 (originally livestreamed on Periscope as "No Hate in Cville").
61. Chris Suarez, "Charlottesville City Council Gives Lee, Jackson Parks New Names," *Daily Progress*, June 5, 2017.
62. Ibid.
63. Lisa Provence, "Response to KKK: 'Don't Take the Bait'—Chief Thomas," *C-ville Weekly*, June 16, 2017.
64. Lauren Berg, "Police Chief Says Use of Tear Gas at KKK Protest Was Appropriate," *Daily Progress*, July 11, 2017.
65. Solidarity Cville, "Solidarity Cville Documents Threats of Violence Planned for August 12," July 17, 2017, https://solidaritycville.wordpress.com/2017/07/17/solidarity-cville-documents-threats-of-violence-planned-for-august-12/.
66. Michael Signer, *Cry Havoc: Charlottesville and American Democracy under Siege* (New York: PublicAffairs, 2020), 170.
67. Chris Suarez, "Unite the Right Rally Sparks First Amendment Questions," *Daily Progress*, July 29, 2017.
68. Ibid. On Bristow, see Southern Poverty Law Center, "Extremist File," https://www.splcenter.org/fighting-hate/extremist-files/individual/kyle-bristow.
69. Ibid.
70. See Heaphy, *Independent Review*. The review notes that "officers failed to intervene in physical altercations that took place in areas adjacent to Emancipation Park. [Virginia State Police] directed its officers to remain behind barricades rather than risk injury responding to conflicts between protesters and counter-protesters. [Charlottesville Police Department] commanders similarly instructed their officer not to intervene in all but the most serious physical confrontations . . . When violence was most prevalent, CPD commanders pulled officers back to a protected area of the park, where they remained for over an hour as people in the large crowd fought on Market Street" (6).
71. Aaron Gell, "Anti-Fascists Are Waging a Cyber War—and They're Winning," Medium, September 9, 2019, https://gen.medium.com/antifas-keyboard-warriors-254f62be2a95. In the aftermath of the insurrection at the Capitol on January 6, 2021, the work of these antifascist online sleuths has gotten more widespread media attention. One of the more prominent ones, Molly Conger, a Charlottesville resident, began this work in the aftermath of A12 and was heavily featured in a major *Washington Post* profile. Robert Klemko, "A Small Group of Sleuths Had Been Identifying Right-Wing Extremists Long before the Attack on the Capitol," *Washington Post*, January 10, 2021, https://www.washingtonpost.com/national-security/antifa-far-right-doxing-identities/2021/01/10/41721de0-4dd7-11eb-bda4-615aaefd0555_story.html.
72. Unicorn Riot, "LEAKED: Chats of #UniteTheRight Charlottesville Or-

ganizers Exposed on Discord App," August 14, 2017, https://unicornriot.ninja/2017/white-supremacists-unitetheright-charlottesville-plans-exposed-discord-app/.
73. Neil MacFarquhar, "Charlottesville Lawsuit Puts Rising Intolerance on Trial," *New York Times*, October 28, 2019, https://www.nytimes.com/2019/10/28/us/charlottesville-civil-rights-trial.html.
74. Neil MacFarquhar, "Jury Finds Rally Organizers Responsible for Charlottesville Violence," *New York Times*, November 23, 2021, https://www.nytimes.com/2021/11/23/us/charlottesville-rally-verdict.html. See also Integrity First for America, "IFA's Charlottesville Case: Sines v. Kessler," https://www.integrityfirstforamerica.org/our-work/case/charlottesville-case. The victory wasn't as sweeping as it could have been, because the jury deadlocked on the lawsuit's federal charges brought by Kaplan and her team, which applied the rarely used 1871 Ku Klux Klan Act.
75. Gell, "Anti-Fascists."
76. Emily G, @EmilyGorcenski, tweet, July 22, 2017.
77. Paul Abowd, "Nazi 'Tyrone' Exposed as US Marine," Al Jazeera, April 17, 2018, https://www.aljazeera.com/news/2018/04/17/neo-nazi-tyrone-exposed-as-us-marine/.
78. See chapter 7. Quoted from Biden's speech at the Democratic Party Convention accepting the presidential nomination.
79. Heaphy, *Independent Review*, 110–11.
80. See for instance Bernard Lafayette, *In Peace and Freedom: My Journey in Selma* (Lexington: University Press of Kentucky, 2013).
81. As noted in the afterword, I participated in that training, but rather than attend the St. Paul's evening service, I went to Congregation Beth Israel's regular Friday night service.
82. UVa Students United, Facebook post, August 11, 2017.
83. A. C. Thompson, "Documenting Hate: Charlottesville," *Frontline*, 2018 season, episode 18, ProPublica/PBS, aired August 7, 2018, https://www.pbs.org/wgbh/frontline/documentary/documenting-hate-charlottesville/.
84. Ransby wrote the prize-winning biography of the SCLC manager and midwife of SNCC, *Ella Baker and the Black Freedom Movement: A Radical Democratic Vision* (Chapel Hill: University of North Carolina Press, 2003).
85. Susan Svrluga, "'Antifa Is Winning': Richard Spencer Rethinks His College Tour after Violent Protest," *Washington Post*, March 12, 2018, https://www.washingtonpost.com/news/grade-point/wp/2018/03/12/antifa-is-winning-richard-spencer-rethinks-his-college-tour-after-violent-protests/. See also Spencer's video, AltRight.com, "College Tour Course Correction," March 11, 2018, https://www.youtube.com/watch?v=SFT9UHytoxI&t=1454s.

86. Tess Owen, "How Boston's Massive 'Free Speech' Rally Fell Apart," *Vice*, August 19, 2017, https://www.vice.com/en/article/zmy8be/how-bostons-massive-free-speech-rally-fell-apart.
87. Dahlia Lithwick, "This Is What Democracy Looks Like," Slate, November 9, 2017, https://slate.com/news-and-politics/2017/11/the-messy-intra-progressive-fight-in-charlottesville-offers-lessons-for-democrats-across-the-country.html.
88. Mikaela Lefrak, "Virginia Grants Cities the Power to Remove Their Confederate Statues," WAMU, April 12, 2020, https://wamu.org/story/20/04/12/virginia-grants-cities-the-power-to-remove-their-confederate-statues/.
89. "Virginia Governor Announces Plans to Take Down Robert E. Lee Statue in Richmond," CBS *This Morning*, June 5, 2020, https://www.youtube.com/watch?v=Vauke8c6JxY&t=110s.
90. Larry Buchanan, Quoctrung Bui, and Jugal K. Patel, "Black Lives Matter May Be the Largest Movement in U.S. History," *New York Times*, July 3, 2020, https://www.nytimes.com/interactive/2020/07/03/us/george-floyd-protests-crowd-size.html.

4. A12

1. Robert Hariman and John Louis Lucaites, *No Caption Needed: Iconic Photographs, Public Culture, and Liberal Democracy* (Chicago, IL: University of Chicago Press, 2007), 27.
2. Ibid., 11.
3. David D. Perlmutter, *Photojournalism and Foreign Policy: Icons of Outrage in International Crises* (Westport, CT: Praeger, 1998), 18.
4. Akiba A. Cohen, Sandrine Boudana, and Paul Frosh, "You Must Remember This: Iconic News Photographs and Collective Memory," *Journal of Communication* 68, no. 3 (June 2018): 455.
5. See chapter 6 for more on how iconic images of the Birmingham campaign have been turned into statues memorializing the 1963 events.
6. Congregate Charlottesville, "1000 Clergy and Faith Leaders Urged to Come to Charlottesville for August 12," https://congregatecville.com/press-release-for-clergy-call?fbclid=IwAR1AP8f4pCXKzBggVqYcU2NoqXDsfx26r_Mbbhhera-ZNfmpe7DnsXRGz4g. See also Abbey White, "A Charlottesville Faith Leader to Unite the Right: 'Love Has Already Won Here,'" Vox, August 14, 2017, https://www.vox.com/identities/2017/8/14/16140506/congregate-cville-charlottesville-rally-protest-interview.
7. Tobin Miller Shearer defines performative prayer as "public prayers employed during civil rights actions to address the immediate political moment

and gathered audience—to create crisis" in "Invoking Crisis: Performative Christian Prayer in the Civil Rights Movement," *Journal of the American Academy of Religion* 83, no. 2 (June 2015): 491.
8. "Selma: Beatings Start the Savage Season," *Life*, March 19, 1965.
9. SNCC activists had made a similar calculation the previous year, inviting and training hundreds of white students from elite colleges to come to Mississippi for its Freedom Summer voter registration and education campaign. The cameras inevitably followed. See for instance Bruce Watson, *Freedom Summer* (New York: Penguin, 2010).
10. Linda Williams, *Playing the Race Card: Melodramas in Black and White from Uncle Tom to O. J. Simpson* (Princeton, NJ: Princeton University Press, 2001).
11. Peter Brooks, *The Melodramatic Imagination* (New Haven: Yale University Press, 1976).
12. Williams, *Playing the Race Card*, 12.
13. Ibid., 9.
14. Brooks, *Melodramatic Imagination*, 35.
15. As I recount in the afterword, I witnessed and took part in some of these sessions. I also saw the chaos as the alt-right and counterprotesters clashed on Market Street. The mass media eventually discovered the role played by Charlottesville clergy as news organizations cast about looking for fresh stories to cover about Charlottesville in the weeks following the August 12 violence. CBS, for instance, focused on the role of activist clergy in a nationally telecast news special.
16. See chapter 7.
17. Brennan Gilmore, "What I Saw in Charlottesville Could Be Just the Beginning," *Politico*, August 14, 2017, https://www.politico.com/magazine/story/2017/08/14/what-i-saw-in-charlottesville-could-be-just-the-beginning-215487.
18. Hawes Spencer, *Summer of Hate: Charlottesville, USA* (Charlottesville: University of Virginia Press, 2018), 14–15. See also Luke Mullins, "The Man Who Sued the Trolls," *Washingtonian*, August 9, 2018.
19. Terrorist vehicle attacks before Charlottesville include, among others, the Bastille Day 2016 truck attack in Nice, France, that killed eighty-six; the December 16, 2016, Christmas market attack in Berlin, killing twelve; and multiple attacks in London on Westminster and London Bridges. Interestingly this CNN piece itemizing such attacks does not include the one in Charlottesville: "Terrorist Attacks by Vehicle Fast Facts," August 25, 2022, https://www.cnn.com/2017/05/03/world/terrorist-attacks-by-vehicle-fast-facts.
20. See for instance the ABC News breaking news item from August 12, 2017, presumably shortly after Gilmore uploaded his cell phone footage to Twitter: https://www.youtube.com/watch?v=Y3_72kSnevM.

21. Sasha Torres, *Black, White, and in Color: Television and Black Civil Rights* (Princeton, NJ: Princeton University Press, 2003), 34–35.
22. Ryan Watson, "In the Wakes of Rodney King: Militant Evidence and Media Activism in the Age of Viral Black Death," *Velvet Light Trap*, no. 84 (Fall 2019): 34–49.
23. Gene Roberts and Hank Klibanoff, *The Race Beat: The Press, the Civil Rights Struggle, and the Awakening of a Nation* (New York: Knopf, 2006), 383.
24. For more on Will.i.am's video "Where Is the Love" featuring A11 and A12 images, see chapter 7.
25. Chapter 7 examines Trump's televised responses to the events in Charlottesville.
26. Jennifer Wenzel, "Is Ryan Kelly's Pulitzer Prize–Winning Photograph an American 'Guernica'?" Conversation, August 17, 2017, updated April 17, 2018, https://theconversation.com/is-ryan-kellys-pulitzer-prize-winning-photograph-an-american-guernica-82567.
27. Steve Hendrix, "It's Still Hard to Look At," *Washington Post*, August 10, 2018, https://www.washingtonpost.com/graphics/2018/local/charlottesville-photographer-pulitzer-prize-photo/?utm_term=.e9f71166fffa.
28. Perlmutter, *Photojournalism and Foreign Policy*, 18.
29. Ibid., 20.
30. Hariman and Lucaites, *No Caption Needed*, 29–30.
31. By reproducing these images this analysis may contribute to further objectifying Walter Gadsden and Marcus Martin. I wish to draw readers' attention, therefore, to chapter 6, which explores how both the Birmingham and Charlottesville communities spoke back to these iconic images of white supremacist violence. I also encourage readers to examine the portrait of Marcus Martin in chapter 6 and my analysis of it. Local activist photographer Ézé Amos shows Martin as a subject in control of his visual representation.
32. Martin A. Berger, *Seeing through Race: A Reinterpretation of Civil Rights Photography* (Berkeley: University of California Press, 2011).
33. Ibid., 35. Of course, as Berger and others have pointed out, the young man, Walter Gadsden, is not actually doing what the photo on first glance suggests. See chapter 6 for more discussion of this photo and its complexities.
34. "They Fight a Fire That Won't Go Out," *Life*, May 17, 1963.
35. Berger, *Seeing through Race*, 26.
36. See for instance Timothy Bella, "Every Day Is August 12 in Charlottesville," *Atlantic*, August 10, 2018.
37. Film and television historian Donald Bogle mapped out the key Black stereotypes in American popular culture, specifically cinema, in his highly influential and frequently updated and revised classic, *Toms, Coons, Mulattoes,*

Mammies, and Bucks: An Interpretive History of Blacks in American Films (New York: Viking, 1973). A fifth edition appeared in 2016.
38. Ibid., 13.
39. One of the most reproduced photos of the civil rights era, it even inspired a book about the two women featured in the photo, their eventual improbable friendship and then falling-out. See David Margolick, *Elizabeth and Hazel: Two Women of Little Rock* (New Haven: Yale University Press, 2012).
40. See the foundational texts on the concepts of the male gaze and female passivity in visual images: John Berger, *Ways of Seeing* (London: British Broadcasting Corporation, 1972); and Laura Mulvey, "Visual Pleasure and Narrative Cinema," in *Visual and Other Pleasures* (Indianapolis: Indiana University Press, 1989), 14–26. The scholar bell hooks, in a classic rejoinder to Mulvey-inspired feminist film theory, problematized the notion of the gaze within the context of Black ways of looking in "The Oppositional Gaze," in *Black Looks: Race and Representation* (Toronto: Between the Lines, 1992), 115–31.
41. On the essential role played by Southern white women as a political force, both in the segregationist cause and also extending into the New Right, see Elizabeth Gillespie McRae, *Mothers of Massive Resistance* (New York: Oxford University Press, 2018). The book features the iconic photo of segregationist mothers on its cover.
42. Alexandra Minna Stern, *Proud Boys and the White Ethnostate* (Boston: Beacon Press, 2018).
43. Ibid.
44. Heaphy, *Independent Review*, 137–38.
45. Greg Palast, "Journalist Facing a Gun Captures a Viral Photo in Charlottesville," truthdig, August 14, 2017, https://www.truthdig.com/articles/journalist-captured-viral-photo-charlottesville-gun-face/.
46. The DeAndre Harris imagery also evokes the Rodney King footage. The visual composition is almost exactly the same.
47. Berger, *Seeing through Race*, 8.
48. Ian Shapira, "Finding the White Supremacist Who Beat a Black Man in Charlottesville," *Washington Post*, August 31, 2017, https://www.washingtonpost.com/local/finding-the-white-supremacists-who-beat-a-black-man-in-charlottesville/2017/08/31/9f36e762-8cfb-11e7-84c0-02cc069f2c37_story.html. Shaun King is considered a controversial figure within the Black Lives Matter movement because he has engaged in what some have found to be shady fundraising activities. See: DeRay Mckesson, "On Shaun King," Medium, September 12, 2019, https://medium.com/@deray/on-shaun-king-351bd812318c.
49. Ian Shapira, "Fourth Attacker Sentenced in Charlottesville Parking Garage Beating of Black Man," *Washington Post*, August 27, 2019, https://www

.washingtonpost.com/local/fourth-attacker-sentenced-in-charlottesville
-parking-garage-beating-of-black-man/2019/08/27/42b7c5a2-c82b-11e9
-a1fe-ca46e8d573c0_story.html.
50. Watson, "In the Wakes of Rodney King," 36–37.

5. VIOLA/HEATHER AND ANNIE/VERONICA

1. The Southern Poverty Law Center honors both Liuzzo and Heyer as martyrs, with Heyer so designated mere days after her death. See Southern Poverty Law Center, "SPLC honors Heather Heyer at Civil Rights Memorial Center," August 18, 2018, https://www.splcenter.org/news/2017/08/10/splc-honors -heather-heyer-civil-rights-memorial-center. I do want to be mindful of the racial dynamics of elevating activist white women in the struggles against racism and how that tends to minimize or efface the work of Black women. While I hope to problematize that dynamic here, this chapter may also perpetuate some of its aspects. A useful aphorism, "Behind every 'woke' white person is the labor of people of color," is applicable here. Thanks to my colleague Dr. Jalane Schmidt for this insight.
2. Mary Stanton, *From Selma to Sorrow: The Life and Death of Viola Liuzzo* (Athens: University of Georgia Press, 1998). See also Gary May, *The Informant: The FBI, the Ku Klux Klan, and the Murder of Viola Liuzzo* (New Haven, CT: Yale University Press, 2011).
3. Aniko Bodroghkozy, *Equal Time: Television and the Civil Rights Movement* (Urbana: University of Illinois Press, 2012), 132–33.
4. Stanton labels Liuzzo as working-class, because even though she lived an economically comfortable life with her second husband, he was a union official. Heyer, with only a high school diploma and raised mostly by a single mother in a double-wide trailer, more clearly fits that designation.
5. Gail Sheehy, "What Heather Heyer Knew," *Cut*, August 31, 2017, https://www.thecut.com/2017/08/what-heather-heyer-knew.html.
6. Timothy J. Heaphy, *Independent Review of the 2017 Protest Events in Charlottesville, Virginia* (Richmond, VA: Hunton & Williams, 2017). See also Hawes Spencer, *Summer of Hate: Charlottesville, USA* (Charlottesville: University of Virginia Press, 2018).
7. Spencer, *Summer of Hate*, 199. As an activist on the streets that day, I was acutely aware of that helicopter, as the continuous sound of its propellers formed a sonic backdrop to everything I experienced.
8. Bodroghkozy, *Equal Time*, 133; "Liuzzo Family Grief Stricken," *Chicago Tribune*, March 27, 1965, 5.
9. "Rights Killing Invokes Anger of Americans," *Chicago Tribune*, March 27, 1965,

5; "Slain Rights Aid Was Crusader: She's Recalled as Fighter for Dropouts," *Chicago Tribune*, March 27, 1965, 5.
10. Stanton, *From Selma to Sorrow*, 55.
11. See for instance Abby L. Ferber, *White Man Falling: Race, Gender, and White Supremacy* (Lanham, MD: Rowman & Littlefield, 1998); Jesse Daniels, *White Lies: Race, Class, Gender, and Sexuality in White Supremacist Discourse* (New York: Routledge, 1997); Abby L. Ferber, ed., *Home-Grown Hate: Gender and Organized Racism* (New York: Routledge, 2003).
12. "Liuzzo File Study Opens in Detroit," *New York Times*, May 16, 1965, 51.
13. There is no indication from her biographies that Liuzzo suffered mental illness, but such imputations made against women who didn't conform to traditional gender norms served powerful policing functions in this era.
14. Stanton, *From Selma to Sorrow*, 171–72.
15. May, *Informant*, 278.
16. Stanton, *From Selma to Sorrow*, 100.
17. May, *Informant*, 278. For images from the notorious publication, see Civil Rights Heritage Museum Online, "KKK Magazine 'Night Riders' about Viola Liuzzo murder," https://blackhistorycollection.org/2014/09/28/night-riders-kkk-magazine-about-viola-liuzzo-murder/.
18. J. Edgar Hoover, head of the FBI, helped begin these scurrilous and malicious rumors. Within days of Liuzzo's death, he was telling President Johnson about needle marks on her body and suggestions of amorous behavior with Moton, all untrue. See May, *Informant*, 169. LBJ, to his credit, ignored the FBI director's comments.
19. *Night Riders: The Inside Story of the Liuzzo Killing* (Birmingham, AL: BRALGO Publications, 1966).
20. May, *Informant*, 190.
21. Ferber, *White Man Falling*, 79–80.
22. Christina Caron, "Friends Recall 'a Strong Woman' Who Stood Up against Discrimination," *New York Times*, August 14, 2017, 14.
23. "Charlottesville: Who Was Victim Heather Heyer?" BBC News, August 14, 2017, https://www.bbc.com/news/world-us-canada-40924922.
24. Spencer, *Summer of Hate*, 230.
25. Amy Erdman Farrell, *Fat Shame: Stigma and the Fat Body in American Culture* (New York: NYU Press, 2011), 64.
26. C. Suarez Rojas, "Assistant Chief Medical Examiner Confirms Blunt Force Injury as Cause of Heather Heyer's Death," *Richmond Times-Dispatch*, December 3, 2018, https://www.richmond.com/news/virginia/assistant-chief-medical-examiner-confirms-blunt-force-injury-as-cause/article_a932c291-e128-5a60-9d65-29d490951e22.html.

27. See Alex Kaplan, "Fringe Media Are Furiously Trying to Absolve the White Nationalist Who Allegedly Killed Heather Heyer," Media Matters for America, September 8, 2017, https://www.mediamatters.org/blog/2017/09/08/Fringe-media-are-furiously-trying-to-absolve-the-white-nationalist-who-allegedly-killed-He/217886. Kaplan's online article provides copious links to examples of alt-right social media sites where the victim-blaming and fat-shaming of Heyer occurred.
28. I have no desire—nor do I believe it necessary—to quote Anglin's words. Readers who wish to see the article can search for it themselves. See Andrew Anglin, Daily Stormer, August 13, 2017.
29. George Hawley, *The Alt-Right: What Everyone Needs to Know* (New York: Oxford University Press, 2019), 46.
30. Kathleen Belew, *Bring the War Home: The White Power Movement and Paramilitary America* (Cambridge, MA: Harvard University Press, 2018), 160. See also Alexandra Minna Stern, *Proud Boys and the White Ethnostate* (Boston, MA: Beacon, 2019), which discusses alt-right anti-feminism and embrace of gender essentialism.
31. See Heather Heyer Foundation, https://www.heatherheyerfoundation.com. In 2022, the Foundation ceased operations, donating its remaining funds to Charlottesville's Jefferson School African American Heritage Center.
32. In 1991 the women of the Southern Christian Leadership Conference erected a marker to Liuzzo at the site of her death. It has had to be protected with steel fencing from defacement by white supremacists. More recently, in 2019 a statue of Liuzzo was unveiled in a Detroit park named for her. Susan Bro, Heather Heyer's mother, attended and was quoted in Detroit media coverage. See for instance: Julie Hinds and Micah Walker, "Detroit Statue Finds a Barefoot, Undaunted Viola Liuzzo Walking Again for Civil Rights," *Detroit Free Press*, July 23, 2019, https://www.freep.com/story/news/local/michigan/2019/07/23/statue-civil-rights-icon-viola-liuzzo-dedicated-detroit-park/1806238001/.
33. Stanton, *From Selma to Sorrow*, 112.
34. Rowe participated in the 1961 beating of Freedom Riders in Birmingham while working as an FBI informant. May's *The Informant* maps this history out well.
35. See for instance John Blake, "The Voting Rights Martyr Who Divided America," CNN, February 28, 2013, https://www.cnn.com/2013/02/28/politics/civil-rights-viola-liuzzo/index.html. See also *CBS Evening News*, July 2, 2014, https://www.youtube.com/watch?v=PldrJhY_C5s.
36. See for instance *NBC Nightly News*, August 16, 2017, https://www.youtube.com/watch?v=tJjNfaFGYu0.

37. "Heather Heyer Remembered at Memorial," CBS News, August 16, 2017, https://www.youtube.com/watch?v=hmdeTv9_OfU.
38. Stanton, *From Selma to Sorrow*, 221.
39. Betty Friedan, *The Feminine Mystique* (New York: Norton, 1963).
40. Susan J. Douglas, *Where the Girls Are: Growing Up Female with the Mass Media* (New York: Times Books, 1994). See also Bonnie J. Dow, *Watching Women's Liberation, 1970: Feminism's Pivotal Year on the Network News* (Urbana: University of Illinois Press, 2014).
41. On fourth-wave feminism, see for instance Nicola Rivers, *Postfeminism(s) and the Arrival of the Fourth Wave: Turning Tides* (Cham, Switzerland: Palgrave Macmillan, 2017).
42. Akasha Gloria Hull, Patricia Bell Scott, and Barbara Smith, *All the Women Are White, All the Blacks Are Men, But Some of Us Are Brave: Black Women's Studies* (Old Westbury, NY: Feminist Press, 1982); Kimberlé Crenshaw, "Demarginalizing the Intersection of Race and Sex," *University of Chicago Legal Forum* 1989, no. 1, article 8, 139–67.
43. This assessment is based on my own extensive viewing of CNN's and MSNBC's coverage in the aftermath of the Unite the Right violence. This viewing was not, however, a systematic study.
44. Juan Williams, *Eyes on the Prize* (New York: Penguin, 1987), 263.
45. Bodroghkozy, *Equal Time*, 120–21.
46. Aniko Bodroghkozy, "Mediating Selma, 1965, 2015," in *The Shadow of Selma*, ed. Joe Street and Henry Knight Lozano (Gainesville: University of Florida Press, 2018), 144–46.
47. The film took some creative license in its portrayal of Cooper's assault on Sheriff Clark.
48. "Selma: Beatings Start the Savage Season," *Life*, March 19, 1965, 34.
49. Kathleen K. Rowe, "Roseanne: Unruly Woman as Domestic Goddess" in *Feminist Television Criticism: A Reader*, ed. Charlotte Brunsdon, Julie D'Acci, and Lynn Spigel (Oxford: Oxford University Press, 1997), 76. See also Natalie Zemon Davis, *Society and Culture in Early Modern France* (Stanford, CA: Stanford University Press, 1975).
50. Bodroghkozy, *Equal Time*, 120.
51. Solidarity Cville, "Join Us to Demand Charlottesville #DropAllCharges against Racial Justice Hero Veronica Fitzhugh," Daily Kos, August 25, 2017, https://www.dailykos.com/stories/2017/8/25/1693174/-Join-us-to-demand-Charlottesville-DropALLcharges-against-racial-justice-hero-Veronica-Fitzhugh.
52. Samantha Baars, "Not Guilty: A Win for Veronica Fitzhugh," *C-ville Weekly*, October 27, 2017.

53. "Susan Bro, Mother of Heather Heyer, Testifies before House Committee about White Supremacist Violence," *Richmond Times-Dispatch*, May 15, 2019, https://www.richmond.com/news/virginia/susan-bro-mother-of-heather-heyer-testifies-before-house-committee/article_60486201-d193-5993-8729-00a32d6491c0.html.

54. Weiyi Cai, Joe War, Juliette Love, Troy Griggs, and Jason Kao, "White Extremist Ideology Drives Many Deadly Shootings," *New York Times*, August 4, 2019, https://www.nytimes.com/interactive/2019/08/04/us/white-extremist-active-shooter.html. See also Justin Ling, "How 4chan's Toxic Culture Helped Radicalize Buffalo Shooting Suspect," *Guardian*, May 18, 2022, https://www.theguardian.com/us-news/2022/may/18/4chan-radicalize-buffalo-shooting-white-supremacy.

6. "THIS IS WHAT COMMUNITY LOOKS LIKE!"

1. I was a leading member of the steering committee that put the project together.
2. Diane McWhorter, *Carry Me Home: Birmingham, Alabama—The Climactic Battle of the Civil Rights Revolution* (New York: Simon & Schuster, 2001), 375.
3. Martin Berger discusses the discrepancy between what this photo appears to signify and what only a closer examination reveals. See Berger, *Seeing through Race*, 35–39. McWhorter discusses it as well. See McWhorter, *Carry Me Home*, 375.
4. In a podcast on this subject, Malcolm Gladwell interviewed a colleague of the deceased Middleton and his German-immigrant wife, who both attested to his lack of racial animus. Gladwell also dug up an obscure interview with Gadsden from the 1990s indicating that the victim of Middleton's dog held quite prejudiced views of his own people. See Malcolm Gladwell, "The Foot Soldier of Birmingham," season 2, episode 4, *Revisionist History,* July 6, 2017 (podcast), http://revisionisthistory.com/episodes/14-the-foot-soldier-of-birmingham.
5. R. Bruce Brasell, *The Possible South: Documentary Film and the Limits of Biraciality* (Jackson: University Press of Mississippi, 2015), 61.
6. bell hooks, "The Oppositional Gaze," *Black Looks: Race and Representation* (Boston, MA: South End Press, 1992), 115–31.
7. McDowell, interviewed by Malcolm Gladwell for the *Revisionist History* "Foot Soldier" podcast, admits as much.
8. Gladwell, "Foot Soldier."
9. Ibid.
10. Louis P. Nelson and Claudrena N. Harold, eds., *Charlottesville 2017: The Legacy of Race and Inequity* (Charlottesville: University of Virginia Press, 2018),

3–4. See also the website Marked by These Monuments, which is based on the walking tours of Charlottesville's Confederate monuments and was created by University of Virginia professor and antiracist activist Jalane Schmidt and Dr. Andrea Douglas, director of the African American Heritage Center: https://www.thesemonuments.org.
11. Schmidt and Douglas, Marked by These Monuments.
12. The most powerful, poignant, and moving statue in Kelly Ingram Park is *Four Spirits*, a memorial to the four little girls killed in the KKK terrorist bombing of the 16th Street Baptist Church in September 1963. At the entrance of the northwest corner of the park and facing the church, it was erected in 2013, fifty years after the bombing. It memorializes how the snuffed-out lives of those four girls continue to matter. Because it is not a monument to the young activists and does not engage with iconic media imagery, as do the *Freedom Walk* and *Foot Soldier* pieces, I have not included it in my analysis.
13. Consider, by comparison, the 9/11 memorial in Lower Manhattan designed around the footprints of the Twin Towers, which opened a mere decade following the terrorist attacks.
14. As of 2022, at the site of the car attack commemorative chalking and knitted sleeves and purple ribbons on poles continue to decorate the area.
15. "Thousands Mark '65 March in Selma, Ala." *New York Times*, March 9, 1975, 50.
16. Selma Bridge Crossing Jubilee: https://www.selmajubilee.com/.
17. I was one of them.
18. Elliott Robinson, "Planning for Charlottesville Unity Days Kicks Off," Charlottesville Tomorrow, March 4, 2019, https://www.cvilletomorrow.org/articles/planning-for-charlottesvilles-unity-days-kicks-off.
19. Inside Out: The People's Art Project, http://www.insideoutproject.net/en/about.
20. "Heyer Memorial Stomped," *C-ville Weekly*, May 1, 2019. Antifascist activists quickly identified Dudley. See: Molly Conger @socialistdogmom, tweet, April 28, 2019.
21. Kayla Epstein, "This Emmett Till Memorial Was Vandalized Again. And Again. And Again. Now It's Bulletproof," *Washington Post*, October 20, 2019, https://www.washingtonpost.com/history/2019/10/20/this-emmett-till-memorial-was-vandalized-again-again-again-now-its-bulletproof/.
22. I was personally involved in all these discussions, debates, and questions as a Unity Days community volunteer. I saw Draine's idea as a media project, and since I'd already been thinking about media treatment of "Charlottesville," I joined the steering committee.
23. The project is archived here: https://www.insideoutproject.net/en/group-actions/usa-charlottesville.

24. A shortened version of this paragraph appeared as explanatory text on the public installation. The steering committee decided that the local community didn't need to be further reminded of the dominant narrative, since they would already be quite familiar with it.
25. In the summer of 2022, Amos built on the impulse behind the Inside Out project with another large-scale public photography installation. Focusing on activists and on community resilience during and after the Summer of Hate, Amos displayed his photos in the trees all along the city's downtown pedestrian mall as a commemoration of the fifth anniversary of the community's fight against the forces of the alt-right and white supremacists. QR codes next to the photos allowed people to hear the stories of those pictured. The project is available also at the following website: Ézé Amos, "The Story of Us," https://www.ourstorycville.org.
26. Berger, *Seeing through Race*, 53; Leigh Raiford, *Imprisoned in a Luminous Glare: Photography and the African American Freedom Struggle* (Chapel Hill: University of North Carolina Press, 2011).
27. Solidarity Cville, "Corey Long Did Nothing Wrong," April 10, 2018, https://medium.com/@solidaritycville/corey-long-did-nothing-wrong-c67a7807dd15.
28. Staff, "Corey Long drops appeal of rally-related disorderly conduct conviction," *Daily Progress*, January 10, 2019. https://www.dailyprogress.com/news/local/corey-long-drops-appeal-of-rally-related-disorderly-conduct-conviction/article_2c7f1bb0-1529-11e9-a6d8-ebed47c50707.html.
29. See for instance this analysis of the power of the photograph: Doreen St. Felix, "An Image of Revolutionary Fire at Charlottesville," *New Yorker*, August 14, 2017, https://www.newyorker.com/culture/annals-of-appearances/an-image-of-revolutionary-fire-at-charlottesville.
30. He was interviewed by CNN's Don Lemon in the immediate aftermath of A12 and gave his account in other media outlets such as: Jeff Farrell, "Charlottesville: Man Pictured Using Homemade Flame Thrower on White Supremacists Speaks Out," *Independent*, August 15, 2017. He did so again a year later following his conviction. See for instance Timothy Bella, "Every Day Is August 12 in Charlottesville," *Atlantic*, August 10, 2018.
31. Donald Bogle, *Toms, Coons, Mulattoes, Mammies, and Bucks: An Interpretive History of Blacks in American Films* (New York: Viking, 1973). This classic study has gone through numerous revisions with a fifth edition released in 2016.

7. FOUR PRESIDENTS

1. Mary Ann Watson, *The Expanding Vista: American Television in the Kennedy Years* (Durham, NC: Duke University Press, 1990).
2. See "John F. Kennedy Civil Rights Address," American Rhetoric Top 100 Speeches, https://americanrhetoric.com/speeches/jfkcivilrights.htm.
3. Steven Levingston, *Kennedy and King: The President, the Pastor, and the Battle over Civil Rights* (New York: Hachette, 2017).
4. Gary May, *Bending toward Justice: The Voting Rights Act and the Transformation of American Democracy* (Durham, NC: Duke University Press, 2015), 118.
5. Miller Center at University of Virginia, "Presidential Speeches: March 15, 1965 Speech Before Congress on Voting Rights," https://millercenter.org/the-presidency/presidential-speeches/march-15-1965-speech-congress-voting-rights.
6. May, *Bending toward Justice*, 122.
7. Ibid.
8. Gary May, *The Informant: The FBI, the Ku Klux Klan, and the Murder of Viola Liuzzo* (New Haven, CT: Yale University Press, 2011), 172.
9. Cory Gardner tweeted: "we must call evil by its name. These were white supremacists and this was domestic terrorism." Julia Manchester, "Republican Lawmakers Criticize Trump Response to Charlottesville," *The Hill*, August 12, 2017, https://thehill.com/homenews/senate/346339-gop-senator-to-trump-we-must-call-evil-by-its-name.
10. Rosie Gray, "'Alt-Right' Leaders Won't Condemn Ramming Suspect," *Atlantic*, August 14, 2017, https://www.theatlantic.com/politics/archive/2017/08/alt-right-leaders-wont-condemn-ramming-suspect/536880/.
11. The popular and frequently memed lyric is from Jay-Z's 2008 song, "My President Is Black": "Rosa Parks sat so Martin Luther could walk / Martin Luther walked so Barack Obama could run / Barack Obama ran so all the children could fly."
12. For a problematizing of the traditional civil rights movement narrative see, for instance, Jacquelyn Dowd Hall, "The Long Civil Rights Movement and the Political Uses of the Past," *Journal of American History* 91, no. 4 (March 2005): 1233–63; and Leon F. Litwack, "'Fight the Power!': The Legacy of the Civil Rights Movement," *Journal of Southern History* 75, no. 1 (February 2009): 3–28.
13. Rick Perlstein, "Exclusive: Lee Atwater's Infamous 1981 Interview on the Southern Strategy," *Nation*, November 13, 2012, https://www.thenation.com/article/archive/exclusive-lee-atwaters-infamous-1981-interview-southern-strategy/.

14. Jesse H. Rhodes, *Ballot Blocked: The Political Erosion of the Voting Rights Act* (Stanford, CA: Stanford University Press, 2017). The Shelby decision determined that the Act's "pre-clearance" mandate, which required states with a history of voter suppression (almost all those of the former Confederacy) to get Justice Department consent to make any changes to local voting laws and practices, was unconstitutional. The result has been a flurry of voter ID laws and other measures that have made it harder for Black people, the poor, and other disadvantaged groups to vote. The nonracist, color-blind rationale that mostly Republican lawmakers have used is to invoke concerns about voter fraud.
15. Eduardo Bonilla-Silva, *Racism without Racists: Color-Blind Racism and the Persistence of Racial Inequality in America* (Lanham, MD: Rowman & Littlefield, 2014), 15.
16. In December 2020, during his final weeks in office, Trump vetoed, but Congress managed to override, a military spending bill that included a provision renaming bases throughout the South. Trump was willing to deny military service members a 3 percent pay raise along with billions in other military spending, because he decided it was important that those bases continue to honor Confederate generals.
17. Neil MacFarquhar, "As Domestic Terrorists Outpace Jihadists, New U.S. Law Is Debated," *New York Times*, February 25, 2020, https://www.nytimes.com/2020/02/25/us/domestic-terrorism-laws.html. When Joe Biden came into the White House, he quickly launched government-wide efforts to combat far-right domestic terrorism, but his administration as of 2022 had not pushed for a law specifically declaring domestic terrorism a federal crime. Unlike during the Trump years, Biden's Department of Homeland Security labeled homegrown violent extremism an area of national priority; however, without a statute on the matter, coordinating federal intelligence and law enforcement has remained a challenge. See: W. J. Hennigan and Vera Bergengruen, "Buffalo Exposes the Limits Of Biden's Domestic Terror Strategy," *Time*, May 20, 2022, https://time.com/6177847/biden-pledged-to-defeat-domestic-terror-buffalo-why-thats-not-enough/.
18. Marisa Iati, "Two Senators Want Antifa Activists to Be Labeled 'Domestic Terrorists.' Here's What That Means," *Washington Post*, July 20, 2019, https://www.washingtonpost.com/politics/2019/07/20/senators-want-antifa-activists-be-labeled-domestic-terrorists-heres-what-that-means/.
19. George Hawley, *Making Sense of the Alt-Right* (New York: Columbia University Press, 2017), 213.
20. Ibid., 214.
21. Larry Buchanan, Quoctrung Bui, and Jugal K. Patel, "Black Lives Matter May Be the Largest Movement in U.S. History," *New York Times*, July 3, 2020,

https://www.nytimes.com/interactive/2020/07/03/us/george-floyd-protests-crowd-size.html.
22. Tessa Owen, "The Alt-Right Love Affair with Trump Is Over. Here's Why," *Vice*, July 9, 2019.
23. Tom Jackson, Paul Duggan, Ann E. Marimow, and Spencer S. Hsu, "Proud Boys Sparked Clashes during Pro-Trump Rally, D.C. Officials Say," *Washington Post*, December 14, 2020, https://www.washingtonpost.com/local/public-safety/trump-rally-violence-proud-boys/2020/12/14/bf2f5826-3e26-11eb-8bc0-ae155bee4aff_story.html.
24. Ben Collins and Brandy Zadrozny, "Proud Boys Celebrate after Trump's Debate Callout," NBC News, September 29, 2020, https://www.nbcnews.com/tech/tech-news/proud-boys-celebrate-after-trump-s-debate-call-out-n1241512.
25. Patrick Healy and Jeff Zeleny, "Clinton and Obama Spar over Remarks about Dr. King," *New York Times*, January 13, 2008, https://www.nytimes.com/2008/01/13/us/politics/13cnd-campaign.html.
26. Julie Hirschfeld Davis, Sheryl Gay Stolberg, and Thomas Kaplan, "Trump Alarms Lawmakers with Disparaging Words for Haiti and Africa," *New York Times*, January 11, 2018, https://www.nytimes.com/2018/01/11/us/politics/trump-shithole-countries.html; Katie Rogers and Nicholas Fandos, "Trump Tells Congresswomen to 'Go Back' to the Countries They Came From," *New York Times*, July 14, 2019, https://www.nytimes.com/2019/07/14/us/politics/trump-twitter-squad-congress.html.
27. Michael D. Shear, "Trump Retweets Racist Video Showing Supporter Yelling 'White Power,'" *New York Times*, June 28, 2020, https://www.nytimes.com/2020/06/28/us/politics/trump-white-power-video-racism.html.
28. Linda Gordon, *The Second Coming of the KKK: The Ku Klux Klan of the 1920s and the American Political Tradition* (New York: Liveright, 2017), 11. There is some historical controversy over the provenance of Wilson's statement, although his racism is not disputed. See, for instance, Arthur Lennig, "Myth and Fact: The Reception of *The Birth of a Nation*," Film History, no. 16 (2004), 117–41.
29. Gordon, *Second Coming*, 165.
30. Andrea Douglas and Jalane Schmidt, "Marked by These Monuments," https://www.thesemonuments.org/home/#new-page-3.
31. Louis P. Nelson and Claudrena Harold, *Charlottesville 2017: The Legacy of Race and Inequity* (Charlottesville: University of Virginia Press, 2018), xi.
32. Stephen Weinberger, "*The Birth of a Nation* and the Making of the NAACP," *Journal of American Studies*, no. 45 (2011), 77–93.
33. Felix Harcourt, *Ku Klux Kulture: America and the Klan in the 1920s* (Chicago, IL: University of Chicago Press, 2017), 27.

34. Ibid., 26.
35. See Steven Levitsky and Daniel Ziblatt, *How Democracies Die* (Cambridge, MA: Harvard University Press, 2018).
36. Dan Balz, "Biden Makes His Opening Bid: It's All about the President," *Washington Post*, April 25, 2019, https://www.washingtonpost.com/politics/biden-makes-his-opening-bid-its-all-about-the-president/2019/04/25/8b78ba6a-6770-11e9-82ba-fcfeff232e8f_story.html.
37. Joe Biden, "We Are Living through a Battle for the Soul of This Nation," *Atlantic*, August 25, 2017, https://www.theatlantic.com/politics/archive/2017/08/joe-biden-after-charlottesville/538128/.
38. Lauren Feeney, "Two Versions of John Lewis' Speech," *Moyers & Company*, July 24, 2013, https://billmoyers.com/content/two-versions-of-john-lewis-speech/#original.
39. Thomas Gentile, *March on Washington: August 28, 1963* (Washington, DC: New Day, 1983), 172, 178–81.
40. May, *Bending toward Justice*, 125.
41. Kevin Robillard, "Charlottesville Activists Don't Want Joe Biden To Use City as a Campaign 'Prop,'" Huffington Post, April 26, 2019, https://www.huffpost.com/entry/charlottesville-activists-dont-want-joe-biden-to-use-city-as-a-campaign-prop_n_5cc200d2e4b0e56130eeaafd.
42. Veronica Stracqualursi, "Mom of Woman Killed in Charlottesville Says Incident Must Be Part of Political Dialogue," CNN, April 26, 2019, https://www.cnn.com/2019/04/26/politics/heather-heyer-susan-bro-charlottesville-joe-biden-cnntv/index.html.
43. I am mindful that this book, with its copious use of media imagery from A11 and A12, and my analytical work on those images may be received by some activists and survivors as a kind of theft as well, or a recirculation of their ongoing trauma.
44. Even in 2022 in a major speech kicking off the midterm congressional election season in which he warned about "MAGA Republicans" and their threat to democracy, Biden reminded voters of Charlottesville: "I made a bet on you, the American people, and that bet is paying off. Proving that from darkness—the darkness of Charlottesville, of Covid, of gun violence, of insurrection—we can see the light." "Remarks by President Biden on the Continued Battle for the Soul of the Nation," White House, September 1, 2022, https://www.whitehouse.gov/briefing-room/speeches-remarks/2022/09/01/remarks-by-president-bidenon-the-continued-battle-for-the-soul-of-the-nation/.
45. Marita Sturken, *Tangled Memories: The Vietnam War, the AIDS Epidemic, and the Politics of Remembering* (Berkeley: University of California Press, 1997), 26.

CONCLUSION

1. "Man Gets Life plus 419 Years in Deadly Charlottesville Car Attack," CBS News, July 15, 2019, https://www.cbsnews.com/news/james-alex-fields-jr-charlottesville-car-attack-sentenced-life-plus-419-years-today-2019-07-15/.
2. Joe Walsh, "'Crying Nazi' Christopher Cantwell Sentenced to 41 Months for Extortion," *Forbes*, February 24, 2021, https://www.forbes.com/sites/joewalsh/2021/02/24/crying-nazi-christopher-cantwell-sentenced-to-41-months-for-extortion/?sh=250dd2b44652.
3. Counter Extremism Project, "Extremist Leaders: Matthew Heimbach," https://www.counterextremism.com/extremists/matthew-heimbach.
4. Mark Greenblatt and Lauren Knapp, "Extremist Heimbach to Relaunch Hate Group, Says He Supports Violence," Newsy, July 20, 2021, https://www.newsy.com/stories/extremist-heimbach-to-relaunch-hate-group-supports-violence-3/?sourceid=1066251&ms=blast&emci=d317bedf-4eea-eb11-a7ad-501ac57b8fa7&emdi=d8e8b4e1-5cea-eb11-a7ad501ac57b8fa7&ceid=8442024.
5. Chris Schiano, "Neo-Nazi 'American Identity Movement' Disbands," Unicorn Riot, November 2, 2020, https://unicornriot.ninja/2020/neo-nazi-american-identity-movement-disbands/.
6. Neil MacFarquhar, "Charlottesville Lawsuit Puts Rising Intolerance on Trial," *New York Times*, October 28, 2019, https://www.nytimes.com/2019/10/28/us/charlottesville-civil-rights-trial.html.
7. Integrity First for America, "Federal Court Grants Evidentiary Sanctions against Neo-Nazi Hate Group National Socialist Movement in IFA's Charlottesville Suit," June 23, 2021, https://www.integrityfirstforamerica.org/newsroom/federal-court-grants-evidentiary-sanctions-against-neo-nazi-hate-group-national-s.
8. Drew DeSilver, "Turnout Soared in 2020 as Nearly Two-Thirds of Eligible U.S. Voters Cast Ballots for President," Pew Research Center, January 28, 2021, https://www.pewresearch.org/fact-tank/2021/01/28/turnout-soared-in-2020-as-nearly-two-thirds-of-eligible-u-s-voters-cast-ballots-forpresident/.
9. See for instance Saachi Koul, "There's a Straight Line from Charlottesville to the Capitol," BuzzFeed News, January 7, 2021; Caleb Ecrma, "The Eerie Charlottesville Echoes of Trump Supporters' Capitol Coup," *Vanity Fair*, January 7, 2021; Deena Zaru, "Why Trump's Response to Capitol Siege Evokes Memories of Charlottesville," ABC News, January 8, 2021; Lois Beckett, "From Charlottesville to the Capitol: How Rightwing Impunity Fueled the Pro-Trump Mob," *Guardian*, January 8, 2021; Elle Reeve, "For the Mob That Stormed the Capitol, a Lesson from Charlottesville," CNN, January 13, 2021;

Patrice Taddonio, "'Enabling It to Happen Again': How Charlottesville Led to the Capitol Attack," *PBS Frontline*, January 26, 2021.
10. Peter Herman, Marissa J. Lang, and Clarence Williams, "Pro-Trump Rally Descends into Chaos as Proud Boys Roam D.C. Looking for a Fight," *Washington Post*, December 13, 2020, https://www.washingtonpost.com/local/public-safety/proud-boys-protest-stabbing-arrest/2020/12/13/98c0f740-3d3f-11eb-8db8-395dedaaa036_story.html.
11. Talia Jane, "Washington, DC, Activists Brace for 'Klanuary' as Trump Supporters March on City," *Teen Vogue*, January 6, 2021, https://www.teenvogue.com/story/washington-dc-activists-klanuary-trump-supporters-march. See also: Delia Goncalves, "'Your Silence Is Violence': Black Lives Matter DC Calling on Nearby Hotels to Shut Down for Upcoming Protests," CBS-WUSA9, December 30, 2020, https://www.wusa9.com/article/news/community/equality-matters/black-lives-matter-dc-demands-hotels-shut-down-and-condem-pro-trump-protestors/65-5a5a4747-8f4e-4648-980c-febccd0167be.
12. As this book goes to press, it is still difficult to draw conclusions about the degree of planning and orchestration of the insurrectionists' actions. FBI research indicates clear coordination between Proud Boys and the Oath Keeper militia group (both of whom were present for the Unite the Right rally). The Congressional House Select Committee investigating January 6 attack hearings (ongoing as this book goes to press) have also shown that Trump and his associates coordinated the attempt to stop Biden's certification as president and that Trump wished and expected to be taken to the Capitol with his "Stop the Steal" supporters. Considering Trump's media-imagery savvy, one can only imagine the "Trump at the Capitol" images the defeated president may have envisioned.
13. Linda Williams, *Playing the Race Card: Melodramas in Black and White from Uncle Tom to O. J. Simpson* (Princeton, NJ: Princeton University Press, 2001); and Martin A. Berger, *Seeing through Race: A Reinterpretation of Civil Rights Photography* (Berkeley: University of California Press, 2011).
14. See for instance *CBS Evening News*, "Officer Hailed as a Hero for Leading Capitol Rioters Away from Lawmakers," January 11, 2021, https://www.youtube.com/watch?v=SFzx1FJia94.
15. On February 6, 2021, CNN broadcast the newly released cell phone interview. See "New Video of Capitol Rioter: Trump Is Still Our President," https://www.youtube.com/watch?v=cO8tqpJW3WE.
16. Craig Timberg and Drew Harwell, "Pro-Trump Forums Erupt with Violent Threats Ahead of Wednesday's Rally against 2020 Election," *Washington Post*,

January 5, 2021, https://www.washingtonpost.com/technology/2021/01/05/parler-telegram-violence-dc-protests/.
17. See Alexandra Minna Stern, *Proud Boys and the White Ethnostate* (Boston, MA: Beacon Press, 2019).
18. Rachel Axon and Katie Wedell, "'Pics or It Didn't Happen': Experts Explain Why Capitol Rioters Posted Incriminating Videos and Selfies," *USA Today*, January 21, 2021, https://www.usatoday.com/story/news/investigations/2021/01/21/fbi-uses-selfies-social-posts-arrest-u-s-capitol-rioters/4203158001/.
19. Kyle Cheney and Josh Gerstein, "Where Jan. 6 Prosecutions Stand, 18 Months After the Attack," *Politico*, July 7, 2022, https://www.politico.com/news/2022/07/07/jan-6-prosecutions-months-later-00044354.
20. Sam Dorman, "GOP Politicians Condemn Violence at Capitol, Call for an End to Riots," Fox News, January 6, 2021, https://www.foxnews.com/politics/gop-politicians-condemn-violence-at-capitol-call-for-an-end-to-riots.
21. Matt Ford, "Republicans Are on the Brink of Embracing Capitol Rioters," *New Republic*, June 16, 2021, https://newrepublic.com/article/162749/ron-johnson-capitol-riot-gop-false-history.
22. Guy-Uriel E. Charles and Luis E. Fuentes-Rohwer, "The Court's Voting-Rights Decision Was Worse than People Thought," *Atlantic*, July 8, 2021, https://www.theatlantic.com/ideas/archive/2021/07/brnovich-vra-scotus-decision-arizona-voting-right/619330/.
23. "The Capitol Siege: The Arrested and Their Stories," NPR, February 2, 2021, updated July 21, 2021, https://www.npr.org/2021/02/09/965472049/the-capitol-siege-the-arrested-and-their-stories.
24. Alan Feuer, "Fears of White People Losing Out Permeate Capitol Rioters' Towns, Study Finds," *New York Times*, April 6, 2021, https://www.nytimes.com/2021/04/06/us/politics/capitol-riot-study.html.
25. Chris Cameron, "The Anti-Defamation League Calls for Tucker Carlson to Be Fired over 'Replacement Theory' Remarks," *New York Times*, April 9, 2021, https://www.nytimes.com/2021/04/09/us/tucker-carlson-adl-replacement-theory.html.
26. Trump was permanently banned from Twitter, his favorite social media platform, shortly after the January 6 riots, because of his incitement of the mob. He was also removed from Facebook until January 2023, at which point the company will evaluate whether he remains a threat to public safety.
27. John Fiske, *Media Matters: Race and Gender in U.S. Politics* (Minneapolis: University of Minnesota Press, 1996), 263.
28. Sarah Rankin, "Black Contractor Braves Threats in Removing Richmond's Statues," AP News, December 25, 2020, https://apnews.com/article/us-news

-virginia-racial-injustice-richmond-only-on-ap-590bcf679e5940b99ac6ccc fe9354f93. Team Henry Enterprises also helped in the installation of UVA's memorial to enslaved laborers.

29. Michael Signer, *Cry Havoc: Charlottesville and American Democracy Under Siege* (New York: PublicAffairs, 2020), 23.
30. Johns's visibility has been heightened in recent years, especially in Virginia. A statue of Johns is expected to be added to the US Capitol's National Statuary Hall to represent the state. Her statue will replace Robert E. Lee, who along with George Washington represented the Old Dominion for over a century. The Lee statue was removed in December 2020. See Cameron Thompson, "Virginia Is One Step Closer to Getting Statue of Civil Rights Icon Barbara Johns in the U.S. Capitol," CBS-6 News, July 22, 2022. For more on Johns and the struggle to integrate the schools of Prince Edward County, which shut their doors for five years rather than integrate, see: Bob Smith, *They Closed Their Schools* (Chapel Hill: University of North Carolina Press, 1965); and Kristen Green, *Something Must Be Done about Prince Edward County: A Family, a Virginia Town, a Civil Rights Battle* (New York: HarperCollins, 2015).
31. Theresa Vargas, "The Girl Who Brought Down a Statue," *Washington Post*, July 17, 2021, https://www.washingtonpost.com/local/zyahna-bryant-charlottes ville-lee-statue/2021/07/17/9073933e-e688-11eb-b722-89ea0dde7771_story .html.
32. Susan Bro has very consciously worked to steer reporters who come to her for quotes to instead interview Charlottesville activists of color. Personal correspondence with author, June 2021.
33. Aniko Bodroghkozy, *Equal Time: Television and the Civil Rights Movement* (Urbana: University of Illinois Press, 2012). Richard Lentz's analysis of the major newsmagazines suggests the situation was much the same in national print media. See *Symbols, the News Magazines, and Martin Luther King* (Baton Rouge: Louisiana State University Press, 1990).
34. Vargas, "Girl Who Brought Down a Statue." See also Zyahna Bryant, "Charlottesville's Robert E. Lee Monument Is Coming Down Thanks to Me and Black Women Like Me," *Teen Vogue*, July 10, 2021, https://www.teenvogue.com /story/charlottesvilles-robert-e-lee-monument-coming-down-black-women -zyahna-bryant-op-ed.
35. "Charlottesville Removes Robert E. Lee, Lewis & Clark and Sacagawea Statues," MSNBC, July 10, 2021, https://www.youtube.com/watch?v=1W cGp-0Z_aM. See also Katherine Knott, "Statue Removals Bring Joy to Many, though More Work Needs to Be Done, They Say," *Daily Progress*, July 10, 2021.
36. "Statue of Confederate Gen. Robert E. Lee Removed in Charlottesville, Vir-

ginia," CBS News, July 10, 2021, https://www.youtube.com/watch?v=t7rQ5 Tie1jI.

AFTERWORD

1. Congregation Beth Israel, "Holocaust Scroll," https://www.cbicville.org/about-cbi/special-features/holocaust-scroll.
2. Unbeknownst to me, our congregation president had spent much of the service outside in front of the building with our paid armed guard (Charlottesville police refused to provide protection) and watched as three men stood across the street dressed in fatigues and carrying semiautomatic rifles. See Alan Zimmerman, "In Charlottesville, the Local Jewish Community Presses On," ReformJudaism, August 14, 2017, https://reformjudaism.org/blog/2017/08/14/charlottesville-local-jewish-community-presses.
3. The story of Vinegar Hill and its destruction is told in the 2022 documentary by Charlottesville filmmakers Lorenzo Dickerson and Jordy Yager, Raised/Razed. See Virginia Public Media, https://vpm.org/raisedrazed.
4. See for instance Laura Smith, "In 1965, the City of Charlottesville Demolished a Thriving Black Neighborhood," Timeline, August 15, 2017, https://timeline.com/charlottesville-vinegar-hill-demolished-ba27b6ea69e1.
5. Jalane Schmidt, "Excuse Me, America, Your House Is on Fire: Lessons from Charlottesville on the KKK and the 'Alt-right,'" Medium, June 27, 2017, https://medium.com/resist-here/excuse-me-america-your-house-is-on-fire-lessons-from-charlottesville-on-the-kkk-and-alt-right-84aafddca685.
6. I tell my mother-in-law's story of survival at the end of the acknowledgments. Her testimony is archived at Shoah Foundation Institute, United States Holocaust Memorial Museum, https://collections.ushmm.org/search/catalog/vha35665. She also tells some of her story at the Montreal Holocaust Museum, archived here: https://museeholocauste.ca/en/survivors-stories/eva-majerczyk/.
7. Vann R. Newkirk II, "Black Charlottesville Has Seen This All Before," Atlantic, August 18, 2017, https://www.theatlantic.com/politics/archive/2017/08/black-community-charlottesville-response/537285/. A report commissioned by the city and released in 2020, based on data from 2014 to 2016, found marked disparities throughout the criminal justice system between treatment of Black people versus whites. Such disparity, according to the report, "erodes trust among Black residents regarding the justice system." Charlotte Renee Woods and Elliott Robinson, "Questions Remain in the Wake of the Disproportionate Minority Contact Report's Release," Charlottesville Tomor-

row, February 7, 2020, https://www.cvilletomorrow.org/articles/questions-remain-in-the-wake-of-the-disproportionate-minority-contact-reports-release/.

8. Kevin MacDonald, a professor of evolutionary psychology at California State University, Long Beach, provided the trappings of intellectual or scholarly legitimacy to alt-right adherents through a series of books on Jews, arguing that they had developed an evolutionary group strategy to outcompete non-Jews and to destabilize any society in which they inhabited. Antisemitism was, thus, a necessary counterstrategy by whites to ensure they would not be "replaced." See for instance Southern Poverty Law Center, "Kevin MacDonald," https://www.splcenter.org/fighting-hate/extremist-files/individual/kevin-macdonald.

9. Cora wrote her own account of the day. See Cora Schenberg, "What I Saw in Charlottesville on August 12, 2017," *Streetlight*, August 17, 2017, https://streetlightmag.com/2017/08/17/what-i-saw-in-charlottesville-on-august-12-2017-by-cora-schenberg/.

10. We thought it was tear gas. It was pepper spray, apparently dispersed by alt-right forces. See Timothy J. Heaphy, *Independent Review of the 2017 Protest Events in Charlottesville, Virginia* (Richmond: Hunton & Williams, 2017), 130.

11. Alt-right leaders Richard Spencer and Eli Mosley were gassed that day. It seems likely the blubbering man I witnessed was Mosely. An interview with a medic and cell phone video used in the documentary *Charlottesville: Our Streets* (2017) appear to suggest as much.

12. See for instance Charlottesville Low-Income Housing Coalition, *The Impact of Racism on Affordable Housing*, February 2020, https://www.justice4all.org/wp-content/uploads/2020/03/Housing-Report-FINAL.pdf.

INDEX

Italicized page numbers refer to illustrations.

ABC News, 28; Unite the Right car attack coverage of, 94
Abi-Nader, Jeanette, 145
ACT UP, 20
AIDS activists, 20
Ailes, Roger, 29
Alabama Christian Movement for Human Rights (ACMHR), 16
All Out DC, 177
alt-right, 1; in aftermath of Unite the Right rally, 82, 160–61, 173; and antisemitism, 5, 20, 22, 43, 163, 192, 234n8; and Charlottesville media, 26, 41–44, 68; and demography, 5, 20; doxing by antiracists, 74–76; and fat shaming, 118; gender ideology, 37, 107, 119, 127–28, 181; and Heather Heyer, 118–19; and mass shootings, 128, 159, 160; May 13, 2017, Charlottesville rally, 60–64; and media events, 8; media savviness of, 48–49, 54; misogyny of, 118, 119, 127–28; 1965 and, 4–5, 123, 182; origins of, 20–21; and Pepe the Frog, 34–35; social media use of, 20, 26, 30–35, 38, *39*, 40, 62–64, *63*, 67; and Donald Trump, 5, 20–21, 54, 75, 153–54, 157, 161–62, 208n4; and video gaming, 32–33; violence of, 51. *See also* Unite the Right rally
Amos, Ézé, 143, 145, 147; "The Story of Us" photo installation, 234n25

Anderson, Benedict, "imagined community," 172–73
Anglin, Andrew, 37, 43, 48; and Heather Heyer, 119, 120, 123; *Sines v. Kessler*, 75
antiabortion activists, "Summer of Mercy" (1991), 20
Anti-Defamation League, 41
antifa, 25, 54, 159, 180; and Richard Spencer, 82; and Donald Trump, 157, 161; at Unite the Right rally, 92, 166, 193, 194. *See also* antiracists in Charlottesville
Antifash Gordon, 74–75
antiracists in Charlottesville, 1–2, 5, 51, 111; and alt-right May 13, 2017, rally, 60–64, *61*, 66, 177, 185, *185*; in Joe Biden "Charlottesville" campaign video, 165–66, *166*; car attack, *93*, 93–99, *95*, *98*, 166, 195; and clergy, 59, 66, 87–89, *89*, 92, 145, 215n15; community defense, 126; doxing of alt-right, 74–76, 212n71; and Veronica Fitzhugh, 125–27; Inside Out Charlottesville (2019) portraits of, *142–43*, 143–52, *144*, *146*, *147*, *148*, *149*, *151*; Ku Klux Klan rally (2017), 71–73, 177, 191–92; in local media coverage, 41, 43–44, 58–60, 71–73; media savviness of, 52, 53, 57–58, *77*; mutual aid, 76, *77*, 192–94; national media coverage of, 62–63, *63*, 101, *102*, 103; negative response to Joe Biden "Charlottesville" campaign video, 165, 169–70;

antiracists in Charlottesville (*continued*) nonviolent training of, 78, 192; organizing ability of, 24–25, 55, 57–83, 159; and removal of Charlottesville Confederate statues, 184–88; response to Inside Out Charlottesville project (2019), 140–41; social media use of, 60–63, 65–76, 69, 78; and tiki torch parade, 49, 78–82, 80, 179; and Unite the Right rally, 69, 70, 91–95, 95, 177, 192–95. *See also* Gorcenski, Emily; Showing Up for Racial Justice; UVa Students United

Arab Spring, 54–55

Arrington, Richard, Jr., 131

Atwater, Lee, "Southern Strategy," 158, 159

Baker, Ella, 172

Bates, Berke M.M., 114–15, 194

Bates, Niya, 143–45, *144*

Beard, Gloria, *144*, 145

Belew, Kathleen, 119

Bellamy, Wes, 22–23, 57, 124, 186, 190; *Daily Progress* op-ed about, 43–44

Berger, Martin A., 100–101, 103, 105, 108, 109, 133, 145

Biden, Joseph, 5, 29, 122, 153, 161, 176, 226n17, 228n44; *Atlantic* article (2017) on Unite the Right rally, 167, 171; "Charlottesville" campaign video, 164–68, *165, 166, 168*; "Charlottesville" stump speech, 171–72; criticism of Donald Trump response to Unite the Right, 167; and "imagined community," 172–73; negative response from local antiracist activists to "Charlottesville" campaign video, 169–70; support for Charlottesville antiracists, 76, 81, 165–66, 167–68, 173; and Susan Bro, 170; and Will.i.am video of "Charlottesville" stump speech, 171–72

Birmingham campaign (1963), 1–3, 4–6, 23, 51–52, 55, 82–83; and Black radio, 65; Children's Crusade, 17–18, 99–101, 100, 130–35; hostile media coverage of, 60, 65; and John F. Kennedy, 153–54; local activism in, 16–17; as media event, 6–8, 10, 86, 89, 155, 156, 184; memorial statues about, 131–37, *131, 132, 133, 135*; and photojournalism, 99–103, *100, 102*; Project C, 17; and violence, 19

Birmingham World, 130

Birth of a Nation, The (1915), 103; protest against, 163; White House screening of, 162–63

Black, Don, 30

Black Lives Matter, 3, 109, 180; Charlottesville chapter, 66, 68, 124; DC chapter and Proud Boys, 177; Ferguson, Missouri protests (2014), 54, 56, 84–85, 110, 188; and George Floyd protests (2020), 83–84, *84*, 96, 110–11, 160–61, 176, 183; Proud Boys and, 177; Richmond, Virginia protests, 83–84

Black Panthers, 103

BlacKkKlansman (2018), use of Unite the Right rally video footage, 97, 170

Blackmon, Traci, 78, 89

Blair, Melissa, 114

Bogle, Donald, 103

Bonilla-Silva, Eduardo, 158–59

Boogaloo Bois, 161

Boorstin, Daniel, 6–7, 10

Boynton, Amelia, 18–19, 138; media coverage of, 124, 186

Braden, Anne, 56

Bradley, Mamie, 96

Brasell Bruce R., 133

Bristow, Kyle, 74

Bro, Susan, 118, 186; Inside Out Charlottesville portrait of, 145, 146, *147*; media coverage of, 121–22, *122*, 127, 128, 139; at memorial for Heather Heyer, 121; response to Joe Biden "Charlottesville" campaign video, 170

Brooks, Peter, 90

Brown, Michael, 56, 110

Brown v. Board of Education (1954), 186
Bryant, Zyahna, 22, *144*, 191; comparison to female civil rights movement activists, 186; media coverage of, 186–88, *187*

Caine-Conley, Brittany, 89, 146
Camerota, Alisyn, 170
Cantwell, Chris ("Crying Nazi"), 49, 175; in Joe Biden's "Charlottesville" campaign video, 166; *Sines v. Kessler*, 75
Capitol insurrection (2021), 5–6, 10, 176–84, *178, 179, 180, 181*; comparison to Unite the Right rally, 176–77, 178; criminal charges in, 181–82; and Great Replacement ideology, 183; and hypermasculinity, 178, 180–81; iconic images of, 180–81, *180, 181*; and identities of insurrectionists, 182–83; as media event, 161, 178; and Officer Eugene Goodman, 179, *179*; and QAnon Shaman, 180–81, *181*; Republican lawmakers response to, 182
Carlson, Tucker, 30; and Great Replacement ideology, 183
Castile, Philando, 57, 111
CBS News: Susan Bro, coverage of, 121; Zyahna Bryant, coverage of, 186, 188; Annie Lee Cooper, coverage of, 126; Freedom Rides, 16–17; and Viola Liuzzo's death, 115
Cernovich, Mike, 32–33
Chansley, Jacob (QAnon Shaman), 180–81, *181*
Charlottesville (city): African Americans and law enforcement in, 191, 233n7; aftermath of Unite the Right rally, 83; Blue Ribbon Commission on Race, Memorials, and Public Spaces, 22, 145; "a capital of the resistance" rally, 21, 22; clergy, 1; Confederate monuments, 21–24, 136, 184–88; erection of Lee and Jackson statues in, 163; first anniversary (2018) of Unite the Right rally, 137, 139; "happiest city" in American (2014), 21; Heather Heyer Way, 119, *120*, 138, 149; Jews in, 189–90; local response to media coverage, 140–43; police response to Unite the Right, 73–74, 212n70; removal of Black residents from, 136, 163; removal of Confederate statues from, 184–86; response to threat of violence by Unite the Right rally, 73; second anniversary (2019) of Unite the Right rally, 129, 137, 140–41; segregation in, 189–90, 195; and Vinegar Hill, 190. *See also* antiracists in Charlottesville
Charlottesville Center for Peace and Justice, 77
Chesny, Michael, 76
Children's Crusade (1963). *See* Birmingham campaign
Civil Rights Act of 1964, 3, 4, 18, 19, 82, 123, 161; and John F. Kennedy, 154–55, 168–69
civil rights movement: Black churches, 64–65; iconic images of, 86–87, 99–101, *100*, 104–5, *105*, 108–10, *109*, 130–36; impact of, 19–20, 26; and Lyndon B. Johnson, 155–58, 161–62, 169; and John F. Kennedy, 153–55, 157–58, 161–62, 168–69; media savviness of, 17–18, 19, 27, 45–46, 48; monuments about, 131–37, *131, 132, 133, 135*; and post-civil rights "color blind" ideology, 158–59; triumphant narrative of, 158; vandalizing monuments of, 140–42. *See also* Birmingham campaign; Selma campaign
Clark, Jim, 15, 18, 19, 71, 91, 124, 126; and Viola Liuzzo, 115
Clinton, Hillary, 161–62
CNN, 92, 186, 195; and Susan Bro response to Joe Biden "Charlottesville" campaign video, 170

Cohen, Akiba, 87
Colvin, Claudette, 186
Commander, Courtney, 114
Congregate Charlottesville (clergy group), 66, 87–89, *89*
Congregation Beth Israel (synagogue), 61, *61*; Holocaust scroll in, 189; and Unite the Right rally, 189–91, 233n2
Connor, Eugene "Bull," 16–17, 19, 71, 86, 130, 132, 154
conservative media, rise of, 29–30
Cooper, Annie Lee: media coverage of, 124–27, *125*, 186; as "unruly woman," 126
Coulter, Ann, 57
Court Square Park (Charlottesville). *See* Justice Park
Crenshaw, Kimberlé, 124
Crisis: Behind a Presidential Commitment (1963), 28–29
Cronkite, Walter, 9, 115
Cullen, H. Jay, 114–15, 194
C-ville Weekly, 40, 41–43, *42*, 59, 72, 92; Veronica Fitzhugh, coverage of, 127
Cytanovic, Peter, 103–4, *104*, 107

Daily Kos, 66
Daily Progress, (newspaper), 40, 59; car attack photo, 97–99, *98*; op-ed on Wes Bellamy, 43–44, 59; Unite the Right rally reporting, 73–74
Daily Stormer (website), 37, 43, 73, 119, 176
Damigo, Nathan, 157
Daniels, Jesse, 26, 30
Davis, Natalie Zemon, 126
D'Earth, John, 194
democracy: African Americans' contributions to, 3–5; and Capitol insurrection, 5–6, 161; and demography, 5; and 2020 election, 176
de-platforming, 57, 159
Discord (app), 26, 38, *39*, 40, 78

Documenting Hate (PBS/Pro Publica), 79, 81
Douglas, Andrea, 136
Douglas, Mrs. Paul, 125
Douglas, Susan J., 29
doxing, of alt-right, 74–76
Draine, Lisa, 140, 143
Drake, James, 134
Dudley, Dustin, 140
Duke, David, 30, 97
DuVernay, Ava, 124

Eckford, Elizabeth, 104–5, *105*
Edmund Pettus Bridge. *See* monuments; Selma campaign.
Emancipation Park (Charlottesville), 22, 23, 130, 185, *185*; alt-right May 13, 2017, rally in, 60–63, *63*; Occupy protests (2011) in, 55; Unite the Right rally, 92, 93, 146, 166
Eyes on the Prize (1987), 158

Facebook. *See* social media
Face the Nation (CBS), and George Wallace, 29
Fairclough, Adam, 7–8
Fairness Doctrine, demise of, 29–30
Farrell, Amy, 118
Ferguson, Missouri, protests in (2014), 54, 56, 84–85, 110, 188. *See also* Black Lives Matter
Fields, James, 75, 94, 97, 127, 148; conviction in car attack, 175
Finn, Kristen, 143, 145, 150
First United Methodist Church (Charlottesville), 194
Fiske, John, 7, 10, 183–84
Fitzhugh, Veronica, 125; Charlottesville media coverage of, 59, 126–27; as "unruly woman," 126–27
Floyd, George, 3, 83–84, *84*, 110–11, 161; and media event, 96–97
Foreman, James, 169

Fox News, 29, 183
Freedom Rides (1961), 2, 16–17, 18, 78, 154, 169
Friedan, Betty, 123
Furie, Matt, 34. *See also* Pepe the Frog

Gadsden, Walter, 99–100, *100*, 101, 130–31, 134–35, 152, 216n31
Gamergate, 32–33, 37, 38, 48
Gardner, Corey, 156
Garner, Eric, 110–11
Gathers, Don, 66; Inside Out Charlottesville portrait of, 145, *146;* negative response to Joe Biden "Charlottesville" campaign video, 170
Gavin, Kathy, 71, 72
Gilmore, Brennan, 93–95, *93*, *95*, 97
Gladwell, Malcolm, 135–36
Goodman, Eugene, at Capitol insurrection, 179, *179*
Gorcenski, Emily, 65, 70, 81–82, 93, 171, 181; infiltrating Unite the Right organizing, 72–78; and Ku Klux Klan rally (2017), 71–73, *72;* and Richard Spencer, 74; tiki torch parade, 79, *80*
Graham, Hannah, 53, 190
Great Replacement ideology, 8, 107, 119; and antisemitism, 192; and Capitol insurrection, 183; and mass shootings, 160; and Donald Trump, 162
Green, Charlene, 140
Greenberg, David, 29
Griffith, D.W., 103, 162–63

Hahner, Leslie A., 33–35
Hallin, Daniel, three spheres schema of, 41
Hamer, Fannie Lou, 169, 187
Hannah-Jones, Nikole, 3–4
Harcourt, Felix, 27, 163–64
Hariman, Robert, 86–87, 99
Harris, DeAndre, 107–10, *108*, *110*
Harris, Kamala, 171
Hart-Celler Immigration Act of 1965, 4

Hatch, Orrin, criticism of Donald Trump response to Unite the Right, 156–57
Hawley, George, 160
Heather Heyer Foundation, 121, 220n31
Heimbach, Matthew, 43, 175; *Sines v. Kessler*, 75
Helber, Steve, 101, 103
Heyer, Heather, 2, 75, 97, 99, 111, 112, *113*, 129, 147; in Joe Biden "Charlottesville" campaign video, 166, 170; and Susan Bro, 121–22, 127, 145, 146, 170; decision to protest Unite the Right rally, 116; fat shaming of, 118; and feminist movement, 122–23; legacy of, 119–20; memorial for, 121, 138, 140, 149; and whiteness, 127
Highlander Folk School, 56
Highlander Research and Education Center, 56
Hitler, Adolf, 94
Holland, Maxine, 150–51, *151*
Holocaust, the, xiv–xvi
hooks, bell, 134
Hoover, J. Edgar, and Viola Liuzzo, 120–21, 219n18
How Democracies Die (Levitsky and Ziblatt), 6
Hudson, Bill, 99, 130, 134
Hudson, Jennifer, 172

identitarianism, 20
Identity Evropa, 4, 31, *31*, 37, 46, 49, 157; demise of, 175
immigration, 4, 182; and Donald Trump, 163. *See also* Great Replacement ideology
Inside Out Charlottesville (photography installation), 129, 184; Black Lives Matter motif in, 143–44; Black Power salutes in, *144*, 145, *146;* installation of, 148–49; and Cory Long, 149–52; origins of, 140–43; portraits of Charlottesville activists, *142–43*, 143–52,

Inside Out Charlottesville (*continued*) 144, 146, 147, 148, 149, 151; public statement of, 142–43; response to, 149
Inside Out: The People's Art Project, 140, 141, 143, 152
internet, white supremacists' use of, 30–32
Invictus, Augustus Sol, 23
It's Going Down (news collective), 78

Jabara-Heyer No Hate Act (2021), 122
Jackson, Jimmie Lee, 19; killing of, 114
Jackson Park (Charlottesville). *See* Justice Park
January 6, 2021. *See* Capitol insurrection
Jerry Springer Show, The, 30
Jet (magazine), 96
Johns, Barbara, 186, 232n30
Johnson, Lyndon Baines, 4, 153, 161–62, 164; criticism by SNCC on voting rights bill, 169; seating of Mississippi Freedom Democratic Party (1964), 169; support for Selma voting rights activists, 167, 173; voting rights televised speech, 155–56, 164–65
Johnson-Reed Immigration Act of 1924, 4, 163
JR (photographer), 140, 141, 152
Justice Park (Charlottesville), 23; alt-right May 13, 2017, rally in, 60–62, 185, *185*; history of, 136; Ku Klux Klan rally in (2017), 24–25, 67–69, 191–92; removal of "Johnny Reb" statue from, 83; and Unite the Right rally, 194

Kaplan, Roberta A., 75
Kelly, Ryan, 97–99, 100, 103, 111
Kelly Ingram Park (Birmingham), 17, 65, 130; civil rights statues in, 131–37, *131*, *132*, *133*, *135*, 141, 148, 152; *Four Spirits* statue, 223n12. *See also* Birmingham campaign
Kennedy, John F., 18, 28, 60, 153, 157, 162, 164, 173; civil rights televised speech of, 154–55, 156, 164–65; criticism by John Lewis at March on Washington, 168–69; Cuban Missile Crisis televised speech of, 154
Kennedy, Robert F., 28, 145, 154
Kessler, Jason, 20–22, 24, 25, 26, 38, 66, 73–74, 137; alt-right May 13, 2017, rally, 61–62, *62*; and Charlottesville antiracists, 57–59; coverage in local media, 40–42, 43, 59; and Veronica Fitzhugh, 126–27; and Heather Heyer, 118; *Sines v. Kessler*, 75; social media use by, 62, 210n35
Khan, Humayan, 21
Khan, Khizr, 21
King, Coretta Scott, 138
King, Martin Luther, Jr., 1, 7, 15, 17, 19, 27, 46, 56, 87–88, 96, 113, 125, 137, 158, 161, 168, 188; and J. Edgar Hoover, 121; hostile media coverage of, 60, 130; "Letter from Birmingham Jail," 17, 23, 51, 56, 68; and martinlutherking.org, 30; media savviness of, 58, 67; Montgomery Bus Boycott, 64; respectability politics of, 59–60, 121, 187; response to Lyndon B. Johnson's voting rights speech, 156; and SNCC, 169. *See also* Southern Christian Leadership Conference
King, Rodney, 96
King, Shaun, 109–10, *110*, 217n48
Klein, Adam, 30–32, 33
Kline, Elliot. *See* Mosley, Eli
Ku Klux Klan, 46, 97, 136; gender politics of, 115, 123; and Lyndon B. Johnson, 156; and Viola Liuzzo, 113, 115–17, *117*, 118–19, 156; March on Washington (1925), 44–45, *45*, *46*; media savviness of, 27, 204n5; miscegenation fears of, 116–17; "second coming" (1920s) of, 163–64
Ku Klux Klan rally (2017), 24–25, 43, 67–69, 191–92; and antisemitism, 192; and Veronica Fitzhugh, 126–27; social

media coverage by Emily Gorcenski, 71–73, *72*

Ladies' Home Journal, negative coverage of Viola Liuzzo, 116, 123
Lafayette, Bernard, 18, 78, 81
Lawson, James, 78, 81
League of the South, 107
Lee, Spike, 97, 170
Lee Park (Charlottesville). *See* Emancipation Park
Lentz, Richard, 60
Leo (dog), *100*, 130–31, 134
Lewis, George, 64
Lewis, John, 18, 19, 25, 29, 78, 81, 138; beating on Edmund Pettus Bridge, 108–10, *109*; criticism of Kennedy Administration at March on Washington, 168–69; death of, 110, 138, *139*; and Selma campaign, 90–91
Life (magazine), 28; Birmingham campaign coverage, 101, 134; Selma campaign coverage, 88, 96, 125
Limbaugh, Rush, 29, 30
Liuzzo, Viola, 2, 90, 219n13; fat shaming of, 118; J. Edgar Hoover smear campaign against, 12–121; involvement in Selma campaign, 112–13, 120; legacy of, 120–21, 220n32; and Lyndon B. Johnson, 156; mass media coverage of, 115–17, 118, *119*; and misogyny, 115–17; monument of, 141; murder of, 113–14; and second wave feminism, 122–23
Long, Corey, 101, *102*, 103, 149–52, *151*
Love, Yeardley, 190
Loyal White Knights of the Ku Klux Klan, 67. *See also* Ku Klux Klan rally
Lucaites, John Louis, 86–87, 99
Lyon, Danny, 145

Majerczyk, Eva, xiv–xvi, 191; murder of family, xvi; Shoah Foundation testimony of, 233n6; as slave laborer, xv–xvi; in Warsaw ghetto, xiv
March on Washington (1963), 55, 169, 172; media coverage of, 45–46; and respectability politics, 59–60
Market Street Park (Charlottesville). *See* Emancipation Park
Martin, Marcus, *98*, 99–100, 111, 216n31; Inside Out Charlottesville portrait of, 147–48, *149*
Martin, Trayvon, 84–85
Massery, Hazel, 104–5, *105*
mass media: and Black brutalization, 111; and Susan Bro, 121–22, 170; and Zyahna Bryant, 186–88; and Charlottesville clergy, 88–89, *89*, 146–47; and Heather Heyer, 118; liberal bias in, 29; and Viola Liuzzo, 115–17; and segregationists, 58, 64; as "technologies of memory," 172. *See also* photojournalism; television news
May, Gary, 116
McCrory, J. Brian, 68
McDowell, Ronald, 134–36, 152
McMichael, Pam, 56
McWhorter, Diane, 130
melodrama, and Black suffering, 90, 96–97, 100–101, 103, 108, 179
memes, 26; alt-right use of, 33–35, 67; Charlottesville antiracists' use of, 67–69, *69*; Richard Spencer with torch, *63*; tiki torch rally, 50, *50*. *See also* Pepe the Frog
Metapedia (website), 31
Michigan State University, shutting down of Richard Spencer, 82
Middleton, Dick, *100*, 130–31, 134, 135
Montgomery Bus Boycott, 55; use of communication platforms, 64–65
monuments: and alt-right, 21, 37, 60–63; in Baltimore, 21; and Wes Bellamy, 22–23; Birmingham civil rights statues as, 131–37, *131*, *132*, *133*, *135*; and Zyahna

monuments (*continued*)
Bryant, 22; and Charlottesville (city), 136, 184–88, *185*; Confederate, 21–24, 37, 83, 136, 163, 184–88, *185*; Edmund Pettus Bridge as, 138; Heather Heyer Way as, *120*, 138, 139; in New Orleans, 21; in Richmond, Virginia, 83–84, *84*, 184; and Team Henry Enterprises, 184; Virginia General Assembly (2019) legislation on, 83. *See also* Inside Out Charlottesville; Kelly Ingram Park
Mosley, Eli, 38, 78; *Sines v. Kessler*, 73, 175–76; teargassed at Unite the Right rally, 193–94, 234n11; and tiki torch rally, 46, *46–48*, 203n39. *See also* Identity Evropa
Moton, Leroy, 113, 116–17
MTV Video Music Awards, 121

NAACP, 46; and *The Birth of a Nation* (1915), 163; and March on Washington, 48
Nash, Diane, 78, 81, 124, 186
National Organization for Women (NOW), 123
NBC News, 27; Zyahna Bryant coverage of, 186–87, *187*
New Right, "Southern Strategy," 158, 159
Newsweek (magazine), 29; Birmingham campaign coverage of, 60; negative coverage of Viola Liuzzo, 116
New York Times, 29, 84; and Heather Heyer, 118; negative coverage of Viola Liuzzo, 115–16; and Selma campaign, 124
Night Riders: The Inside Story of the Liuzzo Killing (1966), 116–17, *117*, 118–19
Nixon, Richard, 29
"Normie's Guide to the Alt-Right, A" (Anglin), 37

Oath Keepers, 161, 182
Obama, Barack, 29, 56, 161, 164; and "birther" conspiracy, 159; at Edmund Pettus Bridge (2015), 138; second inaugural speech, 2, 197n2; and Will.i.am "Yes We Can" video, 171
Occidental Dissent, 22, 31, *32*, 118
Occupy Wall Street protests, 54–55; organizing power of, 55

Pape, Robert, 183
Parker, Rosia, 150, *151*
Parks, Rosa, 56, 158, 186
Pathé News, newsreel coverage of Ku Klux Klan, 45
Pelosi, Nancy, 180
Pepe the Frog, 26, 34–35, *34*, *35*, 37, 48, 69
Perlmutter, David, 87, 98–99
photojournalism: Birmingham campaign, 17–18, 71, 86, 130–36; brutalizing of Black bodies in, 99–103, 104–5, 108–10, *109*; car attack (Charlottesville), 97–100, *98*, 111, 147–48; and Charlottesville counterprotesters, 101, *102*, 103, 150–52; civil rights movement, 15; George Floyd protests (2020), 84; iconic characteristics of, 86–87, 98–99; Little Rock school integration crisis, 104–5, *105*; March on Washington (1963), 45–46; and media events, 7–8; and segregationists, 58, 63–64, 104–7, *105*, *107*; Selma campaign, 96, 108–10, *109*, 138; as "technologies of memory," 172; tiki torch rally, 48–49, 103–4, *104*, 107; Unite the Right rally, 86, 101, *102*, 103; women segregationists, 106, *106*, 107
Poland, Bailey, 32
Proud Boys: burning Black Lives Matter flags, 177; and Capitol insurrection, 161, 176, 182; confrontations with DC Black Lives Matter after 2020 election, 177; hypermasculinity, 107, 181; and Donald Trump, 161; Unite the Right rally organizing, 59, 126